RACHMANINOFF'S CAPE

'George Rousseau's compelling memoir narrates the extraordinary story of one woman's search for the meaning of her own life, marked by loss and strife, in the fate of the great pianist and composer Sergei Rachmaninoff. In so doing, it illuminates the underexplored and much misunderstood condition of nostalgia in the post-Romantic age.'

Simon Pawley
Russian History, University of Oxford

,

'If biography means the writing of a life, then the facts pertaining to the life of Sergei Rachmaninoff are clear and well-established. Yet how is a biographer to sound the mysterious inner life of Rachmaninoff as a creative artist? And how can facts alone account for the impact of his music on listeners to this day? As sensitive as it is erudite, as intuitive as it is reasoned, *Rachmaninoff's Cape* attends to the melancholy and nostalgia that are so central to the composer's musical language. And in its intertwined narratives of Rousseau's own life, and the touching story of Evelyn Amster's fatalistic fascination with the life and works of the Russian émigré composer, it offers its readers a tale of doublings, revenants, symmetries and serendipities that lingers like one of Rachmaninoff's own haunting melodies.'

Philip Ross Bullock
Professor of Russian Literature and Music, University of Oxford

'Finally, a deeply moving book about Rachmaninoff the man and his inner world. Rousseau penetrates to the heart of the milieu of aspiring American pianists and their teachers in twentieth-century New York City.'

Dr Norland Berk
New York psychiatrist

RACHMANINOFF'S CAPE

A Nostalgia Memoir

by

George Rousseau

Virtuoso Books

Also by George Rousseau

Books

This Long Disease My Life: Alexander Pope and the Sciences
Goldsmith: The Critical Heritage
The Renaissance Man in the Eighteenth Century
The Letters and Private Papers of Sir John Hill
Tobias Smollett: Essays of Two Decades
Medicine and the Muses (translated into Italian and Japanese)
Perilous Enlightenment: Pre- and Post-Modern Discourses--Sexual, Historical
Enlightenment Crossings: Pre- and Post-Modern Discourses— Anthropological
Enlightenment Borders: Pre- and Post-Modern Discourses--Medical, Scientific
Gout: The Patrician Malady
Marguerite Yourcenar: A Biography
Nervous Acts: Essays on Literature, Culture and Sensibility
The Notorious Sir John Hill: The Man Destroyed by Ambition in the Age of Celebrity

Edited Books

The Augustan Milieu: Essays Presented to Louis A. Landa
Tobias Smollett: Bicentennial Essays Presented to Lewis M. Knapp
Organic Form: The Life of an Idea
The Ferment of Knowledge: Studies in the Historiography of Science
Science and the Imagination: The Berkeley Conference
Sexual Underworlds of the Enlightenment
The Enduring Legacy: Alexander Pope Tercentenary Essays
Exoticism in the Enlightenment
The Languages of Psyche: Mind and Body in Enlightenment Thought
Hysteria Before Freud
Framing and Imagining Disease in Cultural History
Children and Sexuality: The Greeks to the Great War

Anthology

English Poetic Satire

George Rousseau

GEORGE ROUSSEAU is a professor of history at Oxford University and was, until 2013, the Co-Director of its Centre for the History of Childhood. A native New Yorker, he has been called a remarkable polymath for the range of his knowledge and depth of his scholarship in several fields. Professionally he is an internationally known cultural historian who works in the interface of literature and medicine, and emphasizes the relevance of imaginative materials – literature, especially diaries and biography, art and architecture, music – for the public understanding of medicine, past and present. He trained in New York, like his protagonist Evelyn Amster, to become a concert pianist and then crossed over into academic life, eventually holding professorships at Harvard, UCLA, Aberdeen, and Oxford. He had been writing historical books for four decades until something happened. His friend's mother died and left him a large trunk filled with remarkable diaries and papers enabling him to chronicle her fascination with the great Russian pianist-composer Sergei Rachmaninoff (1873-1943). In the process, Rousseau was able to recreate New York City's musical life in the early twentieth century, as well as explore the much-misunderstood condition of nostalgia among immigrants who came to America, like Rachmaninoff, in the nineteenth and twentieth centuries. Now he has written a gripping memoir – *Rachmaninoff's Cape* – telling the whole story. How the Jewish Evelyn Amster herself almost made it to the concert stage, how her obsession with Rachmaninoff developed at an early age, and – most intriguingly – why our received sense of Rachmaninoff's life is inadequate for understanding the man and his music.

For Evelyn Amster, whose story enabled me to understand my own

Contents

Author's Note

Readers of *Rachmaninoff's Cape* should not be duped by its first section into thinking it a work of fiction. This opening can appear to be novelistic, yet read on for a few dozen pages and you realize the narrating 'I' has begun his task of retrieval to prepare the way for the ensuing memoir: a double story about Evelyn and George who craved a new biography of the Russian composer Sergei Vasilyevich Rachmaninoff (1873-1943). If the narrator's ('George') portrayal of Evelyn employs fictional techniques, this is because I have tried to ensnare the reader into Evelyn's conflicted world as quickly as possible. Once captured, the reader can probe the parallel universes of all three subjects: Evelyn, George, and Rachmaninoff himself. My most pressing task has been an adequate description of nostalgia's complexity. But I also aim to describe what a new life of Rachmaninoff, based on his own nostalgia, would amount to; demonstrating that 'lives' always entail more than conventional selves packaged in standard biographies. The memoir incorporates the powerful responses of two of these figures – Evelyn and George – who were jointly immersed in Rachmaninoff's life from the 1940s to the present time. And it further construes Rachmaninoff's creative nostalgia for his homeland in ways we are just beginning to understand in the aftermath of the Cold War, the collapse of the Iron Curtain, and the migrations since 1989 of millions of emigrants who fled their country – as Rachmaninoff did – because they could no longer imagine life inside it. If my literary form, devised to vivify this nostalgia since the colossally liberating effects of 1989, appears to masquerade as fiction in parts of this book, it is an illusion. Nostalgia remains one of the least understood yet most universal of human sentiments. All the figures in *Rachmaninoff's Cape* are biographical and walk, or once walked, the same earth as you and me: aspiring concert pianist Evelyn Amster (1918-1989), academic scholar George Rousseau (1941-), and great Russian composer Sergei Rachmaninoff.

I have written because readers today crave deeper understanding of nostalgia than they currently possess; not the commodity versions bombarding them in the media and on the Internet, or the journalistic varieties that present it as the 'politics of nostalgia', but its more universal shapes commensurate with other life-giving forces: birth, death, love, marriage, and the broad spectrum of emotions without which human experience would be unrecognizable. And readers seek to understand what nostalgia is emotionally, psychologically, culturally, and especially why it is so globally distributed, cultivated and compromised throughout cultures Western and Eastern, the nostalgia whose profile is still silent. They want to compare their own shades of nostalgia with that of a famous composer like Rachmaninoff and an obscure but harrowing American lady like Evelyn. I could not have enabled this knowledge through the construction of an impersonal, third-person narrative parading itself as a 'history of nostalgia', as I explain in the dialogue with Helen at the end of Part One.

Furthermore, if music is the most sublime of the arts, it also sets the perfect context for conveying this still poorly understood constellation of nostalgia-emotions. And some of its most common forms with which non-specialist readers are familiar are indeed musical, as in the affective responses many people have to their favorite types of music. Few composers could be better exponents for a memoir about nostalgia than Rachmaninoff because he spans the gap between highbrow classical music and popular Hollywood versions. Viewed beside Evelyn, in contrast to whom he was as famous as she was obscure, Rachmaninoff spans nostalgia's broad register, embodies its psychological and aesthetic depths, and appeals to a wide range of readers extending from scholars and specialists to the more generally curious and educated. Configured in this sense, nostalgia poses challenges of a biographical, cultural, historical, and literary nature, but none more so than the double-genre bind between memoir and biography.

George Rousseau
Oxford, England

Part 1: Evelyn and Rachmaninoff

A FEW MONTHS BEFORE HER DEATH during the Thanksgiving holiday in 1989 Evelyn Amster packed a large trunk with her notebooks and papers. She had been fading for several years, playing snippets of Rachmaninoff's music on her wooden upright piano in the bay window of her *adobe casita,* as she called it, while dozing off to Pacific sunsets. The tall trunk stood to the right of the piano, and she filled it meticulously. A few items each day, bundling small, medium, and large files together, until it was jam-packed.

Then Evelyn phoned the FedEx people and asked them to ship it to me across town in the Hollywood Hills. That was in mid-November 1989, and we had not seen each other for almost a year. She was unaware I was on sabbatical leave in New York to continue my research on the history of nostalgia – an intricate subject to disentangle – and sent the trunk to my California address. My neighbour Stella was looking after the post, forwarding urgent items, and apprising me of impending crises on the property. Stella took a few days to retrieve the trunk; when she did, its sender and contents mystified her.

Stella telephoned me in New York the day before Thanksgiving to wish me a happy holiday. During that phone conversation she summarized November's arrivals: '… also, a large, old-fashioned, wooden trunk from Evelyn Amster with a Venice Beach address, too big and heavy to carry.' My questions revealed that Stella could not lift the big trunk alone into the boot of her car. So she left it in the downstairs hallway of my house.

I recognized the name and suspected the worst. Evelyn Amster was seventy-one, had slowed down, and was probably dead. 'Keep it there,' I instructed Stella during that same phone conversation, and before thinking about what I had just spurted, I said 'I'll probably fly out for her funeral.'

My curiosity did not end here. I asked Stella to open the trunk, canvass its contents, and phone me back the next day.

Stella phoned on Thanksgiving morning. 'It's stuffed with little notebooks, handwritten sheets, annual diaries filled with comments and doodles, dozens of small yellow pads also filled, packages of letters tied with string, many sheets crumbling, so they must be old.'

Exactly what I expected. Evelyn had lived on her own in Venice Beach for twenty years and became reclusive; the *other* Venice, as Angelinos often referred to it, where muscle men display their physical prowess on the worm-eaten LA boardwalk. She had migrated there around 1968 'in search of Sergei Rachmaninoff,' as she used to say in an adopted posh inflection to offset her thick New York City accent; the great pianist-composer who cut an unprecedented figure in the American consciousness of the last century. Rachmaninoff's name was as difficult to say and spell as his piano music was hard to play, but Evelyn had her reasons.

She lived quietly, and as she faded made ever more jottings in her pads. She wrote for hours; nothing sustained, not even long letters, just compiled these drafts, impressions, scribbles, saying that before she died she wanted to know 'the truth' about the greatest pianist of her generation, Sergei Rachmaninoff.

During that same phone call I asked Stella whether there was a return address on the FedEx mandate and she said yes, 'an apartment 1D in Venice Beach.' I begged Stella to drive over to Venice – a thirty-minute drive from my house in the Hollywood Hills – and discover what she could about Evelyn. No use in my phoning Evelyn if she was dead. But I gave Stella Evelyn's phone number just in case she were alive. That was on Thanksgiving Thursday, the holiday when Americans commonly phone each other.

Stella drove to the shabby apartment block on the boardwalk that weekend; knocked on Evelyn's door, had no reply, spoke to neighbours, discovered that 'the eccentric lady' had indeed died about a week ago. One woman in the small block, who seemed acquainted with Evelyn, said the funeral was next Wednesday, December 2, which Stella reported in her telephone call to me that night.

I flew out by a non-stop flight the day before the funeral, the Tuesday after Thanksgiving, December 1, the first flight I could get after the holiday; as curious about the trunk's contents as I was distraught by Evelyn's death. 'It would have been so good,' I kept reminding myself on the flight, 'to see her just once more, to ask her what she finally learned about her great idol, Sergei Rachmaninoff, and to thank her for what she had done for me forty years earlier.' Although I had not seen much of Evelyn in recent years I never ceased to marvel at her generosity when I was eight years old, nor could I forget it.

Stella was unable to provide the funeral parlour's address, so I realized I would have to become proactive if I were going to attend it in time. I rented a car at LAX and drove straight to Venice Beach, only fifteen minutes by the coastal route hugging the Marina. I had lived in LA myself for two decades and knew its roads like the back of my hand.

I located Evelyn's apartment manager, the very caricature of a Jewish geezer riddled with arthritis, wearing trainers and a baseball cap, and told him the story; mentioning the trunk and my long association with Evelyn, telling him that I was a professor at UCLA on sabbatical leave in New York City and had just flown in for the funeral, which I hoped I had not already missed.

'No', he said with a Yiddish accent, 'not yet, tomorrow, Wednesday. You are in time, young man.' He also ushered me into the unlit flat vacated by my friend Evelyn who lay dead in the morgue.

The place was reasonably tidy, just Evelyn's books scattered about. There were no pads or papers – perhaps all had been stuffed into the tall trunk awaiting me in the Hollywood Hills.

The manager also told me Evelyn left instructions that her funeral should be held in a wood-dappled funeral parlour in Venice. He had trouble pronouncing 'wood-dappled' and turned out the 'w' as a 'v'. There must have been discussion of the funeral parlour Evelyn had chosen or, perhaps, the local residents, most of them elderly, already knew the place and its crumbled furnishings. He commented that only a few people would attend. 'We Jews bury quickly, no time to invite everyone, and Thanksgiving interrupted. Besides, Evelyn only knew three or four people.'

Armed with these essential facts and an address and having seen Evelyn's empty apartment for myself – proof she really *was* dead – I carried on driving to my house. I sped through Venice on to Highway 10 and further up into the Hollywood Hills.

Once home I was too jetlagged to rummage through the tall trunk's contents but I could not go to sleep without exploring it. Stella had already described the jottings in our telephone conversations, but there is nothing – I said to myself – like seeing for yourself. Just as I suspected: most of the notes pertained to Rachmaninoff and were interspersed with abundant comments and pages about her son's life. I opened a few pads, browsed their jottings, recognized Evelyn's hand, closed the wooden lid and slid into bed.

I awoke early on Wednesday, had a double shower, went out for a big breakfast, and drove to the Jewish funeral parlour in plenty of time for the noon burial. The landlord was right: six people showed up, all women, one rather fancy, plus the rabbi.

The rabbi spoke compassionately, said Evelyn was a woman of vast learning and great presence of mind who played the piano beautifully and had been a concert pianist when she was young. The hearse was taken to a nearby cemetery in Culver City, which Evelyn had prearranged. Four of us followed it. Prayers were said at the graveside, we tore our undershirts and tossed hand-shredded remnants into the grave, said kaddishes for Evelyn, and watched the coffin lowered. Nothing followed on from the service; no food, no remembrances, no conversation – just four of us dispersed.

I started the engine of my rented car with a dry, numb taste in my mouth wondering if this were the way I would some day vanish from the world – with just five people and a rabbi to say goodbye. Then I drove to Stella's place in Runyon Canyon to describe the funeral. Stella cooked a marvellous sardine-based pasta with decorative anchovies; we drank two bottles of red wine and talked, mostly about Evelyn, until past midnight.

I had known the curve of Evelyn's life for a long time: how she grew up in Queens after the First World War, the only child of Jewish immigrants who became wealthy; her father a successful, charismatic, and moustached European merchant; how she failed as a young concert pianist, then married Sam Amster, had one child – Richard – a musical prodigy who played the cello.

All this was old hat to me, but the funeral also elicited vivid memories of that traumatic day forty years earlier, in the spring of 1949 when I was eight years old, and I could not stop telling Stella about the 'catastrophe' while we ate and drank.

Evelyn's son Richard was then seven, a year younger than me. We had met at Chatham Square Music School, in Manhattan, where we both had scholarships. Pianists and string players, even of that tender age, were paired to accompany each other, and Richard was my partner. We got on well, and one Saturday that autumn – the day of the week the students usually spent at Chatham Square – Mrs Amster invited me to the family home in Queens for a weekend, my first time there. It was Richard's eighth birthday.

My parents lived in Brooklyn and did not own a car; so my father took me on the subway to Flushing, where the Amsters lived. Sam Amster collected us at the subway station, my father introduced himself and after a few minutes said goodbye, entrusting me to this man who drove me to their house about a mile away. My understanding was that my father would come to fetch me on Sunday afternoon.

To me as an eight-year-old boy their house seemed a large brick structure several stories high. Evelyn was at the front door, daintily dressed in something with a floral pattern, waiting to greet us, and on entering I smelled a hot lunch cooking. She took me upstairs to a small bedroom, invited me to drop the little suitcase I had brought, and said I should go into Richard's music room where he was practicing.

I had no difficulty identifying the right room on the landing because I could hear Richard's cello playing. It was a large and handsome room, book-lined and hung with curtains of thick fabric over the windows and had high ceilings. A large brown concert piano stood in the middle and next to it I found my friend seated, playing his cello.

Richard stopped when he saw me enter, and rose holding his cello. I walked over to him, not so much to greet him with a hug – I was only eight and did not hug other boys – but out of some type of curiosity about this new setting; perhaps the awe of being in this beautiful room with these ornate pieces of furniture and this polished concert piano; the sight of Richard and his ancient cello in this setting which lay in such huge contrast to the stark white walls of our Saturday practice room at Chatham Square. Chatham's very small practice rooms were bare except for an upright piano and piano stool.

Yes, it must have been bewilderment at seeing my friend in this setting that elicited this sense of wonder. For I had stood close to Richard's cello many times before in music school; might even have touched it. I knew what beautiful wood it was made from and how old it was. But I had never viewed it, and its player, in such an ornate setting.

After this my memory goes blank … I do not remember how it happened, or – perhaps – the shutting down of memory has shielded me from a wound too painful to recall as an adult. The next thing I remembered, as I told Stella on the night of Evelyn's funeral, was that Richard's cello lay broken on the floor. A huge crack ran down its front.

Richard was as shocked as I was and stood motionless, as if stunned to the marrow. My heart beat faster and faster, and I recall wanting to run away, to escape anywhere. Although I was only a boy my whole world crumbled and was undone. All I could think was 'I didn't do it, I didn't do it, it fell.'

Evelyn was cooking downstairs and must have heard the cello's heavy thump. Within seconds – no more than that – she rushed into the room to behold the catastrophe before her.

She looked at her inert son; she gazed at my terror but not my tears for I don't remember crying. I was in shock and do not know if my memory speaks accurately, but this is what I recall after four decades:

Evelyn walked over to me, put one hand on my shoulder, the other on my back, and sweetly whispered to me – a boy of only eight from a tenement house in Brooklyn – 'don't worry sweetheart, Richard has *another* cello'.

She spoke those words slowly, with such sincerity she could have rended your heart. I cannot speculate what Richard made of the exchange, but I was bowled over and calmed down. I don't remembering saying anything at all. Not a word.

Memory has also obliterated the first few hours after the catastrophe. For example, I have no recollection of that lunch or whether I ate anything, or whether Richard's father was present. I can only recall attentively watching Evelyn's cheerful face in their formal dining room, which also had similar heavy curtains and a high ceiling, and wondering how anyone can act so kindly.

By late afternoon Richard and I were practicing together in the music room on his *other* cello. I don't remember pleading with him or crying. My heart was beating normally again. I must have slept that night for I do not recall lying awake in fright. And by the time my father collected me on Sunday afternoon the broken cello receded somewhat in my consciousness.

Neither Evelyn nor her husband said anything about the catastrophe to my father – just handed me over as if the weekend evolved uneventfully. I dared not mention it to my father on the subway, but once back in the tenement in Brooklyn I told them.

My mother grew alarmed: 'you broke his cello?' I was compelled to expatiate and did. I said I wasn't sure whether I broke it or Richard did. One of us may have slipped. Nothing was certain about the moment itself. 'Your father,' pointing at him and raising her voice, 'will need to take a second job to pay for it.' On and on she nagged about the horrors that would follow from my reckless behaviour.

Did I explain to them Evelyn's remarkable charity? How could I account for the fact that *nothing* would be paid for the calamity? The Amsters were a different breed of people from us, both mothers and fathers. They forgave people.

Evelyn could have ruined me on that day; could have demanded that my strapped family pay for a new cello and heaped such guilt on my conscience for the catastrophe that years of psychoanalysis would have been needed to recover. Instead, she worked her magic in two sentences accompanied by impeccable restraint and unimaginable charity. My father would have extracted retribution and torment. He had behaved as a tyrant when I lost my eyeglasses at six; said that if I lost them again he would never buy me another pair and I would grow up blind without learning to read or seeing other people.

Is it any wonder I grew up, instead, imagining Evelyn as the kindest woman who ever lived and idealizing her? At least until the events I now recount mellowed my view and deepened my understanding of poor Evelyn who now lay dead inside a coffin in the earth.

I returned to Richard's ornate music room many times during the next few years without ever hearing again about the broken cello. Within weeks of the catastrophe the Amsters led me to think they bought Richard another spare cello to replace the one I broke.

Evelyn also said something else during that weekend. She told me I was Richard's best friend. At eight I was too young to understand what she meant, but in time I understood the comment to signify that she herself, in addition to Richard, liked me. At the time I thought she identified some quality in me, even at eight, extending beyond that of a future accompanist for her son. But I later intuited her logic: if Richard liked me, she must too, for she and Richard were almost one and the same person.

I must stand aside to recreate how she came to disclose this principle of ultimate sympathy among the three of us: two Amsters – mother and son – and myself. It alone explains why I dropped everything to fly out to her funeral, as well as why her papers had such significance for me and compelled me to reconstruct her life.

Evelyn and Rachmaninoff

Eight years after the accident I began to correspond with Evelyn as the result of another calamity, this one far more tragic than the catastrophe with the cello; then, around 1968, she migrated from Long Island to California and we slowly lost touch. Our letters grew infrequent, recompensed only by midnight telephone calls two or three times a year when we tried to recoup lost time and stayed on the phone for an hour.

Evelyn never returned to New York but we were lucky. I took an academic post at UCLA around the time she migrated; these were independent events but permitted us occasionally to see each other. I saw her mellowing, gracefully greying, insouciantly growing handsomer, more stoical too than I remembered her in Queens. Her sixtieth birthday in Venice, in 1978, was a small affair; a few ageing bohemian locals prepared corned-beef, cole-slaw, and drinks. Predictably she said a few words about Rachmaninoff's life, the man who mattered so much to her.

I knew perfectly well why she headed out to Beverly Hills. 'To find Sergei Rachmaninoff and understand his plight,' she said at the time – as she would often later on – the great Russian who died in 1943 when Evelyn was twenty-five. Before she migrated I tried to talk her out of this ludicrous pursuit but got nowhere. She was adamant; kept insisting it was the 'only purpose of her life now that she was alone.'

Evelyn meant 'in search of Rachmaninoff's footsteps:' to understand his life after he fled the Bolsheviks in 1917 and emigrated to America. If she could reconstruct his emigration from Russia to New York and California, its dates, causes, reasons and effects on his musical composition, especially its unparalleled emotion of incessant yearning and longing, she imagined she would understand her own loneliness – this was her weird logic: from *Rachmaninoff's* yearning to *her* loneliness. But by 'plight' she meant something else; she meant '*her* plight about *Richard.*'

How did Richard fit in and why did Richard die?

This was the question and it took me years to understand how everything fit together: Evelyn's life, her son Richard's life and his illness, and Rachmaninoff's life. Not the *facts* of Richard's early death, which I shall divulge momentarily – they were straightforward if also pathetic – but her sense that her finger ended where Richard's finger began, and the way this connective bond swept over her each year like some tidal wave. So much so that the pre-Richard Evelyn – the Evelyn who existed before she was mother to this boy – was transformed from the person she had been when aspiring to be a concert pianist. And, later, the post-Richard Evelyn, who became a different person again after she left New York and migrated to California.

It wasn't a simple matter of establishing the *facts*, although the facts were crucial before I could understand anything; the harder part resided in penetrating her rich mental orbit that intuitively constructed parallel universes between Richard and Rachmaninoff.

I would more accurately have said *Evelyn and Rachmaninoff*, for she herself had been, as I have said, an accomplished pianist early in life and well knew how her youth had overlapped with Rachmaninoff's adulthood; not that she ever concertized or became famous but they were near contemporaries. Yet I did not view her parallel universes in the way she did for a long time, and eventually I rejected them. But that was not until I had reconstructed – for the sake of clarity – not two but *three* lives: her son Richard's, Rachmaninoff's, and her own. I had harboured suspicions, of course, but the tall trunk stuffed with papers and diaries provided the missing links.

Inside it I found fifteen large notebooks, one for each year of Richard's life beginning in 1942, plus oversized folders brimming with notes and filled pads, each labelled with a year from the time Evelyn migrated. The last envelop, half empty, was dated 1988. 1989, her last year, did not exist. Written in tiny handwriting nothing was edited or deleted; the entries copied as if she had dictated them or spoke them into a tape recorder as an audio diary. Occasionally she annotated an error of fact or chronology, or expunged and replaced it in the margin; otherwise the handwritten version was the final product of whatever these jottings were intended to be. She must have discarded hundreds of pages along the way. Binned thousands of scribbles.

Within a few months I realized she had viewed both her own life, and Rachmaninoff's, as allegories of the pain of memory. As if neither life could 'forget loss' – this was their commonality. Not the jussive 'speak, memory', as Nabokov has written, but the equally hortatory 'memory, forget;' or, the impossibility of forgetting. She was not flaunting her belief; just trying to resolve what her notebooks continually referred to as 'RR', *Rachmaninoff's riddle*. The abbreviation recurs hundreds of times in her notes.

Riddle? As a quondam keyboard performer myself I understood how this puzzling Russian composer could occupy that niche in her mind; how she came to idealize him, by turns and twists, so extravagantly that she imagined she *was* him. Rachmaninoff, like her son Richard, also developed an early illness: a creative block for which he was treated in 1900, which almost finished him off. But Rachmaninoff allegedly conquered his malady whereas Richard did not. Out of collapse Rachmaninoff produced his celebrated second, 'come-back', piano concerto, and remained vigorous for two decades until the revolutionaries terrified him and he packed up, fled Russia for the West, emigrated to America, and ended up in California. He was Russia's foremost pianist and, by the 1930s, the West's too. Evelyn would also end up in California and, like Rachmaninoff, die there. I discovered that the dual universes of *Rachmaninoff* and *Richard* were more enigmatic.

Evelyn's notebooks compiled columns comparing *two* lives, Richard's and Rachmaninoff's – not that Evelyn herself could ever compose those lives; but they were laid out as a beginning novelist might prepare her notes in sequential notebooks covering many years. Except that she herself was missing: there was no dedicated diary or journal about *her*, nothing entitled 'Evelyn', just annual diaries indicating where she went and who she saw. These annotated calendars extended as far back as 1941, when she married Sam. Someone intimate with New York City, where she lived until she migrated, and the musical milieu there in which she was raised, could reconstruct her pre-1941 biography, from her birth in 1918, but it would be an ordeal.

Rachmaninoff's life was something else. It had not had a major revisionary biography written in English since 1956 – thirty-three years before I inherited Evelyn's trunk. A trained musicologist with knowledge of Russian archives and Russian history was needed to assess it. A new biography of Rachmaninoff could be suggested, based on new knowledge or new approaches, but it would need to propose concrete new avenues and lines of thought.

Evelyn always wrote in the first person and tried to begin at the beginning, describing her privileged upbringing compared to the children of other immigrant, often unprosperous, Jews, and explained her responsibility in raising a son who was doubtlessly 'an extraordinary musical talent'. But she abandoned all her accounts and descriptions after a few paragraphs and left no coherent narrative. Except for two jottings: an extended account of Richard's death and a draft of 'The Nurse's Tale,' which pertained to the end of Rachmaninoff's life.

Richard's death at fifteen, in 1957, nearly deranged her; left her stranded in the universe and made it impossible for her to complete any other accounts she may have started of the parallel universes of these two men. Nor could she understand herself after Richard's death beyond the exigency of the moment. After that everything became too traumatic.

I SPENT THE NEXT THREE YEARS, 1989-1992, immersed in the tall trunk's contents. My sabbatical came to an end but I ploughed on studying her jottings. The surprise I discovered was the light it shed on my own pursuit after 1992. By then I was frantically chasing the medical history of a condition no longer recognized today as one: *NOSTALGIA, longing for the home*. Or, as the dictionaries say, *yearning for past times or past places*. A huge academic book on this topic would break new ground. But it was Evelyn's tantalizing parallel universes, not scholarly books in libraries, which ultimately enabled me to conceptualize the largest stakes implicit in a broadly based historical and psychological condition of nostalgia.[1]

---

[1] Some readers will wonder what this 'condition' is and why it matters. Or, in a more historical key, what it was and what it has become. The word *nostalgia* was coined in 1688 by an Alsatian military doctor (Johannes Hofer) from two roots: *nostos* (home) and *algia* (suffering for), which he combined to describe a longing for home. Hofer noticed that his patients were symptomatic, sleepless, lost their appetites, and even attempted suicide; he diagnosed the root cause of their common misery as separation from their homeland. Most of his patients were young Swiss mercenaries, and he wondered how they could become so disaffected only a short distance – in Alsace – from their native ground. He found the answers when they described to him the different sights, sounds, smells, diet, quality of air, even the different taste of milk between one Swiss valley and another. Hofer realized how spatially localized his newly invented *nostalgia* was and described these miniscule differences in the treatise he published describing his newly identified malady. Throughout the next two centuries (1688-1888) physicians continued to comment on nostalgia as a medical malady. Dozens of medical treatises were printed about it, and it slowly seeped into popular culture as a less medicalized condition, i. e., as the state of longing for another place or time even without medical symptoms. The Romantic poets were particularly attracted to nostalgia for its creative inspiration, and Victorian writers, in Britain and on the Continent, constructed whole swathes of their literature based on its psychological effects. Nevertheless, nostalgia retained its symptomatic medical profile, and even during the American Civil War large numbers of soldiers suffered from its effects and were described as 'suffering from nostalgia' in the medical literature of the 1860s. But the rise of psychiatry and psychoanalysis at the end of the nineteenth century temporarily halted its medical credibility when European doctor after doctor – Charcot, Jaspers, Freud, Jung – debunked its status and claimed its symptoms were owing, instead, to forms of psychological melancholy that required treatment. By the time the Great War of 1914 erupted, few soldiers presenting with the same symptoms as Hofer's mercenaries were diagnosed as 'nostalgic'. These were some of the complex transitions I was aiming to document in my research.

Early in the twentieth century nostalgia faded from military domains and entered broad psychological realms often thought too amorphous to categorize: i. e., the politics of nostalgia, the collective nostalgic temperament, nostalgic desires for past times and past things, and – among geographically displaced persons – nostalgia as the longing for a lost physical homeland. Hofer's original *maladie du pays* became a *mal du siècle*: broadly asymptomatic but mentally incurable, transformed from defined space to indefinite time, and removed from an emotional state capable of description to yearning for the impossibility of mythical return. Even in its new, amorphous embodiments it was concurrently described as instilling tension in

With this caveat: Evelyn believed Rachmaninoff never recovered. This view inhered in her shorthand 'RR', the nostalgic riddle she identified. What she worked out for herself was that his 1900 recovery was fleeting, unlike his irrevocable escape from revolutionary Russia, but that the man who lived on for another three decades with the pain of memories he could not obliterate – memories so powerful they overcame him – was a chronic and lifelong nostalgic. It took me a decade to understand that this was the essence of her notes about 'RR'. Whether true or false I had to assess them, and that occupied another decade.

I studied the tall trunk's contents and melded it with the literature and biographical material about Rachmaninoff. Evelyn's files always

---

individuals and compelling them to lead parallel lives between real and imagined worlds; or, to exist in transitional psychological states between *real* presents and *imaginary* pasts. Russian poet Andrei Voznesenky wrote a poem about this tension entitled 'Nostalgia for the Present' ('Nostalgiya po nastoyashchemu').

In parallel, during the nineteenth century nostalgia had become a source of creative enrichment to writers and thinkers, from the French symbolists, Proust and Joyce forward, who constructed much of their oeuvre based on its enchantments, as in Proust's masterpiece, the *Remembrance of Things Past*. Nostalgia in this sense was positive, invigorating, even magical. The resonance nostalgic artists sensed could be energizing as well as thrilling, and exceeded the quest to reclaim enigmatic lost homes. Nostalgic moods provided imaginary windows into exotic realms and foreign places, and propelled many writers and artists, composers and painters, to explore unknown pasts. In this sense nostalgia extended Romanticism into a latter-day Modernism these artists often claimed to renounce. But the political realities of twentieth century life – war, nationalism, holocaust, dislocation, mass migration, genocide – also produced such large waves of displacement that new 'maladies of nostalgia' were engendered despite the lack of valid medical vocabulary to describe them. And they continue today, whether in the guises of any number of post-traumatic stress disorders, many also originating under conditions of war and displacement, or as suffered by asylum seekers who continue to weep with loneliness while they miss far-away families, as millions do today. It was this varied heritage of rugged nostalgia from Hofer to the present I was especially aiming to retrieve: such a large chunk of cultural and intellectual history that I found the task daunting, as my memoir explains. I was 'writing out' nostalgia because it occupied a universal place in human history and mattered both to human health over the ages and to the genesis of human creativity. Nostalgia is important because it can never be banished, not even from the healthiest human psyche.

proved to be touchstones for my understanding. For example, they contained dozens of clipped photographs of Rachmaninoff and reviews of his concerts. These were always the *public* face of the great pianist, who permitted few familiar, domestic photographs to be published showing him in private life. Evelyn's archive consisted of black and white photographs showing a sombre countenance unable to smile or laugh. The surviving images, like the one of him reading in a hammock in his garden in New Jersey, present him fully clothed in jacket and tie, as if about to perform at the keyboard. Evelyn became obsessed with these photographs of a 'cape-man' decked out in concert attire, like the famous one taken in New York during his first American concert tour. Her notebooks comment profusely on his black coat and its shiny satin lapels as 'his secret.' This was his legendary black cape, which he seems never to have doffed on the concert stage.

By 1995, six years after Evelyn's death, I began to construct parallel chronologies of their lives – Evelyn's and Rachmaninoff's – as a prelude to the task at hand. By recreating Evelyn's life I hoped to understand Richard's too, the friend I liked so much.

Besides, by 1995 I was a well-established academic historian who never proceeded without detailed chronologies and checklists. Everything had to be documented. So I started at the beginning and filled the gaps. I believed my readers – if I ever finished writing these parallel lives within the parallel universes of one woman's mind – would be grateful for whatever clarity I could bring.

I provide the parallel chronologies below: Evelyn's in regular font, Rachmaninoff's italicized.

CHRONOLOGIES

c 1870   Evelyn's paternal grandparents, the Abramovicis, born in
               Moldova

1892-93   Mihaela and Cezar Abramovici, Evelyn's parents, born

1873	*Rachmaninoff born in Novgorod, Russia; his best friend Chaliapin born three weeks earlier*
1876	*Prince Alexander Golitzyn born at Petrovskoe*
1877	*Cousin Natalia Satina, Rachmaninoff's wife, born[2]*
1879	*Cousin Sophia Satina born, Rachmaninoff's sister-in-law*
1881	*Nurse Olga Mordovskaya born at Petrovskoe*
1885	*Rachmaninoff moves into Nikolai Zverev's house; biographer Sergei Bertensson born in Russia, twelve years younger than Rachmaninoff*
1887-8	*Rachmaninoff distressed by piano teacher Zverev's attitudes*
1889	*Rachmaninoff leaves Zverev's house and moves to aunt Varvara Satina's large house in Moscow*
1890	*Rachmaninoff's flirtation with the Skalon sisters at Ivanovka*
1891	*Rachmaninoff composes furiously under the direction of Siloti and Tchaikovsky*
1892	*Rachmaninoff imagines himself in love with Natalia Skalon; Tchaikovsky pronounces Arensky and Rachmaninoff the two most promising composers in Moscow; his first melancholic bouts set in*
1893	*Zverev dies in January, Tchaikovsky in October, two events producing emotional turmoil in the young Rachmaninoff*
1894	*Twenty-one year old Rachmaninoff meets cellist Lodyzhensky's gypsy wife, Anna Alexandrovna*
1895	*Rachmaninoff in love with Anna, furiously composing and dedicating works to her*
1896	*Rachmaninoff dedicates The Crag to Anna*
1897	*Rachmaninoff's first symphony, dedicated to Anna, is premiered in Petersburg and savaged by the critics*
1898	*Rachmaninoff becoming emotionally ill; meets Chekhov*

---

[2] The family name was Anglicized as 'Satin' despite retention of their Russian patronymic as 'Satina'. I follow this designation throughout this book: i. e., the Satin family, Natalia Satina, Sophie Satina, etc.

1912	Evelyn's parents marry in Moldova where they were born
1912-3	Regional wars and famine compel the Abramovicis to migrate
1914	The Abramovicis arrive at Ellis Island, New York; their passports record their surname as Abrams
1914-18	the Abramses settle on Orchard Street on Manhattan's lower East Side, learn English, and adjust to America
1918	Evelyn born on Christmas Day, six weeks after the end of World War One
1921	Mihaela gives birth to a second child, Benjamin
1923	Evelyn enters Kindergarten on the East Side and commences piano lessons with Irene Bonamici, a neighbourhood teacher

Evelyn and Rachmaninoff

1897-1900	*Rachmaninoff intermittently depressed*
1899	*Rachmaninoff begins to write the Second Piano Concerto*
1900	*Rachmaninoff breaks down*
1900	*Rachmaninoff hypnotized by Dr Dal*
1901	*Rachmaninoff again working on his Second Piano Concerto[3]*
1902	*Rachmaninoff and cousin Natalia Satina married*
1903	*Rachmaninoff's first daughter Irina born, a sickly child*
1907	*Rachmaninoff's second daughter Tatania born in June*
1917	*Prince Alexander and Lyubov Golitzyn flee St Petersburg, travel eastwards towards Manchuria with Nurse Olga Mordovskaya, age thirty-six*
1922	*The Golitzyns migrate from Harbin to Seattle with Nurse Olga*
1924	*Irina Rachmaninoff marries Prince Wolkonsky*

---

[3] So much of *Rachmaninoff's Cape* aims to explain the creative and emotional investment Rachmaninoff placed in this work that I have set it off in upper cases – Second Piano Concerto – to distinguish it from his other piano concertos. His love affairs, emotional collapse, rehabilitation through hypnosis, and eventual completion of the concerto over the years 1899-1901 synthesized the romantic melancholy and temperamental nostalgia he brought to bear on this composition so formative in establishing – together with the *Prelude in C-sharp minor* – his fame as a composer.

1926	Cezar recruited to sell fur coats for Marc Kaufman Furs, Manhattan's oldest fur retailer
1927	Cezar begins to earn steep commissions selling furs to the rich
1927	Daisy Bernheim born on Elm Drive, Beverly Hills
1928	the Abramses move to Queens; Evelyn takes piano lessons with Mrs Honoré, makes remarkable progress
1930	Evelyn auditions for impresario Samuel Chotzinoff, is assigned to teacher, the young Adele Marcus, a Texan-American concert pianist
1934	Evelyn becoming a star pianist, studying at the Juilliard School; the Great American Depression reaching a nadir but Cezar growing rich
1935	Adele Marcus decrees Evelyn is headed for the concert stage
1937	Evelyn's concert debut planned at Manhattan's Town Hall
1938	Evelyn is twenty on Christmas Day
1939	Evelyn's debut on January 14 at age twenty-one
1940	fallout of Evelyn's failed debut concert, stops practicing, casting about; her grandparents die in Moldova
1941	Evelyn meets Sam Amster and soon marries him
1942	Richard Amster born on 22 November in Queens
1942	Daisy Bernheim hears stories about the famous pianist arriving on her street, watches the moving vans as they unload
1943	Richard Amster is one year old; Daisy Bernheim is sixteen when Rachmaninoff dies on 28 March

1925   *Prince Wolkonsky kills himself, age twenty-eight, weeks before their child is born; Rachmaninoff's granddaughter, Princess Sophia Petrovna Wolkonsky, daughter of the widowed Irina, is born*

1926-36 *The Rachmaninoffs live in five countries, build a summer house in Switzerland, and he tours the world giving concerts*

1939   *Rachmaninoff spends summers at his villa Senar on Lake Lucerne in Switzerland until war breaks out, then permanently moves to the USA*

1941   *Rachmaninoff moves to California and meets the Golitzyns, who are his own age, and Nurse Olga Mordovskaya*

1942   *Rachmaninoff moves to Tower Road, Beverly Hills in June and shortly afterwards to 610 North Elm Drive*

1942   *several of Rachmaninoff's friends die in August; Nurse Olga Mordovskaya, age sixty, moves to Elm Dr*

1943   *Rachmaninoff plays his last recitals in January-February, Nurse Olga Mordovskaya with him at his death on 28 March*

1944	Daisy remembers Natalia Satina selling her house, Rachmaninoff's pianos are moved out of the house
1948	Richard Amster begins to play the cello at six, guided by his mother, advances quickly, declared a musical prodigy
1949	George meets Richard at Chatham Square; the catastrophe over the cello
1950	Richard appears older than his eight years, diligently practices the cello
1952	Richard studies with Leonard Rose at Juilliard
1953	Evelyn notices Richard's first grey hair
1953-54	Richard's peak years playing the cello
1954	Richard's body physically altering, medically diagnosed
1955	Richard's first visit to Children's Hospital in Boston
1956	Richard in and out of hospitals
1957	Richard dies on November 23 at fifteen
1958	George leaves New York to attend Amherst College
1959	Sam Amster leaves Evelyn for Joyce; Evelyn alone in Queens
1959-67	Evelyn returns to playing the piano and reconnects with her earlier musical life
1960	Evelyn's obsession with Rachmaninoff crystallizes; she begins to read widely about his life and times, annotates Sergei Bertensson's biography, and fantasizes about Rachmaninoff's 'secret'
1963	Sam Amster dies in New York
1965	Cezar Abrams dies in New York
1967	Mihaela Abrams dies at seventy-six in New York
1968	Evelyn migrates to Beverly Hills in search of Rachmaninoff

1951 *Rachmaninoff's wife, Natalia Satina, dies of cardiac failure in Manhattan on 17 January*

1951 *Dr Golitzyn dies in Los Angeles (wife Lyubov died in 1948)*

1956 *Bertensson publishes his biography in English of Rachmaninoff*[4]

1961 *Tatania Rachmaninoff dies in July*

1962 *Sergei Bertensson dies in Los Angeles*

---

[4] This benchmark biography is by Sergei Bertensson and Jay Leyda, *Sergei Rachmaninoff: A Lifetime in Music* (Bloomington: Indiana University Press, 1956), and has not been superseded in almost sixty years despite the appearance of many look-alikes containing little new material or fresh insights. David Butler Cannata's introduction was added in 2001. All further references appear as 'See Bertensson'.

1968-89	Evelyn lives in California for two decades and compiles diaries
1973	Evelyn, now fifty-five, reads Victor Seroff's reissued biography of Rachmaninoff
1975	Evelyn, fifty-seven, meets Daisy Bernheim on Elm Dr, her own age, who tells her about a Russian nurse who attended to Rachmaninoff on his death bed
1978-80	Evelyn turns sixty, becomes obsessed with Rachmaninoff's ties to the 'old Russian nurse' mentioned by Daisy; starts to make notes and drafts her 'Nurse's Tale', moves from Beverly Hills into an apartment on the boardwalk in Venice Beach
1983	Evelyn is sixty-five ad compulsively drafting notes
1988	Evelyn is seventy and fading
1989	Evelyn is seventy-one, sends the tall trunk with notebooks to George in November just before her fatal heart attack over the Thanksgiving holiday
1989-92	George immersed in Evelyn's diaries for three years
1993	George awarded a three-year national grant to study the history of nostalgia
1994	George migrates from New York to London

Evelyn and Rachmaninoff

1968   *Rachmaninoff's granddaughter the Princess Sophia Petrovna Wolkonsky Wanamaker dies at forty-three in the Bahamas*

1969   *Sophia's mother Irina, Rachmaninoff's oldest daughter, dies within months of her daughter*

1975   *Rachmaninoff's sister-in-law Sophia Satina dies in New York at ninety-six*

EVELYN'S FATHER CHATZKEL WAS A ROMANIAN JEW whose family traded in furs and spruce woods in Upper Moldavia. These forests supplied wood to the great makers of German concert pianos – Blüthner, Beckstein, Steinway, and Bosendörfer – that made Romania rich. When 'Cezar' – as the family sentimentally called him – turned twenty, wars loomed in the surrounding Balkans, and his father, Yefim Abramovici, urged him to find a loyal girl and elope with her to America. Cezar quickly did. They arrived on Ellis Island in July 1914 shortly before the first gunshot was fired in Sarajevo, which killed Prince Ferdinand and sparked the largest European conflagration in memory. After that moment it would have been too late to flee the Balkan Wars, the result of Bulgarian collective madness to form an empire encircling the Aegean, and – now in 1914 – the larger pan-European menace.

The nickname 'Cezar' (indicating 'severed from others' in Romanian) described the fiery young furrier's temperament and self-reliant manner from youth, but he was christened 'Liviu': far indeed from Chatzkel, already an assimilated Yiddish form of the Hebrew Ezekiel, and now further transformed into the grandiose Cezar. He never spelled Cezar with an 's' and was no gypsy or charlatan; just the opposite – he was hard working if uneducated, and the bride he found was Mihaela, a Jewish tailor's daughter in nearby Barlat. Papa Yefim kissed his son's bride Mihaela, and pressed into her warm palm a grey velvet pouch full of gold coins after three days of farewell festivities; he wept, knowing he would never see them again. Grandmother Rahelusha stood ruefully inert at her son Yefim's side, weeping as the horse-driven wooden strap pulled out of the pebbled path. Their only grandson, courageous Cezar, was voyaging to the New World – sailing into the unknown.

Years later Mihaela remained tight-lipped about the ocean crossing, as if the subject was taboo. Evelyn later wondered if the prospect of crossing a European Sea and fierce Atlantic Ocean instilled in her mother some type of sleeping sickness. Only a year earlier the Titanic had sunk on the same crossing. Mihaela choked up as if retreating into amnesia – claimed to have forgotten the crossing; Evelyn speculated whether her mother had been so delirious with joy at both marriage and flight to freedom that she shrouded the memory of crossing the ocean as a deep secret in a silent box.

Mihaela vividly recalled the queues on Ellis Island and medical check-ups – she and Cezar were declared robustly healthy. This is what she understood the officer to say: 'robust health' meant 'good body.' Once on land, husband and wife used the silver chips the officers gave them to pay for a horse-driven strap, and found a single room on the ground floor of a tenement with dark staircases near Orchard Street on the East Side of Manhattan, the New World's largest ghetto of immigrant Jews. They had been filling up the vicinity since the 1890s, which looked like any Eastern Europe city with its ramshackle outdoor stalls and wooden stands. Vendors, stationary and mobile, pushed their wares in every language except English. There were small shops – tailors, groceries, hardware stores – and delicatessens emitting smells of 'hot dogs' (frankfurters) and 'latkos' (fried potato pancakes). The rows of brownstone houses had long since been vacated by the Manhattan rich, who migrated to the upper East and West side and to the country. By the 1890s these brownstones were being converted into dreary, walk-through tenement flats for the poor.

The newly named 'Abramses' opened their two trunks and set out to learn the basic words of English. They found a nearby Romanian pawnbroker who exchanged Yefim's gold pieces – and the velvet pouch too – for worn green dollar bills. Then they learned the names of nearby streets and shops. They were industrious and optimistic – and free: willing to work all hours of day and night to settle into this new homeland. But they possessed no knowledge, least of all the language of this new country, other than what Yefim had taught Cezar about furs and spruces.

Cezar said he would never have children until he found a job and could provide for Mihaela. A Hungarian in his tenement who liked him – an older immigrant from Timisoara – taught him to become an overnight tailor without speaking English. It was a sort of gypsy trick: you put out a small table and chair in front of the window, display scissors and a few roles of thread on the table, roll up the window shade, and magic! – people pass by, tap on the window, you wave beckoningly, you are a tailor.

Cezar stitched and sewed for a few months, and joked (*shatzped* and *kibbitzed*) with passing clients from whom he began to learn English, while affecting a dozen other languages. He spoke Greek to this customer, Italian to the next. Mihaela shopped, cooked, cleaned, and paid the next week's rent. She neatly folded the cash bills into an envelope and walked down to the manager's apartment. Managers collected weekly rent in fear that tenants might disappear overnight; there were no contracts or leases, just one week's advance rent.

One day a well-dressed middle-age man tapped on the window. He had heard about Cezar and needed a full-time tailor in his shop on Orchard Street, near Delancey Street. He could guarantee regular work and pay Cezar a dollar a day. He spoke fluent Romanian and told him he emigrated from Bucharest. This good luck seemed remarkable to Cezar and Mihaela – a Romanian boss – now they could have a baby without worrying about learning English or finding money. But Mihaela did not get pregnant. Was she too frightened of the new country? Cezar stroked her head, kissed her ears passionately, told her not to worry, and continued to upgrade his English from sounds to words, and into semi-grammatical sentences.

Five years later Evelyn was born on the first of May 1918: Evelyn Ruth Abrams. Evelyn for Mihaela's mother (she was Evelyn Adamescu in Barlat), Ruth for Cezar's grandmother Rahelusha, Abrams from Abramovici, a name Cezar took at Ellis Island when the officer persuaded him it was more 'American'. Two years later, early in 1920, Benjy was born. They seemed a happy little family growing up on New York's lower east side during the 1920s, moving from one tenement to a larger one, provided for by a dashing father who was prospering as a tailor and who now spoke minimal English and told jokes while he flirted with the neighbourhood women during those years of massive inflation.

Later Mihaela told her daughter that when she was five, in 1923, Evelyn asked her for piano lessons. Cezar was ecstatic: his beautiful, dark-eyed little girl would play the piano. Neither he nor Mihaela were musical, but Cezar's grandparents and cousins played the cimbalom and *doba*, a large double-headed drum, and danced to it on their farms outside Barlat. Thrifty Mihaela complied: she saved a quarter a week from her food allowance and located a dark brown upright piano for eight dollars around Evelyn's sixth birthday. Three burly men carried it up the stairs to their second-story apartment with two full bedrooms they now occupied. Cezar found Irene Bonamici to give his daughter weekly piano lessons; her Italian mother had tapped on the window and became one of his best customers. He spoke Italian to her and stroked her back.

Irene was about twenty and seemed a fully mature lady to little Evelyn. She wore thick lipstick and had developed breasts. She displayed lovely soft hands and an aquiline Italian nose that made her appear sublimely beautiful. Irene bought Evelyn a spiral notebook, and at each lesson wrote down the keys she should play and taught her to read notes.

Irene instructed Evelyn for one year, then relocated. Evelyn could date Irene's departure because shortly before she left, Evelyn's tonsils were removed in a Brooklyn hospital across the Williamsburg Bridge. Afterwards, the Abramses themselves moved from the East Side to Brooklyn. A few months later Mihaela took her daughter on the subway to a music school where Evelyn auditioned for a couple of ladies. They asked her to step outside the room, where Mihaela was waiting, and then one lady came out to tell mother and daughter that Evelyn was accepted as a student.

Evelyn's new teacher was Mrs Honoré, a thin, tallish lady who spoke English with a thick French accent Evelyn could not understand. Each week Mihaela brought her daughter on the same subway from Flatbush, where they had moved, to this music school on Atlantic Avenue. Evelyn nagged to come alone but Mihaela refused. The trolley car whizzed down Ocean Avenue past Prospect Park, then slid down Flatbush Avenue to the music school; a low, dilapidated grey building with aseptic smells inside. Mrs Honoré was less personable than Irene; wrote in no notebooks. She opened the sheet music to the page where Evelyn was supposed to play and listened; then she said things Evelyn could not understand and the lesson was finished. She assigned Evelyn little preludes and fugues by Bach, and only lit up when giving her Debussy's music for children – then her eyes shimmered, like twinkling stars, and she became funny and very French.

Cezar announced another move, this time to Queens. He had been recruited to work for a company in Astoria that supplied hand-tailored furs to the finest shops in Manhattan. The boss – a fellow Romanian Jew named Moshe – hired him. They catered to rich clients and required his expertise. Someone who could cut mink into perfect slices of 7 millimeters, or about a quarter of an inch thick, then use the most up-to-date sewing machines of the 1920s to create a checkerboard of diamond and micro-chevron patterns.

'European wisdom', Mihaela called it, slowly, in porridge-thick pronunciation, recently having learned more English and shaking her head up and down in approbation that her husband had finally been recognized. She continued to babble on to Evelyn what a gruelling process it was.

'Your father has patience and a very steady hand,' she said.

Moshe turned out not to be the boss but the import manager. He and Cezar often spoke about the pelts of fox and minx Cezar had seen as a boy in Romania.

Then Cezar found a one-bedroom apartment in Jackson Heights, a small commute to his warehouse on the overland train (the underground subway within Queens opened later than 1928). Mihaela said it was too far to travel weekly to Atlantic Avenue for piano lessons. Evelyn protested – she would go alone. Cezar took his daughter's part: he would take Evelyn on Saturdays, his day off. So, lessons with Mrs Honoré moved to Saturday mornings, in a weekly trek Evelyn loved. Daddy and daughter together on the overland line, laden down with sandwiches and pickles, changing twice – on Grand Street and Fulton Street – in a two-hour journey. 'Four hours', Mihaela shrieked, when she heard the first time. 'No, Evelyn, we will find you another piano teacher.'

'YOU KNOW VITA ON THE FIRST FLOOR,' Mihaela thumped to Evelyn before they moved out of Flatbush, as if a paid actress at the Delancey Street Vaudeville, 'her husband has left her. She has no money. What will she do? Her son Murray will starve. *We* have landed on our feet. *Cezar* is such a good man.'

Vita was considerate and spoke dainty English; Murray was three years younger than Evelyn. Once, when he was six and his cheeks blushed, Murray kissed Evelyn. But Josephine, who lived in the next apartment, a strange older woman with a thick German accent who wore darkly coloured dresses and stilettos, objected. She had no children of her own, and told Mihaela Murray was 'sick.' 'Did he also touch her breasts?' Josephine demanded. Evelyn avoided her because Josephine had complained that her piano practicing was a nuisance, that Evelyn was a 'p-p-pest.'

'What will the new place be like?' Evelyn asked Mihaela.

'It has two bedrooms and is on the second floor. You will have your own room in Jackson Heights – Benjy can sleep with us.'

'Will the upright piano come with us?'

'Silly, silly', Mihaela coyly replied, 'of course the piano will come with us.'

Jackson Heights seemed far away to Evelyn. The piano was transported with the sofa and two armchairs, and Evelyn's room was so large it could have accommodated a much bigger piano. Evelyn at ten basked in the glory of her new sanctuary. Her mother installed thin, white, lace curtains and a cot. Evelyn found a flower vase and cut dandelions from the small green patch near the basement entrance. She walked to school, PS 69 on 37th Avenue, and rushed home to practice for her Saturday lesson. Mrs Honoré required her to practice two hours each day, loading her up with ever more Bach and Debussy – until suddenly, out of nowhere, Honoré proclaimed that Evelyn must audition for another teacher, 'a pianist of note'.

Mihaela rejoiced: 'our Evelyn becomes a celebrity, like her father.' Max, Mihaela's younger brother who had by now, in 1928, migrated to America with his wife, Adriana, and whose English was non-existent, chimed in that Chanukah: 'Evelyn, booboola, you're gonna make your mama so happy some day.'

Evelyn was a smart girl also learning academic subjects in school – reading, writing, arithmetic, geography, history – but she wasn't sure what lay in store. Nothing new occurred for three months, except the doubling of trips to Atlantic Avenue. Mihaela left Benjy with Vita and took Evelyn to the Wednesday lesson; Cezar kept to their Saturday expeditions. Then Mrs Honoré announced an 'audition' would take place in a fancy suite in Manhattan.

Mihaela and Cezar accompanied her. But nerves overtook Evelyn who grew frightened while the lift climbed, seemingly without end. It stopped on the top floor, where a tall woman in a red suit awaited them. 'Was this lady the pianist of note,' Evelyn wondered? The tall woman ushered them to an expansive room with high windows overlooking Manhattan. A youngish woman with wavy black hair and soft brown eyes was reclining on the sofa.

'This is Adele Marcus', the tall lady said, 'one of the judges'.[5] Adele smiled, and Evelyn noticed her butter-thick lipstick. 'She wants to hear you play. Do, please, all sit down.' And with this, she left the room.

---

[5] Adele Marcus (1906-95) became one of the star teachers at the Juilliard School of Music after the Second World War and one of America's most renowned coaches of young pianists. Her ferocity towards female students was legendary and the pianists she produced almost all male. Two years before Evelyn auditioned for her Marcus had played a concerto with the Juilliard School orchestra. She was then only twenty-two, pretty, and curvaceous, and the men on the faculty relished her. A much later photograph of her of the 1950s still reveals her physical difference from the other, much older and less prepossessing, women on the faculty: Rosina Lhevine, Olga Samaroff, and Ilana Kabos; see Andrea Olmstead, *Juilliard: a History* (Urbana: University of Illinois Press, 1999), p. 97. Marcus formally joined the Faculty of the Institute of Musical Arts (as Juilliard was then known) in 1936, five years after it moved to its new building at 130 Claremont Avenue, at 122nd St. in Manhattan, where Evelyn would take lessons. Before 1936 Marcus gave lessons there privately. The young Evelyn learned that her teacher was more successful with male students than female for reasons that remain unclear. Marcus' pedagogical views are explained in Adele Marcus, *Great Pianists Speak with Adele Marcus* (New York: Paganiniana, T.F.H. Publications, 1979). A large literature exists about Marcus' cruelty to female students, perhaps none more eloquent than music commentator Greg Benko's revelation about a young female prodigy who was *not* Evelyn: 'About Adele Marcus – in the 1960s I knew a prodigy "piano valkyrie" who seemed to me to have the talent to turn into a new Teresa Carreño. Her well-

Before anyone could move, Adele began to talk to the Abramses in a sincere manner that did not exclude Evelyn. She explained that her performing schedule allowed her to teach very few students – she was often away from Manhattan. But she was persuaded that if the most gifted students could be identified early, they could learn to play well – this was why she was devoting herself now to teaching the young, and if her itinerary let up she would only teach children under twelve.

The Abramses were bowled over by this magnanimity, their chins nodding to each other as if acknowledging how wrong they were to think their daughter would be summoned to the piano without further ado; and even more impressed when this affectionate Adele – who had sized them up from their accents and appearances – continued to talk about herself. How she was the thirteenth and last child of Jewish-Russian immigrants who settled in Kansas City at the turn of the century, began to play the piano at four and soon found herself studying with acclaimed pianists – Artur Schnabel and Joseph Lhévinne, how she had moved to Manhattan in 1929 after winning a big piano award whose prize was a recital in Manhattan's Town Hall, her debut concert.

Mihaela and Cezar took all this in as if they must remember a *Who's Who* biography – but Evelyn sat nervously in awe of the great lady: so charming, so polished, so restrained. She had never met anyone so captivating, certainly not Irene or Mrs Honoré. 'Would you

---

meaning but misguided parents put complete trust in Juilliard and Adele Marcus – a huge mistake. The psychological abuse heaped on this girl by Marcus was more than she could bear, and she ended up in an institution. In the very hour before her graduation recital Marcus was a virago, screaming at her that she was worthless and presumptuous to suppose she was ready for the appearance … in so vicious and intense a manner that the poor girl had a breakdown and did not play the recital – or ever again anywhere. I suppose the intent of Marcus's tirade was to produce the opposite effect.' See http://www.artsjournal.com/slippeddisc/2013/02/when-curtis-was-known-as-the-coitus-institute.html, citing an article by Robert Fitzpatrick on the abuse of students by famous piano teachers at Juilliard and Curtis (accessed 13 March 2013). I am grateful to Dean Elder, former editor of *Clavier Magazine*, for verifying that Evelyn Amster's name is absent in the list of formally matriculated students at Juilliard during the 1930s and 40s.

like to play something?' Adele asked, as if the answer could go either way. Evelyn arose, walked on the thick purple carpet to the large, shiny, ebony grand piano with enormous belly, its cathedral lid already lifted, embossed in gold with the word 'STEINWAY' on its belly-side. She began to play Bach.

When she finished Adele asked her if she had anything else prepared. 'A Schubert impromptu and Chopin waltz,' Evelyn replied, and played them too, without anyone flicking an eyelid. Adele thanked her when she finished and asked her to step out of the room. She explained to the Abramses that their daughter was hugely talented; but she had not been well taught and it would be expensive to undo her bad habits. Would Evelyn make the commitment to practice three – four, five, six – hours a day?

Mihaela's inner voice sounded alarm bells about this 'commitment's cost;' while Cezar already imagined *his daughter* as a great pianist. A glamorous and commanding woman of twenty-five – his imagination soared – her long red-blonde hair flowing, her face illuminated under spotlights, her magical fingers playing to packed houses. He could mind-read Mihaela's money angst, which washed off his back: he would turn up the charm and sell more furs to his socialites.

'Think about my proposal,' Adele stated matter-of-factly. She could not give Evelyn more than one lesson a month, but would make provision with another teacher in Manhattan, described as an 'assistant', who would teach Evelyn at least twice a week. 'Think about it for a few weeks', she said as she gave them a purple card, and then write to me care of my concert management with your answer.'

They 'thought' profusely and consulted each other on the train back to Jackson Heights. '*You* might become one of *them*,' Cezar merrily quipped to Evelyn, seemingly having made his decision before Evelyn finished her sentence, while simultaneously studying the other passengers to ascertain whether they understood the significance of what had transpired today.

Who was *them?* – not the subway riders. 'That woman speaks like a go-ddess,' he said, weighing down on the d's, his vocabulary now expanded despite the flawed diction.

'She speaks so little,' he continued in awe. 'Her words are few, she says only what is *important.*'

As Cezar pontificated Evelyn stared into space, as if conversing with denizens of the unknown. Mihaela wasn't listening: she tossed her head sideways, quietly back and forth, away from her family, and pressed her nose to the cold window-pane, quietly dreaming that her daughter had been singled out for greatness. The cap of her nose was piqued by the pane's temperature. The two Abrams parents were confused and excited.

'You can ride up yourself,' Cezar said, looking in Evelyn's direction. 'You already take subways alone.'

But Mihaela sensed that Adele's proposition was larger than anything they had faced.

'It is a giant leap step,' she announced.

Inside, Evelyn stirred – all this talk augured an adventure she could not imagine avoiding, nor was she frightened at the prospect of tutelage.

They debated for two weeks and eventually wrote affirmatively. They sent drafts to Vita Attie, who turned them into grammatical English:

> 'November 10, 1930
>
> Dear Miss Marcus
>
> We would be honoured if Evelyn could study with such a distinguished teacher like you. Evelyn can also attend the lessons with your assistant. We are able to pay thirty dollars a month for the combined lessons. Do you think this amount will be sufficient?
>
> We are very grateful to you for your interest in our Evelyn.
>
> Very truly yours,
>
> Cezar Abrams

The first lesson was arranged for early January. Mihaela alerted Vita who replied with a terse sentence on a yellow three-cent postcard: 'Interviews, reporters, commissions, your darling Evelyn will be famous, Mazeltov', the words in red pen surrounded by hearts and kisses.

'We will not move again,' Cezar thumped, repeatedly supporting the idea that Evelyn could take the subway by herself to Manhattan.

'She's *Jewish*', Mihaela bleated in full-throated assurance.

Adele's religion was the last thing on Evelyn's mind, who did not even know what kind of Jew she herself was.

'A woman named Marcus,' Mihaela rolled the 'a's' in Maarrcus, 'must be Jewish.'

The lessons were not held in the skyscraper but in a small studio room on East 56th Street containing a grand piano and two identical wooden chairs with tiered backs. Adele was a born pedagogue who moved slowly, first gaining the trust of her charge, and then laying down the law that the acquisition of technique was a serious, lifelong endeavour. The lessons cost five times Mrs Honoré's fee but Cezar gracefully paid it, and Evelyn concocted the idea that she herself could take a few students aged seven to ten to contribute – 'kids in the neighbourhood,' Mihaela said cunningly, 'who cannot find piano teachers.' Mother and daughter were in banded league over this plan.

By the second year Evelyn was teaching a few kids for thirty cents a lesson. All went well until Gloria, eight years old, told her mother Evelyn bit her. Mother and daughter confronted Mihaela with the evidence: a red mark on the meaty side of the girl's palm. Mihaela was horrified to think her thirteen-year old Evelyn would commit such a crime. Evelyn did not cry but felt cheapened; ashamed in her own uncertainty whether or not she bit. She was learning to be a severer taskmaster than Adele.

But calm ensued. Evelyn learned what Adele wanted and produced it: technical mastery delivered in driblets. Adele taught her what a melody was and how to phrase it; how to differentiate any number of different crescendos and diminuendos; how you established a tempo and kept it, or lost it at your peril. To deliver these goods she practiced hours every day – did little else than attend school. She also became inward looking, just when a pubescent fourteen year old might display opposite traits.

Adele now mattered to her more than anyone: trying to please her, which she rarely felt she did, learning from her, being praised. Her high-school work did not suffer despite ever more piano practice. Her interior life, pervaded by Adele's commandments, which were being built on the type of trust only masterful teachers can forge in their students, was also growing.

Yet Mihaela worried that her daughter was changing out of recognition. 'Evelyn,' she said, 'let's talk as mother and daughter; what's the matter darling? You play so beautifully. ... that Chopin waltz. Is something wrong?'

'No, no, mama, everything is fine, I just wish I could please Adele more.'

'Then something is wrong with *Adele*. Listen, my darling, to how much better you play now than with Mrs Honoré. I wish we had a recording machine so you could hear,' thinking at the back of her mind she would never mention one to Cezar lest he try to buy one.

'It's ok, mama, really. My body is changing ... this has nothing to do with Adele. Adele is fine.'

Evelyn persuaded Mihaela but not herself. She did play better now – she knew that – her hands were growing, her fingers too; her technique becoming more secure, she could play faster and louder, and softer too. But could she cut the ice? – this predicament stymied her. Could she master ever-more difficult piano compositions the way Adele's older, more proficient students did?

She tried not to fret too much – worrying proved counterproductive. By keeping her nose to the grindstone she progressed from strength to strength with Adele, practiced more and more: Bach, Beethoven, Schubert, Chopin. Her descending scales, ascending thirds, and octaves grew firmer and she awaited the day when Adele would assign her Chopin études similarly to the girl (Marcia Schwartz, from Brooklyn) whose lesson was always before hers.

BEFORE CARRYING ON WITH EVELYN'S TUTELAGE I must explain why all this mattered to me; not merely because Evelyn had saved me from a catastrophe when I was eight, but because my own early life paralleled hers despite having been born a generation later, by which time Evelyn Abrams (née Abramovici) and Sam Amster married.

I was born in 1941 in a tenement house in Brooklyn to the children of Jewish Sephardic Turkish immigrants. My mother told me that at three I begged for pads to write in, and at four, a piano to play. They had no money for pianos during those post-war years. But my mother, like Mihaela, skimped on her weekly food allowance, and saved up twenty dollars. For my fifth birthday she bought me a battered upright piano. I was in heaven: clinking its faded ivories and scribbling in my penny pads. She found me a local piano teacher and before I finished the first decade of life I could really play. Soon afterwards I was 'discovered' and on my way to becoming a child prodigy, not so differently from Evelyn.

Nor from my Sephardic Jewish cousins, some close, others distant, especially the Sedakas (Neil Sedaka) and Perahias (Murray Perahia). The original Sephardic immigrants who came to Ellis Island from Turkey around 1900 knew little about classical music. They intermarried, spoke Ladino (Judeo-Spanish) at home, and rejoiced at their good fortune in having arrived in America. Their children grew up in the first half of the century with the sound of music in their ears: jazz, blues, gospel, country, pop, even classical. It was their children – the generation of Neil Sedaka, Murray Perahia, Richard Amster, myself – who were disproportionately invested in music for reasons that have never been adequately explored.

During the 1930s, the visionary impresario Samuel Chotzinoff ('Chotzi') founded a settlement house for gifted children on New York's East Side, the school Evelyn attended before me. Chotzi was a genius: could play the piano as exquisitely as he could court the great and good, identify talent in unlikely quarters, entice parents to dedicate their lives to their talented children, and fundraise too.[6] But big-time funding was hard to come by during the Great Depression, and wartime deflected it further, so Chotzi's school did not formally open its doors until 1946. The Chatham Square Music School looked like any other neglected tenement house on the north side of Clinton Street, between Houston and Delancey, close to the Abramses' first dilapidated apartment on Orchard Street. When students emerged from its front steps and walked on the pavement down Clinton Street towards Delancey Street, they found themselves at a broad junction of crumbling tenements and the first cable anchors of the Williamsburg Bridge, the world's longest suspension bridge, today leading to some of Brooklyn's most gentrified property.

I soon learned to know every step of this *via romana* delivering me to the BMT subway back to Brooklyn. On Saturdays the streets were

---

[6] Chotzinoff (1889-1964), a near contemporary of Rachmaninoff, was also born in Russia and migrated to New York at seventeen, in 1906, the year of Adele Marcus' birth. His musical talent declared itself early, and by his early twenties he was concertizing with eminent violinists, including the formidable Jascha Heifitz, whose sister Pauline he married. Chotzinoff also wrote fluently: a double flair that gained him an undergraduate scholarship to Columbia University where he learned to write critically and studied music theory and history. Columbia, then an all-male ivy-league university, also brought him into contact with the sons of New York's elite and introduced him to the ways of the City's power brokers, this in a decade (the 1920s) when most sons of immigrant Jews were not being admitted there and instead attended the public university across town in Harlem. By the mid 1920s Chotzinoff had become the music editor of New York's leading magazine, and used his influence in its offices to meet everyone connected to the classical musical world. In 1936, when he became NBC's director of music, he had established himself as one of America's leading arts presences. At NBC he and conductor Arturo Toscanini collaborated throughout the war years, and Chotzinoff wrote the conductor's first full-length life: *Toscanini: an intimate portrait* (1956), then widely reviewed as offering a controversial portrait but nevertheless agreed to be the most informative biography there could be. Chotzinoff was the Prime Mover in the discovery of many young American Jewish concert artists (such as child prodigy pianist Byron Yankilevich whom he discovered, refashioned as 'Byron Janis', and sent to be trained by Adele Marcus). Chotzinoff wrote several memoirs of his life in music, including *A Lost Paradise: Early Reminiscences* (1956) describing his early days in Russia as the son of a Russian rabbi, and *Day's at the Morn* (1956) recollecting his association with dozens of leading musicians, including Sergei Rachmaninoff.

always filled with local 'New Yorkers' of every description, old, young, and mostly foreign; hole-in-the-wall shops the size of a closet and just as dark, brimming with ethnic foods and second-hand clothing; ubiquitous motley sights and pungent smells more reminiscent of Hogarthian scenes in cacophonous eighteenth-century London than post-war urban America. My admission to Chatham, like Evelyn's earlier, came by auditioning for the 'impresario' – 'Chotzi' – who was short and slender, dressed on that day in a pinstriped suit. But I was only ten and to me he seemed Zeus-like; from another planet while I played for him, as he frantically lurched around the room blinking his eyes. This was on a high floor of the newly opened Rockefeller Centre. I had never seen anyone squint so unabashedly or thrash about so nervously. He introduced himself as 'Samuel Chotzinoff', pointed to the lanky woman in a daisy blouse whom he introduced as Caroline Fischer, his assistant. She towered over him and held a yellow pad, ready to take notes. Chotzi asked me a few questions and then jerkily pointed to the piano. I remember tip-toeing to the Steinway and confidently playing Haydn, especially the grace notes.

After my audition I was admitted. To enter the post-war Chatham Square you walked up five stone steps, opened double doors, entered into a small foyer with an office on the left occupied by the tall lady with the yellow pad at the audition. Behind Caroline Fischer's office was a vast room that must have been some socialite's reception room in Edith Wharton's day; now it was the concert room for student and teacher recitals. Upstairs were teaching rooms, on two floors, each containing a grand piano, capped by two further floors composed of very small cupboard-sized rooms where students practiced on upright pianos – perhaps servant's quarters of old.

Vera Maurina Press – 'Madame Press' – was almost indescribable. More than the legendary pedagogue, as I later discovered (Madame Press was not yet there during Evelyn's time), and a native Russian who had been a pupil of the great Ferruccio Busoni. Press studied with him in St Petersburg, then followed him to Berlin when he migrated. The American composer Morton Feldman, who was born a few years after Evelyn and raised in Brooklyn, like me, became Press's student around the time I did, and when Madame Press died in 1970 at ninety, he wrote a eulogistic ensemble for winds in her memory called *Madame Press Died Last Week at Ninety* – and notable American opera composer John Adams still professes to love to conduct it. According to Feldman, Madame Press instilled in him a 'vibrant musicality rather than musicianship.' Feldman was a young man of fourteen when his father, a Jewish immigrant from Kiev who manufactured children's coats, in contrast to Cezar's expensive furs, took him to hear Evelyn's debut at Town Hall, as we shall see, in 1939. But this advances Evelyn's story too quickly.

Flash forward to 1949, about six months before the catastrophe with the cello, and my own mother is nicknaming Madame Press 'the Ancient Vault of Horror' after hearing my weekly accounts of lessons with her. To me Press looked a century old, had white stringy hair that appeared artificially curled, a long, aquiline pasted-on nose, long gaunt fingers that presaged death, and spoke slowly in a raspy voice compelling the listener to imagine the speaker as some remote ghoul. Madame Press was worlds apart from Mrs Honoré: never praised me or smiled. At the second lesson she said I held my hands incorrectly and lurched out with her own right hand to demonstrate. It was ice-cold with large blue veins, a cadaver grabbing my young pudgy one. Press then withdrew, as if reconsidering a slap. She placed a penny on each finger to prevent the wrist from moving when playing, groaning that I would never play well until the pennies were stationary. If they fell off, she threatened to wrap my fingers in bandages as further tests.

Madame Press took me – then a twelve-year old boy – 'off Debussy' (as if the Frenchman were a drug) and set me on a stiff regimen of Bach, Beethoven and Chopin: the *Two-Part Inventions*, an early Beethoven sonata, Chopin preludes. Nothing I did pleased her: everything was wrong, my tones, my rhythm, my dynamics. Either I moved my wrist and the penny fell off, or I played a wrong note or phrased it grotesquely. The 'Vault of Horror' was outraged.

How could I not remember this musical past in my later friendship with Evelyn? I recounted those lessons to her many times in subsequent years, saying how much I wondered whether Press' Russian origins – that inimitable accent and those indescribable fingers – left an indelible impression on me: the wish never to play Russian piano music. And Evelyn sweetly recounted her lessons with 'Adele' and her crazed obsession with Rachmaninoff.

But now flash back to the 1930s, when Evelyn has been admitted to Chotzinoff's pre-formed school and is studying with Adele Marcus. Teacher and student are getting on famously, and Evelyn has been told she is ready to audition for a new radio program. The judges are two great pianists: Joseph Lhévinne and Artur Rubenstein who was then living in Manhattan. Evelyn played six Chopin preludes and is selected as a winner. But she is also a fourteen-year-old girl whose 'life' was on the East Side. She went alone, early, every Saturday morning, for her lesson with Miss Marcus and grew accustomed to turning on the attentiveness at the stroke of the hour. She ate her sandwich with other students who had come for their lessons, attended the required classes in solfeggio, accompanying, music theory and chamber music. She was developing a routine to last a lifetime – and a work ethic that no minute should be empty.

Beethoven sealed Evelyn's fate one Saturday morning in October 1934 when a violinist and cellist – both girls – joined her to play one of Beethoven's early piano trios with the chamber music coach. It was their first time playing together with this coach and she could not remember his German-sounding name – something like 'Mossback' or 'Mossbacker'. He sat imperiously on a green sofa and commanded the three girls to start, yet no sooner had they begun than he laced into Evelyn: 'You do not keep the tempo, my dear;' 'you play too much fortissimo;' 'less pedal;' 'your left hand must be strictly in time with the cello.'

Evelyn wasn't sure whether these were his exact words, for he grumbled and moaned in what seemed a distant wail: his English was of another epoch, his pitch at a level she had never before heard. Evelyn was already formed into a poised adolescent but held back the tears, no less than water ready to burst from its sluice-dam. By the time the wooden clock on the coach's mantel struck the hour and they were dismissed, they had only played the opening measures of Beethoven's trio.

Evelyn ran to the upstairs lavatory, locked the door, and poured out vomit, then tears and sobs. No one heard. She clutched her head in her hands to cover up, grabbed her coat in the lobby and took the subway back to Queens. Mihaela suspected something – Evelyn never returned so early on Saturday afternoons. Mihaela sat silently for a few minutes on the living-room sofa, marched up to Cezar, who was tallying accounts on the kitchen table, and quietly demanded a family conference of three at which Evelyn would be compelled to recount what had occurred. Cezar's view was that she must remain at Chatham Square but her chamber-music teacher must be changed. Mihaela deferred to Cezar, who said they should do nothing until they pondered the consequences.

They followed his precept but the outcome was decided, anyway, at the annual June school concert, Evelyn's third. She played all twenty-four Chopin preludes by heart. Afterwards, there was loud applause and congratulation. Even Adele congratulated her, and Cezar and Mihaela sent her a large bouquet of flowers delivered to the stage by the string-bean Caroline who gave her an icy-stiff kiss. Chotzinoff, always holding court at these annual events, came over and said he wanted to speak with her – soon.

On the day a few weeks later, enshrined in an appointment, he met Evelyn in the downstairs auditorium and asked her to play one of the preludes. His assistant Caroline was not present. Then he showed her a few tricks to play the prelude better. He even called them 'tricks': 'did you realize,' he asked, both eyes squinting, 'that you could reach the same goal more easily by doing it this way?'

He talked and summoned Evelyn to speak freely: 'how do you think you're getting on?' he blinked continuously, his roaming eyes seeming to do the speaking.

'You played remarkably that night,' he said.

Evelyn thanked him and wondered about his drift.

'Miss Marcus,' he said, 'will soon be leaving Chatham Square and moving to the Juilliard School.'

Evelyn was astounded.

'She would like to take you with her.'

Evelyn remained silent.

'If you agree, I will send your parents a letter indicating your lessons will start in about a month. We will try to find a scholarship for you. Despite any scholarship at Juilliard, your lessons would be private and cost twenty dollars each.'

MIHAELA CONSIDERED THE SUM OUTRAGEOUS but Cezar vowed to find eighty dollars a month, then a fortune. The Great American Depression had gripped New York's boroughs, droves of workers were unemployed, yet Cezar was prospering in the fur trade, still selling to rich people. Evelyn had seen mature men wheeling pushcarts with just a few wan looking apples and yellowing oranges around Chatham Square. None of the family's friends in Queens had lost their jobs but Mihaela was constantly lamenting they would. She even wondered if they would be transported back to Europe.

But something changed when she left Clinton Street: Evelyn's lessons with Adele at Juilliard took on a different hue. Adele was the same Adele; the same Texan-American who had lost all traces of any deep Jewish-American drawl, if she ever possessed them; young, modestly dressed, always in bright lipstick, straightforward, already displaying signs of the great pedagogue she would become after the War. Adele laughed and was quick-minded. What contrast there was, Evelyn thought, between her direct approach and Madame Honoré's Debussyian softness. The lithe French lady was restrained and undemanding – charitable and always yielding; Adele was firm and tough without *double entendre*: she meant what she said and the consequences for failure were spelled-out.

As time passed Adele's demands seemed Olympian to Evelyn despite her teacher clearly explaining them: just how many hours Evelyn should practice, how and what she should practice, expectations for her progress and what this trial period of six months amounted to – the 'trial period' Chotzinoff had mentioned which Evelyn tried to forget. Some of Adele's students vilified her while worshipping her teaching. Marcia Heller, another of her students, a year or two younger than Evelyn, shockingly claimed that Adele struck her once and gave her a black eye, a rumor based on gossip, surely, Cezar scoffed, if ever there was one. 'If she ever hits my daughter…' Mihaela warned, shaking her finger in Cezar's face. But Adele never did, and probably not Marcia either. But dissent was percolating between teacher and student.

Still ecstatic that she was at Juilliard Evelyn forgot the 'trial period'; that it would make or break her, nonetheless Adele laid out the plan: Evelyn had six months to prove herself and Adele was under no obligation to retain her if Evelyn failed to measure up. Chotzinoff was out of the picture now, except that he would take some of the 'credit' if Evelyn became a 'star.'

Evelyn worked herself to the bone towards stardom: Chopin, Chopin, and Chopin – the twenty-four études for four, five, six hours a day. Adele assigned little Bach or Mozart; a few Beethoven sonatas were *de rigueur*, as were pieces by Schubert and Schumann. Adele's students gossiped with each other, compared their lessons and experiences, but some students – Evelyn recorded in her diaries – were devious: they told her 'something' to elicit further information. A question such as which études Adele assigned was a ruse to discover how fast you yourself – the *other* student – were advancing. Another asked how many pieces she had memorized, intended to ferret out whether Adele was grooming her for a concert. Evelyn sensed herself being transformed into a 'competitive pagan', the odd phrase she recorded in her diary.

During the spring seasons (when competitions were held) the pressure became unbearable: unrelenting comparisons of repertoires and a who's who of grooming for auditions, rumours about so-and-so getting ahead and who not. Evelyn realized she was in the midst of a competition mill from which no one could escape – except that she was uneasy. She could not articulate her anti-competitive streak to herself but intuited it and accordingly avoided its participants. A few students shunned her as useless. Evelyn did not mind – she just wanted to practice and be alone.

Mihaela and Cezar proved themselves wonderfully supportive throughout this phase and lost no opportunity to encourage their daughter. She spent less and less time on her academic homework.

When the six-month date arrived only Adele listened. Evelyn played reasonably well, by memory and trying to please Adele in her interpretation of every passage and phrase. Adele told her she passed, 'you are seventeen and must win competitions, I will expect you to give a debut concert within a year or two, if you are ready.'

The competitions, Adele said, were similar to auditioning for American radio station WQXR specializing in classical music. You worked up repertories of solo piano and concerto music, came before the judges, and played the parts they wanted to hear. Nerves ruled the day: if you were calm and controlled your mind you could play well; but sometimes your nerves ruled you and your physiology was out of control. Evelyn followed her orders. She won some and lost others. The prizes were little performances here and there – nothing fantastic; just further habituation for the big debut concert Adele mentioned at most lessons.

Evelyn's 'honeymoon' with Adele endured for almost five years. It was late in 1936 – I learned much later from Evelyn's diaries – when Evelyn, having turned eighteen, had her first big blow-out with her teacher. By now she 'loved Adele', as she told her friends and wrote in her notebook, and she felt secure enough to speak her mind to her. Small tiffs had occurred before this one over repertoire and technique, especially Adele's concentration on the way Evelyn held her hands, but this new impasse over the timing of a debut recital for Evelyn was insurmountable. Evelyn thought Adele's recent aloofness precipitated it, but it was based on something else.

Adele had missed a few lessons, said she was concertizing, had become less charitable, spoke more sharply now – 'Nothing I show you can diminish those unnecessary movements' – and once she almost struck her: a gentle slap on the hand making the point about unnecessary motions over which Evelyn seemed to have no control.

Actually Evelyn did not understand the criticism. She moved as little as possible, consciously kept her digital motions to a minimum, but apparently 'movements' occurred beyond her awareness. She even tried to explain the 'unnecessary motions' to Cezar, who was baffled by what she meant. Then Evelyn resolved to renounce them but to no avail, and now this deadlock developing over repertoire.

In fact there were *two* deadlocks: one about the debut, another about repertoire. Adele warned her students not to push for debut recitals until they were ready. 'It's one thing to launch a ship, another to make it sail.' It would be counterproductive, a waste of time and money, she admonished, if the career were not yet capable of taking off. But Cezar saved up a thousand dollars and was nudging his 'celebrity daughter'. Evelyn herself thought the time ripe but could not say why. It would coincide with her twenty-first year; besides, she thought she played as well as Adele's other students. But Adele wanted her to perform composers Evelyn could technically master – Haydn, Beethoven, Schubert – while Evelyn wanted Chopin, Schumann, and especially Rachmaninoff. They reached a compromise of sorts, except for Rachmaninoff, who proved a thorn ripping apart any ententes they periodically reached.

The disagreement over Rachmaninoff festered and brought out the worst in Evelyn. Not that she didn't respect Adele Marcus' views – she did, but because something stirred inside Evelyn when she played Rachmaninoff's piano music. His piano works were difficult, mature, required large hands, but some force welled up in her; adults played it, the 'big names' played it: by scaling its heights, she might become one of *them*. Her reasons were sufficiently egotistical to border on absurdity and had little to do with Rachmaninoff's emotional language. Evelyn was a talented girl: inherently generous and growing up with many types of contradictions; even so, unaware his music was penetrating to her core. Her inner voices, those of a young woman raised as daddy's girl, clamoured in contradictory directions, Rachmaninoff their common springboard, such as:

> 'Rachmaninoff is the most difficult composer – the students who win competitions all play his music'.

> 'Playing Rachmaninoff's piano music is proof that you have reached the pinnacle. Anyone can play Bach and Mozart'.

> 'Rachmaninoff's music captures emotions no other composer does'.

'Rachmaninoff is played by adults for adults, not by children for children'.

She was not ashamed to jot down these half-truths, remembering she believed them as a girl, which I found buried in her notes. I had to reconstruct their contexts to assign them to the battle-months with Adele. Evelyn needed them then to shore up her own confidence, and they probably kept resounding in her mind at most lessons.

But I only construed the full crisis with Adele after Evelyn's death. Having undergone an almost identical education – early scholarship to Chatham Square, piano lessons, scholarships, competitions, the same aspirations for the concert stage – I sensed the tug-of-war and asked Evelyn to explain her memory of it in her last decades of life. She did over a few suppers in Venice Beach, framing everything in terms of 'Evelyn then' and 'Evelyn now': how she had responded *then* in contrast to *now*, as a woman in her late fifties, as she conceded her former stubbornness about Rachmaninoff. But the impasse was then, in the 1930s, no minor laughing matter.

The *older* Evelyn told me the reasons were qualitative, musical, and philosophical. The bottom line, she reasoned, was that Chopin and Schumann were great composers – Adele did not need to tell her this – but Rachmaninoff was something *else*: beyond the compass of most pianists her age, and already branded into her psyche as the result of a weird, indescribable yearning she felt. It was as if she already harbored nostalgia *for* nostalgia's sake; not the depressive type but some indescribably regenerative longing.[7] If she could play

---

[7] I did not, of course, notice this nostalgic strain in Evelyn's character as the little boy who broke Richard's cello. But it became increasingly apparent the closer I became to Evelyn over the years. After I commenced my vast historical study of nostalgia described above (n. 1) I recognized that Evelyn was a nostalgic of the first water and that this was why Rachmaninoff's music attracted her so strongly. But I only let on close to the end of her life. In a long telephone conversation a year or two before Evelyn died I explained my view that nostalgia was ultimately something fundamental in human nature; a universal quality, for mysterious reasons stronger in some persons than others, whose origin could never be precisely pinpointed. We spoke about the melancholic temperament and I rehearsed the vast libraries that

Rachmaninoff's music well at her debut, she would exceed everyone's expectations and be on the road to a career. She could not articulate more than this, nor explain why she felt this way but was certain she did then – at twenty – and would permit no one to talk her out of it.

I remonstrated what an odd position this was for a late adolescent. Evelyn agreed, but there ended the conversations. If I sought to return to the 'unnecessary motions' Evelyn would stop me in my tracks: 'I really don't understand what Adele was driving at'. But if I countered with Adele possibly *imagining* the movements, she'd become defensive and take Adele's part. If I suggested Evelyn's hand was too small to master Rachmaninoff's works, she'd grow offended: 'Well, I didn't try to tackle the Third Piano Concerto!' When I'd offer consolation that she could have omitted its menacing first-movement cadenza, she'd grow fractious.

More was forthcoming: it wasn't merely that Rachmaninoff (with the exception of Chopin) was one of the greatest composers ever to write for the piano – Evelyn retained this view until her death – but that Rachmaninoff understood *her*, *Evelyn* – this was the uncanny part. Rachmaninoff somehow communicated with *her*, guided her through this difficult period of her early life. Later, I remember our visits in

---

had been written about it, of which Evelyn was unaware. I daringly divulged to Evelyn my sense that she had begun life with no conscious awareness whatever of the universal type of nostalgia (as distinct from the medical variety that became symptomatic in some patients). I offered her my sense that after her multiple tragedies – which are coming – she slowly began to understand why Rachmaninoff's melancholic music had been so precious to her as an adolescent, and was perhaps even implicated in the events that occurred at her debut recital. I carried on about the melancholic basis of his sense of melody, far more extreme than anything in Chopin or Schumann. And I told her how grateful I was that she – unwittingly – was crystallizing both medical nostalgia and universal nostalgia for me in the domain of my academic research. Yet I could not have known, when I spoke with her late in the 1980s, how my later reconstruction of her life would further crystallize historical nostalgia for me. Evelyn's death yielded the most suitable subject after years of trying to locate the perfect figure: *Rachmaninoff, the man and his music.* Not merely the man who had affected her so profoundly, but the historical figure I myself could also understand as an aspiring concert artist and professional academic.

the early 1970s when she espoused this extraordinary view and I wondered if she were growing mad.

'He sort of talked to you?'

'Yes', she'd retort, 'I could hear his voice inside my head.'

'Are you sure it wasn't Cezar speaking?'

And then she'd squirt me with lemon juice or cunningly spray aerosol whipped-cream on my head. I could not dislodge her from the view and wondered how she came to believe it. But she always had the same line: 'Are you talking to me *now*, as a fifty-five year-old woman, or to the girl of eighteen?'

I'd concede and implore *both* Evelyns, old and young, to express themselves, now and then, but my thirst to understand made no difference. Nothing would extricate Evelyn's entrenched view. The only difference was her greater current sophistication in maturity in articulating the reasons; by now Evelyn had filled her head with so much memorabilia about Rachmaninoff that she could document her views. The *young* Evelyn had no such knowledge of course – in the 1930s an American girl had nothing to read about *him* – just unspeakable exhilaration when playing his piano music.

What can her life have been like to harbour this position? I'd press her: 'go slower, Evelyn, please, say exactly what it was like, what yearning, why do you think he was so *great*?'

And she'd reply: 'the emotion, the longing, the yearning. Listen to the slow movement of the Second Piano Sonata and your heart breaks a thousand times. There's nothing like it.'

I knew Rachmaninoff's canon of works intimately by now – in the 1970s – and took her on, affirming it was just too darn sentimental, too self-pitying, calculated to wring the heart and shut out other emotions, playful, jovial, comic, but she'd carry on about the value of longing.

'Longing for *what*?'

'You'd know what longing is if you suffered as I have,' was her frequent refrain. How can you doubt a woman who saved you from a catastrophe decades earlier when she discloses this in all sincerity?

Or I'd approach the matter philosophically, apart from Rachmaninoff: 'what is yearning if a composer spends most of his time indulging in it?' This produced charges of ignorance about energy and virtuosity in Rachmaninoff's music. And when I'd complain that virtuosity was beside the point – multiple composers possessed energy and their music required virtuosity – she'd respond that only those who have lost everything know what yearning is.

Some times I'd approach the matter autobiographically, asking her what music she herself heard performed live in the late 1930s, and knowing well that it must have been limited as there were only expensive long-playing records at that time. She'd come back with Cezar – always Cezar as explanation – and reiterate how well off they were. Could Cezar have understood how she felt about Rachmaninoff's yearning?

Before her debut recital Cezar bought her a privately made recording of several Rachmaninoff preludes and a movement of his Second Piano Concerto played by Rachmaninoff himself performing with Leopold Stokowski and the Philadelphia Symphony Orchestra. A client told him the RCA Victor Company was about to introduce vinyl LPs; they would be very expensive but he said he would buy one for her birthday. That October, in 1938, Cezar took her to hear Rachmaninoff playing his famous Prelude in C-sharp minor at Carnegie Hall. (Years later Evelyn scribbled a red note in her diary's marginalia for that year: 'did papa Cezar ever understand my gravitational attraction to SR?')

I could not refute Evelyn's sense of the Abrams' degree of economic comfort while the rest of America grovelled in the Great Depression. Instead I appealed to her memories of Adele: 'what were the lessons with Adele like? What balance was there between technique and musicality? Did she encourage you to play so much Rachmaninoff?'

At one lesson, Evelyn said, Adele explained what a debut concert was: a presentation of yourself to the musical world, especially to the critics. You dressed exquisitely, you must look ravishing and move as gracefully as the lovely debutantes being presented to society on Park Avenue or on Beacon Hill in search of suitable husbands. Your hair was perfect, your carefully selected jewellery personalized to bring out your complexion. Your shoes were of great importance as the audience watched you pedal. Every eye was on you; careers were made and broken at these debuts, so your gown and make-up had to be chosen as carefully as the musical works you played. Was this really Adele's manifesto?

Adele had not yet become the most famous piano teacher in America nor trained the cluster of concert pianists she would after the War: Byron Janis, Van Cliburn, Stephen Hough, Garrick Ohlsson, and others. She told Evelyn her story: how she had been the youngest of thirteen children, her father a Russian immigrant rabbi who never learned to speak English; how Joseph Lhévinne taught her in the 1930s and, very recently, Artur Schnabel at Juilliard; and recounted what taskmasters they were. Lhévinne had been, she said, in the same class at the Moscow Conservatory with Rachmaninoff and Scriabin; and Schnabel, a Jew, fled Berlin and the Nazis, and ran away to America.

To young Evelyn these were ongoing Friday afternoon epic events, history and music lessons, which she usually related to Mihaela who parlayed the summaries to beaming Cezar.

'Then they are *all* Jews, Evelyn,' Mihaela exclaimed to her daughter, pointing her pinkie finger up toward heaven, as if God were listening.

'I suppose so, mama, but Rachmaninoff and Scriabin weren't Jews!'

'But *you* are a Jew, that's why she took you. You're one of her people', Mihaela said leaning on the '*people*' word.

'She took me for my *talent*.'

Mihaela wasn't listening, threw up her hands: 'Imagine, to be in the company of such famous Jewish people.'

Defeated Evelyn countered with 'Adele's father was a rabbi.'

'Was he a cantor? Then she must have grown up with music.'

'She's tough but a really good teacher.'

Meanwhile the former renegade tailor Cezar, now prospering furrier with an aspiring concert pianist daughter, was dreaming of something else: the gown. Ever since he realized Evelyn had to wear one it lingered in his imagination. The big day would make him prouder of his daughter than if she were getting married – anyone could marry, but to think he had left Barlat with pennies in his pocket and would soon be presenting his ravishing and talented daughter, Evelyn Abrams, to the world.

Where? In Town Hall on 43rd Street in Manhattan. Adele herself had recently played a concert there, one of her many New York recitals. The place had plush red-cushioned seats and a big stage with a huge Steinway concert grand piano. Evelyn would sit up there all alone, Cezar mused, for two hours, with every eye fixed on his daughter.

Evelyn grew anxious as the big day approached. Her parents dealt with her gown and wardrobe – shoes, jewellery, perfume – while fastidious Adele concentrated on her musical repertoire. Yet something unpredictable intervened to raise everyone's temperature: Sergei Rachmaninoff.

Adele and Evelyn, as has often been noted, disagreed about the programme for some time. Adele impressed on Evelyn it had to be planned with utmost care: an exact number of minutes, not more than seventy in two halves. It must reveal the young artist's strengths while also displaying sufficient breadth to make apparent the player's range.

An all-Beethoven concert might do for keyboard veterans, Adele advised, but not for a young woman making her Town Hall debut. Evelyn must start with a short classical piece to warm up, perhaps Bach or Scarlatti; continue with a Beethoven sonata to demonstrate ability with a major musical form; after the interval a display of technique and virtuosity, perhaps in Chopin or Schumann or Liszt, and then the encores.

Prokovief would serve well, Adele thought, for the last slot: he was now 'in'. Many debutantes were playing his dazzling toccata as a display of bravura to finish off a concert, but Evelyn wanted to finish with Rachmaninoff, her favourite composer. In fact, she wanted the second half to be devoted entirely to Rachmaninoff, especially the preludes, and finish with the C-sharp minor prelude, the 'world's most famous piano piece', as Cezar kept calling it.

To Adele's shock, Evelyn wanted to include Rachmaninoff's second sonata over which her student was struggling. Evelyn agreed to start the second half with Chopin and Liszt but would not surrender Rachmaninoff. This was the most difficult piece in the whole repertoire, to no avail and despite all her reasons.

'Evelyn,' she pleaded, 'the second sonata takes twenty to thirty minutes to perform, even in the short Horowitz version. It will hog the whole second half of the programme.'

'I know Adele, but I love it so much.'

'Then you cannot also have the Rachmaninoff preludes.'

'But if the first half is short can't I make the second half longer?' Evelyn pleaded.

'The halves should be equal in time.'

' … but I like the preludes.'

'Evelyn, don't put all your eggs in one basket, it's not wise. Rachmaninoff is technically too demanding. Something can go wrong, you'll forfeit everything.'

'Rachmaninoff is my favourite composer.'

'That doesn't matter, this is your *first* concert,' Adele weighed in, becoming vexed.

Her pronunciation of words always charmed Evelyn; even now it enticed her despite disagreement, and Evelyn listened attentively, as if to a wiser mother than Michaela.

'Better take a smaller risk by dividing the programme among three Romantic composers, perhaps ten minutes each.'

Evelyn took on board her savvy mentor. She was ardent and determined but not headstrong. She had never forgotten her first little recital at Chatham Square – the liberation she felt. If only she could do that now, combining her newly acquired virtuoso technique with her passion for the Russian, she could impress the critics.

Three strong reviews, as Adele kept telling her, would decide her fate; three negative ones and the show was over: an open and shut case, black and white. There would be no second chance.

Evelyn had attended several debut concerts in Town Hall; Adele told her students they must. She analysed their programmes and concluded that many selected repertoires were too diverse and failed to persuade the audience that the recitalist was special. Some quality of Rachmaninoff's music, some *je ne sais quoi* of the melodies, harmonies, and unrelenting yearning kept drawing her back. She could not name the quality beyond this.

One grey November day, about three months before the debut, Mihaela carried on about Evelyn's shoes. They had to be sufficiently comfortable to pedal but made of patent leather so they shone in the light's reflection – the audience would then be unable to take their eyes off Evelyn. Adele had no time for such trivia, but Mihaela decreed they must be patent-leather pumps. Then she drastically changed the subject and asked Evelyn, out of the blue, whether she was interested in boys.

Evelyn had no boyfriend. Boys amused her in passing but nothing romantic ever came of one.

'Evelyn, darling, some day you'll get married; you *must* start to think about that now – you're turning twenty.'

'I won't get married for years, why should I think about it now?'

'You must start somewhere, Evelyn; like the piano, you begin at the beginning.'

'I have a career to make mama.'

'Careers' – how Mihaela pronounced that formidable word forcing the r to roll – 'car-reers are not mutually exclusive from boys.'

'I don't have time, mama, I must practice, there's Adele.'

'Oh Evelyn, Evelyn, you don't understand what I'm trying to say; did Cezar forget us during the years when he became an expert furrier?'

'Furriers are not concert pianists.'

'You can't make love to a piano; even Clara Schumann had Robert who gave her about a dozen children,' Mihaela pouted.

'I'm not Clara Schumann, I'm me.'

'And after the debut? There's more to life than concerts, Evelyn, even if you *make* it.'

'I'll worry about that after the debut.'

'Don't underestimate love, Evelyn, don't.'

'I don't, but right now *my* love is the *piano*.' Evelyn placed a crescendo in her voice to show how earnest she was.

'Love cannot be for objects; love is for living creatures, living things...

While Mihaela offered her pronouncement as if philosophical cetainty something snapped inside Evelyn: suddenly, more clearly than earlier, and whether or not arising from a principle of adolescent rebellion or spurting contrarily from the heart of a girl already attuned to pain and poignancy, Evelyn knew she would play the Rachmaninoff Second Sonata because that was what *she* loved. She would explain her further reasons to Adele at the next lesson, especially as the concert programmes were scheduled to be printed before Christmas.

Adele listened, fidgeted and frowned. She herself never played Rachmaninoff in public (Evelyn only learned the reason many years later). Adele tolerated a few minutes of her cocky student's harangue, and then, when she no longer could abide the pretension – a travesty – she cut her off with this type of rebuttal): 'Evelyn, your programme is treacherous, crazy, ridiculous. You are being pig-headed. You're acting out. OK, the Chopin ballad, Liszt's 'Mephisto Waltz', a couple of Rachmaninoff preludes from opus 23 or opus 39, but no Second Sonata.'

Evelyn was decided: why should she lie to herself more than anyone else about the piano music she really loved most? A great piano sonata was not an 'inanimate object,' as Mihaela ineptly thought; it was a living, breathing organism, and she had a relationship with it, negotiated by the piano's live wood, which was as alive and sentient as any living creature or animal. Evelyn obeyed Adele in everything else, and had for years, but for the first time she was unprepared to surrender on this point.

And that was how she described her tussle with Adele to me in Venice Beach in the 1970s. I listened incredulously, breathlessly. I could never have done that at her age.

JANUARY 14 1939 ARRIVED TOO SOON for everyone and found all the Abramses in a frenzied state of preparation. Mihaela had been ticking the days on her new World's Fair calendar. Even Benjy, now seventeen, fitted a three-piece suit and topcoat. Cezar and Mihaela dressed as if they were remarrying, and the twenty or thirty friends they had invited to Town Hall were also dressed up. Cousin Jojo – whose real name was Hazdja without anyone able to spell or pronounce it and whose parents had arrived from the Old Country a generation ago and given him a fancy education at Columbia University and made him into a Wall Street stock-broker – Jojo promised to bring rich clients; if they liked what they saw (he did not say 'heard') they might invest in Evelyn's career. Vita, the Abramses' neighbour from Orchard Street who spoke so histrionically, also attended, proclaiming each time they saw her that Evelyn might become a glamorous movie star. 'Interviews,' she blurted, throwing out her hands, 'reporters, press releases – Mihaela, your daughter's gonna be famous – famous!'

Evelyn rehearsed in her full concert attire so many times that she felt thoroughly comfortable manoeuvring around it, gesturing, crossing-over hands, running up and down the keyboard, especially in the Rachmaninoff sonata. Her outfit included a narrow Rheingold-studded tiara to hold up her hair in a bun, small, matching, bejewelled earrings, the black patent-leather pumps Mihaela had insisted on, and – most crucially – a red beltless gown flowing down to the floor without covering her shoes.

Cezar presented these gifts, and many predecessors too, gifts large and small to his darling Evelyn. Now, as the big day loomed, Cezar also made a case for Evelyn to wear a small fur wrap – one of his own specially cut – but mother and daughter dissuaded him. No one, Mihaela said, wore fur stoles at debut concerts. The idea was as preposterous as wearing rings or bracelets – a pianist's hands and arms must be completely free.

14 January was bitterly cold and clear. The wind was biting and temperatures remained freezing. Evelyn knew she'd have to wear gloves until the moment she walked out on stage. Icy fingers were the kiss of death. Her three pairs of woollen mittens were tucked into the

sheet music under her arm, just in case she needed to consult the score while waiting. She had practiced on the Town Hall Steinway a few days earlier and felt she could command the piano, but had no idea how loud or soft her playing would sound to the audience.

Adele had tutored her in the five basic rules of concert performance, which she wrote out a dozen times and memorized: (1) remember that every movement you make will be seen by the audience, so no faces or sighs and as few sways of the torso as possible; (2) if the piano moves pretend it is not rolling and quietly adjust your piano bench; (3) continue no matter what happens, even if the lights go out or the stage curtain wraps around you; (4) wear no perfume because you could have an allergic reaction and sneeze; (5) if people cough ignore it and pretend you do not hear them. The hall manager told Evelyn he would summon her from the artist's room at the right moment. He found her warming her hands in woollen mittens.

Once called she leapt up, threw down the gloves, stood up erect, and marched out like a princess; walking on stage feeling exhilarated and thinking only one thought: where was Adele sitting? Evelyn would recognize Adele if in the front row. Evelyn bowed, slowly sat at the Steinway, evened out her red dress, adjusted the piano-bench knobs, dusted the keyboard with her white silk handkerchief, lifted her hands to begin the short Bach toccata, and for one fleeting moment turned her head right toward the audience.

What a universe she saw. Huge, cavernous, everywhere black except for the few stars – the reflection of a rhinestone, the glitter of a ceiling light – in its firmament. The world stared at her, the galaxy, the constellations, and their earthly representatives in the form of teacher, parents, family and friends, and fellow students. In a flicker she wondered what she was doing here. Creating another universe, officiating some religious ritual, soaring to the moon?

Then the demon struck. Icy shafts of galactic freeze. Time stopped. She blanked out, froze up. Not her fingers or hands but her brain – her whole head was numb, and eyes too. It was as if she lost consciousness and had been transported to some nighttime realm where black is the only colour. The cavernous Town Hall seemed metamorphosed into a galaxy, or at least planetarium, its dim lights distant stars in the firmament. She saw no people sitting in the rows, just a vast galaxy of sparkling stars that obliterated all memory of why she might be there. She had an eerie sense that her fingers were no longer attached to her hand. Her body grew numb, as frozen as icicles in the polar north.

Evelyn remained frozen in this position for about two minutes, then regained a fraction of her former composure and repeated the well-rehearsed routine; readjusting the piano bench again, dusting the keys, lifting her arms towards the keyboard, until thinking Cezar would catch her in the front row, where the family was sitting, if she fell off the stage.

She thought nothing now except Cezar: '*daddy where are you?*' Gone was Rachmaninoff, gone Adele, gone the world, just Evelyn alone on Town Hall's stage awaiting daddy's warm arms. She was so cold. Freezing. The only thought she could muster was that she could not play. Nothing could make her come unstuck.

She waited another minute, then stood up, smiled at the audience – a plaintive grin informing the gazer something is drastically wrong – then turned right and quietly walked off the stage, back to the artist room by the identical route in reverse.

Evelyn's vomit hit the plush blue sofa before she could slam the door behind her. Out it came, as she ran to the toilet; into the washbasin and then the bowl. Her cheeks were burning, earlier dexterous ice turned to tropical blaze. The room was empty, lights still on. Evelyn walked back to the door and bolted it; turned the key that might lock it and switched off the light, closed her eyes, took a deep breath, and fell into the cushioned armchair.

Her diary says she could never remember how long she reposed there: eyes closed, mouth agape, heart pounding. The next thing she recalled Mihaela and Cezar were rubbing her hands – one on each arm – and Benjy looked on amazed, as if someone had died and his parents were trying to resuscitate them.

'Don't worry darling,' tearful Mihaela kept saying, shaking her head back and forth, 'it's not the end of the world. We're gonna take you home now to sleep.'

Cezar himself looked numb, like Evelyn, the way he was when the transatlantic ocean liner decades earlier docked at Ellis Island. He observed Mihaela minister to her daughter, as if almost dead, and could only think to say, 'I have a taxi waiting outside. We're going home.' Softly, he kept repeating it as if shivering.

Evelyn remembered no taxi ride, nor falling asleep in her bed, but when she awakened the next day was dazed and had no desire to play Rachmaninoff again. She stared at her piano as some alien object and wondered what happened.

'Did I play?' she kept asking herself. 'Have I forgotten that I played? Where are the reviews? Why do I remember nothing?'

The family doctor came around noon to examine her, found nothing, and advised Mihaela that 'Evelyn will be fine in a few days, but give her these tablets if the crying continues.'

Evelyn had not yet cried – that would come, with her hands holding the bed rails. She remained in her room for about five days, could not eat without Mihaela forcing food down with a spoon, holding down her tongue with her finger. Evelyn just wanted to be alone and sleep. All she could think was *Adele*; Adele perched in the front row of Town Hall, her mighty right hand – that hand Evelyn knew so well in her lessons – resting on her chin, chiding her about the Rachmaninoff sonata. It was the jinx – Evelyn was sure – but no 'Red Peril': Stalin's Great Purge frightened many Americans during those years and sprawled over American newspaper headlines. Evelyn heard about it in her history class yet was incapable of blaming anyone but herself for the disaster. She kept telling herself it did not happen because the programme was filled with Russian music. No, she had brought this misery on herself.

She did not contemplate killing herself – was too balanced for that. Mihaela and Cezar would survive the debacle. After all, they had not pushed her to become a concert pianist.

She regained some normalcy after a week and returned to her high school, the School of Performing Arts, which I – as I will explain – attended two decades later. But she dodged her Friday piano lesson and could not bear the thought of confronting Adele.

Adele spared her the agony. A letter arrived from Juilliard requesting Evelyn's presence in the office of the Chairman of the Piano Faculty who broke the news to her at a brief interview. Adele would no longer be teaching Evelyn; there was no need to proceed to another lesson. Evelyn was at liberty to discuss the termination with the Piano Board, who would consider assigning her to another teacher, but Adele's decision was final.

The sudden rupture crushed Evelyn even more than blacking out in stage fright: the idea that she had somehow betrayed Adele, disobeyed her, recklessly refused her advice about Rachmaninoff, and wilfully insisted on playing what she alone wanted. All was finished, Evelyn thought, her world shattered. She alone would live with the fallout for the rest of her life.

Years later, Evelyn told me she learned Adele had her own 'issue' with stage fright, as she did with piano teachers who chased her around the room (she had been one of the first young attractive American women to be taught by legendary Russian immigrants who migrated to America around the turn of the twentieth century; pianists like Joseph Lhévinne must have relished giving her lessons) – small wonder she was so adamant about Evelyn's avoiding the Rachmaninoff Second Sonata. Evelyn found out in a dentist's office in Venice Beach California after migrating there. A Russian man, about forty, with a thick accent, sat next to her in the waiting room. They struck up a friendly conversation; he told Evelyn he was a pianist who had studied with Adele Marcus at Juilliard in the 1960s. His own concert career never took off but he attended several of her recitals in New York where she was so nervous she had repetitive memory lapses. He said it afflicted her early in life and that's why she started to teach, and the critics panned and chastised her for it. He described her looking white as a ghost when she walked out on stage. 'A great teacher but no performer,' he said, 'by a long shot.'

Evelyn and Rachmaninoff

THROUGHOUT THE SPRING OF 1939 Evelyn picked up the pieces. In their Flushing house everyone was tight-lipped; at Performing Arts her classmates responded as if they heard nothing. Mihaela comforted her daughter with saccharine words wrapped in maternal syrup; Cezar kept praising her other talents, saying she'd make some handsome Jewish man a wonderful wife; and Benjy was deflected by other things on his mind, although Evelyn detected shame in his expression whenever he looked at her. Indeed, she thought he was avoiding her altogether.

Evelyn never opened the piano now; her intuitive recovery depended on identifying some new purpose. She had never matriculated in a college other than Juilliard and had no desire to teach. Encouraged by Mihaela she enrolled in an expensive secretarial course but rarely attended. The reality that gnawed at her, instead, was that she had failed to play a debut; her concert career had been over before it started. When Rivka – Mihaela's friend, a generous woman who really cared for Evelyn as if she were her own daughter – fixed her up with a blind date, Evelyn thought 'why not'. She admitted to herself to being twenty-plus going on twelve in dating pedigree, and might as well start now.

Joel Feingold bored Evelyn when they met. They had little in common and no chemical attraction, so Evelyn did not want to see him again. He was tall and pleasant but boring, she told her mother. Rivka, when she heard, interpreted her failure more poignantly than Evelyn did and never again offered to match-make, but other dates followed from Mihaela's contacts. Evelyn was not looking for a husband – what she knew was that she had to push ahead to survive. She had come close to the wire on that concert stage; now she must avoid further 'flings with death'.

Cezar raised the prospect that she might spend a few years at a liberal arts college. 'Any daughter of mine should have a degree' was his newly found position. Mihaela wasn't sure: 'maybe she wants a family or hopes to return to the piano'. She secretly hoped Evelyn would mount another debut but dared not say so. Her daughter was confused more than anything. The void created by Adele's removal hit Evelyn hard; nothing, it seemed, could fill it.

The dogwood bloomed and receded that 1939, replaced by July heat, and during that month Evelyn took a job at a camp in Connecticut that paid her well. Her sole task was to give piano lessons to the campers, which would buy her more time. When she returned in August, Cezar's eyes were red and swollen. A letter had arrived from an aunt in Barlat announcing the death of both his parents. His father died first: a peaceful demise at seventy, the old man blissfully surrounded by all the Old World Abramovicis; followed within five days by his ailing wife, both having asked to be buried in the same grave.

Mihaela wept: how father-in-law Abramovici had pinched her for good luck when tucking the gold-filled pouch under her blouse before they shipped out. But now Cezar stared into space as if greeting them in some eternal beyond. He was a fiery man, quick on the take, but could be as silent as he was confident and ebullient; now, in bereavement, he seemed to be pondering the location of the beyond itself: the terrestrial globe beyond New York, beyond America, beyond the Atlantic, even the beyond of his daughter's recently forfeited career. Loss surrounded him. Cezar pinched himself to prove how many thousands of miles away from Barlat he was. Evelyn never before saw her father in this sombre pose.

Never to meet your grandparents is one of life's greatest losses, yet Evelyn was not prepared to embrace its consequences: instead she dwelled on her own loss and prayed for rejuvenation – intuitively craving passage to the ordinary world or, magically, return to Adele and the glittering world she symbolized.

The Jewish holidays settled down on 'Jewish Flushing', as Mihaela called it, in late September 1939. The four Abramses drove to Temple Sinai in Forest Hills, and then marched on foot to the Glicks – their oldest friends since moving to Queens – to break the Yom Kippur fast with them and three other families. A cousin's son, from Brooklyn, was visiting: Sam Amster, a few years older than Evelyn. He struck her as square, but square with an expressively warm face. Evelyn used the word 'warm' in her diary: warm in the sense of aroused emotion, as in the dominant mood of a classical piece of music. Sam was fair-skinned, of medium weight and several inches taller than Evelyn; shy and withdrawn at first but Lily Glick seated him next to Evelyn at the long supper table sparkling with her best china and he opened up.

He told her he graduated from City College that June with a degree in business administration and after the holidays would start to work in his family's business importing and exporting fabrics. His father gave him a car as his graduation present and promised him a good entry salary; if all progressed to plan he'd succeed him as one of the directors. He had two younger sisters who went to friends to break the fast. The Amsters lived in Brooklyn, in a big house on Bedford Avenue near Prospect Park, had a live-in maid, a St Bernard dog, and a vintage white Cadillac parked in the driveway.

Sam wasn't boasting but Evelyn grasped the point: the Amsters were ultra-comfortable. Somewhat philosophically he conveyed the point that during a period – the summer of 1939 – when the Great American Depression crested and millions of Americans were still unemployed, his family was 'comfortable'. (Evelyn's diary notes that he leaned on the word as if well aware of how privileged the Amsters were, or had become).

Now that he had a degree, a job, and a car, he only lacked a girlfriend to complete himself. Evelyn certainly wasn't instantly attracted but felt comfortable in his presence, even safe. He seemed decent, even modest, despite their 'comforts.'

Mihaela silently watched them from her end of the table. The Abramses were barely outside the Glicks' front door when she began to harangue Evelyn with questions, which she herself answered before Evelyn could. In Mihaela's vivid mind they were already walking down the altar. Cezar was more hesitant, his recalcitrance now prevailing as an opposite state of his characteristic ebullience, but even he perked up at Mihaela's plain insinuations.

One date led to another and before Evelyn could catch her breath she was 'dating Sam'.

'He's such a lovely boy,' Mihaela kept repeating. Even Benjy changed his tune from his former blithe unawareness of the romance.

Evelyn felt she had no choice. Fate sealed her in its book: 'married to a husband rather than a piano', a benign resolution in which she had acquiesced as a willing participant. She was an intelligent woman who grew increasingly self-reflective since her 'tragedy'. She could not produce a single reason to herself, not one, to reject Sam, except that – and of this she was sure – she didn't love him.

She was still a virgin. Mihaela had often lectured her that Jewish girls must remain virgins until their wedding night; if a Jewish girl's fiancé discovered she was not a virgin, he would abandon her, abrogate the engagement, and announce the marriage proposal off. These ridiculous customs bewildered Evelyn yet she told herself she was also a willing, if complicit, virgin. Her mind was bending. She began to configure herself as potentially married, physically married, eventually divorced, Sam and 'the piano' the arch rivals in this new psychomachy. She was aware of the absurdity of these musings but knew Adele would understand the meaning of 'losing your virginity to the piano' or 'be divorced from the piano.'

They dated all winter and spring in 1941, Sam's decency, Evelyn thought, increasing with each date. He never pushed or rushed her; he kept promises and seemed to possess a golden character. Sterling was the word she began to associate with him. He kissed her, more than once, and held her too, but never tried to seduce her. She was becoming the aroused participant.

Her thoughts, not just her body, involuntarily migrated to sex for the first time in her life. On a few occasions she became aggressive, initiated heightened lovemaking, which he rebuffed. 'He wanted a wife', he said, 'not a slut'. After he said the word she strangely felt more secure with him and began to divulge her life at Chatham Square and – later on – at Juilliard with Adele. She described the freeze in Town Hall, her sense that she was falling off the precipice of the world. Sam was in awe of Evelyn's pain; even found ways to calm her when agitated in her memories.

One day Sam implored her to play for him. She protested – she had not been practicing – but Sam persisted and she imagined he might disbelieve that only a little over a year earlier she was on the stage of Town Hall about to dazzle the world with Rachmaninoff. They made a pact: she would practice for a few weeks, and only then play for him. On the day she was nervous; not the stinging nerves of public concerts, of Town Hall, but anxious by dint of bearing her soul naked to him in this intimate way. Sam liked classical music but was unfamiliar with its composers or their styles. She played Chopin to warm up and then Rachmaninoff. He was awed, tearful, and said this was a new window to her soul; he was suddenly persuaded she *must* be his wife even if his parents dissented (how could they not in light of the fiscal imbalance?), and also said that when they were married Evelyn must teach their children music – then they would inherit their mother's gifts.

By spring Sam proposed, shortly after Passover 1941; they married that Chanukah, on Sunday 14 December 1941, exactly one week after the Japanese bombed Pearl Harbour. Sam's parents wanted time to plan their only son's wedding. In most Jewish families it was customary for the girl's father to foot the bill, but Sam modestly relayed his parent's wish for a large wedding of several hundred people and said the Abramses could not be expected to pay for it.

Cezar and Mihaela were relieved; had been apprehensive that money would queer the deal. They had savings but the late 1930s had recently dented Cezar's earnings: rich people continued to buy his furs until 1936 but dropped off afterwards, and by 1939-40 his profits plummeted. He saved up to rent Town Hall for Evelyn and its related fees, especially her velvet gown, and for the manager's concert fee if Evelyn's debut proved successful, but did not have the extra few thousand for a glittering wedding.

The war looming in Europe silently gnawed at him. His parents were recently dead but he still had aunts, uncles, and cousins there, and almost anticipated the Nazi pulverization of the Balkans and its Jews. Evelyn's diary records his exhortations verbatim, as if for historical verisimilitude rather than distraction from her engagement. Cezar had always identified with Romania, Mihaela not at all; she considered herself 'American'. Still, Cezar sparkled and kissed his daughter when he heard the good news about the setting of the wedding date: 'my daughter will give me my first grandchild.' It was such a restrained kiss his daughter could mind-read him: a paternal version of Sam's half-kisses when they parted on dates. Sam tiptoed like Cezar, Evelyn thought, because he too was a gentleman, even at twenty-three.

Evelyn and Rachmaninoff

That summer Sam gave her a diamond necklace, complemented shortly afterwards by sighting of the wedding ring: a modest but pure 18-karat diamond set in dappled gold. They took a Greyhound bus from Manhattan to Key West Florida for their honeymoon on the 15th, and moved into a small but elegant two-storey brick house on Dartmouth Street in Forest Hills after they returned before the New Year. When the real estate agent unlocked the front door for Evelyn's very first visit, Evelyn peered in and could see a new black Steinway grand piano wrapped in a huge red ribbon. 'To Evelyn, love Sam, 27 December 1941', printed in Georgian vermillion.

FROM THIS TIME EVELYN'S ANNUAL DIARIES are erratic. They record that eleven months later, on 22 November 1942, the Sunday before that Thanksgiving, Richard Amster was born, the same day the Soviets encircled the Germans at Stalingrad. Few places on earth can have been further from Evelyn's mind than Russia, no matter how intensely she had invested herself earlier in Rachmaninoff's piano music. And Thanksgiving, an American holiday she took for granted, held no symbolism; certainly not that a son had just been born to her on the previous Sunday. For Evelyn November 22 was a joyous day that not even the memories of a receding concert freeze could tarnish. She had panicked on the concert stage, of course, but Richard's birth proceeded like clockwork, from the moment Evelyn went into labour and Sam whisked her off to Flushing Hospital. The pudgy, healthy baby of normal weight was soon in Evelyn's arms, his large brown eyes and pink skin curiously peering up at her. His once-upon-a-time concert-pianist mother noticed that his tiny, putty fingers were like cake mix, animated to her touch with a moist grip that clutched her.

Sam was less ecstatic, just cautiously watched Richard grow up. He had predicted Richard would resemble his mother and he did: in looks, facial expression, gesture, disposition, and body language. Richard fixed his eyes on Evelyn when she played the piano before he was a year old. By two, he himself was tinkling wantonly at the keyboard, and by three Evelyn giving him lessons. Evelyn practically wept at his progress; even Sam was stunned.

Evelyn also learned to be a 'mother' apart from Mihaela's and Cezar's constant tutelage. Two years earlier motherhood was the furthest thought from her mind; now she was learning its ropes, for example how playing the piano made her less anxious than otherwise about Richard and soothed her sense of deficiency. Sam's business increased, now that the USA had declared war against Japan, his salary doubling in just two years since 1939 – they had no money worries nor would they throughout the war. Her other preoccupation – the memory of gruelling stage fright – also receded; her crying baby took precedence over its former grip, and even her marriage – her growing affection for Sam – did. She kept telling herself that despite the nerves that had wrecked her career she must learn, again, to play for musical friends.

Those months in 1943 and 1944 flew by, the joyous mother amazed at how her beautiful child quelled the shame she concealed about her former career. Her country was at war, men dying, families broken: she had no right to indulge herself in this stupid preoccupation with personal loss. Her fortune had reversed, motherhood agreed with her; and even if her husband was a stranger to most of the ideas swimming in her head since Richard's birth – especially the sense that someday she might retrieve lost ground – Sam was a good man. Still, she caught herself in interior dialogues fantasizing about returns to the concert stage: ridiculous, she knew, but she could not eradicate the fantasies by their roots.

So she practised again while an inquisitive Richard occasionally listened. 'Is that a Rachmaninoff prelude you are playing, baby?' Of course it was; wonderful Sam, to recognize it. A year later, in 1947, Richard was almost five when she judged him ready for piano lessons, taught by her. When he responded positively beyond all expectation, she also decided to buy him a string instrument, an expensive miniature cello. Within two years Richard was playing well. If he could become proficient they would play duets – mother-and-son – and eventually perform with other instruments. Evelyn assessed the plan as less selfish than restorative for the young family of three. Even neutral Sam, who played no instrument, fancied the notion of a cello-playing son: he was taking over his father's business and had become a workaholic. Domestic music making would relax him.

The war made little impact on husband or wife. Sam was ring-fenced from active military duty by virtue of his baby. They followed the Nazi menace on the radio, were horrified like most Americans at the atrocities reported, most of which they could not believe. Evelyn had hoped she would live long enough to travel to Rachmaninoff's birthplace; the war rendered this aspiration impossible, she thought: a ravished Europe was the last place she would ever visit. The battles and death camps were geographically so far away she wondered why she and Sam should be concerned apart from the American 'boys' being called up to active service. Even Mihaela showed little interest, now that her parents were dead. They had died early in 1940, before Romania entered the war on the Axis side. Mihaela assured Evelyn her grandparents were spared the German occupation of their homeland.

Richard's musical progress was phenomenal. He swiftly took to his baby cello and amazed his teacher, a local woman in Queens who had been trained at the Mannes School in Manhattan. At six mother and son began to play duets. This was around the time Richard asked his mother for a teacher other than herself to give him piano lessons.

Evelyn was flustered by his request. What if he learned bad habits? The first year or two, as she well knew, were crucial for the future. What if his talent was dented or derailed? She poured over the implications of Richard's request with Sam. She spoke to his cello teacher and several knowledgeable friends. Eventually Evelyn decided to take him to Chatham Square, now more firmly established than it had been in her time there before the war. This was in 1949.

Sam drove them to Manhattan one Saturday afternoon early in October. The auditions now were less personalized than they had been in Evelyn's time. Three string teachers listened to Richard play for ten minutes and told Evelyn and Sam on the spot that their son was admitted. They would need to pay for his lessons because the form they completed indicated they could afford to. Scholarships were based on need.

Richard was assigned to a middle-age Czech immigrant, expert in the teaching of very young students. Evelyn took Richard for his lessons on the IND subway – the new addition to the New York subway system after the BMT and IRT – every Saturday from Queens to Clinton Street, just as she herself had travelled almost two decades earlier.

Richard was seven, the youngest student enrolled at Chatham Square. I have already recounted how Evelyn invited me to their house at the time of his seventh birthday and described the ensuing catastrophe. The fallout for me, as I recognized later in life, was boundless gratitude to benevolent Evelyn, especially as Richard and I grew to be friends.

Richard's trajectory was more remarkable than mine. At ten he played a recital at Chatham Square that amazed the great and good who attended those student evening concerts. Chotzinoff, leading the school, wrote to the Amsters telling them their son was a phenomenal talent; they had had a moral obligation to foster him to his full potential. He well remembered Evelyn, he confirmed, although he was hazy about why she dropped out of the performing world.

Evelyn was sceptical, anxiously cautious: history might repeat itself. Richard might fail. Anything could become an obstacle. They debated what to do and then trudged off to Chotzinoff's office a few weeks later to weigh up the possibilities. Chotzinoff proposed Richard should be taken to Leonard Rose (1918-84) at Juilliard, the premier cello teacher in America who had begun to teach a couple of years earlier in 1947. The lessons would be expensive but – Chotzinoff tactfully insinuated – the well-off Amsters could not obstruct their son's career just because his mother once froze up on the concert stage.

Chotzinoff's words stung Evelyn. They bit her. So everyone knew, everyone remembered, even this famous music critic, a household name in America. Her failure was public knowledge – an open secret.

Evelyn and Rachmaninoff

Leonard Rose had just turned forty and was America's leading cello teacher. He had already played under Toscanini's baton and as principal cellist of America's great orchestras. His parents, like Evelyn's, were immigrants from Kiev in the Ukraine, and teacher and parents schmoozed about being the children of illiterate Eastern European immigrants. Did Rose know, the ashamed Evelyn painfully mused to herself? He had tactfully referred to her at Richard's lessons as a 'considerable pianist' but she wondered whether he knew the whole story. In any case the ten-year old boy who, Rose said, must be nurtured but not deprived of a childhood, awed him. 'Let Richard take his own course, let him develop at his own pace, don't rush him or you'll make him old before his time.' He repeated the advice at several lessons.

Sam took a backseat in all this nurturing while Evelyn coped well with their son's extraordinary talent. Evelyn was a reflective and sensitive woman; the last thing she consciously wanted was to push Richard into 'a career'. But inner demons also controlled her more than she knew, when she least expected; not merely the shame at what had happened to her but her sense of enduring failure. If Richard's talent was as phenomenal as Chotzinoff portended and Rose confirmed, Richard would find his way; she knew he would. If not, she'd settle for a healthy son. This was the rationale she told herself.

Her marriage to Sam was never as important as Richard. It wasn't loveless but Sam had never really understood her, she thought, nor she him. You have a husband, you have a son: each signifies something else. In your heart of hearts a reflective person like Evelyn recognizes their literal and symbolic difference. Now, astonishingly to Evelyn, Sam said he wanted another son who might some day help him in business. They had tried without success a few years' earlier and pondered adoption, but that was over with and Evelyn mistakenly believed they were resigned. In fact she dreaded becoming pregnant again or adopting. Richard was the only offspring she ever wanted.

Richard was her whole life. 'She had started over', she ecstatically whispered to herself, was practicing more piano now and playing with local chamber musicians too, and entertained the notion that if she formed an ongoing quartet she might one day perform again, which would serve as a model for the aspiring Richard. Sam also acted as if she had refreshed herself, as if he had found a newly recovered wife-pianist and was campaigning for an adopted son (it must be a boy). In his leisure he was playing ball with Richard, riding their bicycles together. 'Father and son', the Flushing neighbours nodded. Yet in his heart Sam was more intent than Evelyn on an ordinary childhood for Richard's. Evelyn wanted a prominent cellist – everything she had lost.

Richard was ten in 1952 and growing into a promising young man; healthy in body, quick of mind, unwittingly sardonic for a boy of ten, and emotionally stable. He had not formed friendships, except for the boy from Brooklyn – George – who broke his cello.

Evelyn's domestic life settled into satiety: a husband who loved her, who adored their son, who provided handsomely for them. In 1951 they moved into a larger house in Forest Hills, where she had her own spacious music room. Sam's parents also bought them a place in Florida where they were spending a few weeks each Christmas. What more could she want? Mihaela and Cezar turned sixty and moved to Atlantic City on the Jersey coast. All four grandparents basked in the promise of their 'aspiring cellist', although the Amsters saw little of them. They referred to their grandson Richard as their 'celebrity' on birthday cards.

Leonard Rose proved to be a model teacher, considerate, expert, tactful. He was not only a famous cellist but also a patient mentor for the young. Evelyn's diaries comment on Richard's lessons, each lesson described, what he played for Rose and what he learned from him. Richard quickly caught on but did not practice in the compulsive way his mother had during her childhood. He did not need to: he had ten times Evelyn's talent. To prepare for the spring recital at Juilliard he merely worked diligently. This was 1953 when he was eleven and a half. The student concert was a triumph: no nerves, no surprises, solid brilliance and everyone clapped. Rose smiled and said Richard would soon be ready to enter competitions.

ONE MORNING IN THE SUMMER OF 1953, when bringing toast to the breakfast table, Evelyn happened to stop directly in front of Richard's head and noticed a grey hair. Just one. She scanned the compass of his scalp and found no others. Do eleven-and-a-half year old boys get grey hair, she wondered? Sam made light of it but Evelyn wasn't convinced. This discovery got her going ... the more she began to inspect every inch of her son, the stranger the signs she detected.

She noticed his voice rising in pitch, its timbre slowly growing thinner and weaker. At first glance – a few months earlier – she shrugged off the observation; but now she linked the grey hair with it and put herself on red alert.

She also noticed a different body odour, like rotting fish. She said nothing to Sam but kept sniffing Richard when she could get close to him without arousing his suspicion. She had read that parents and children throughout the mammalian kingdom have in-built senses of each other. She and Richard came into close proximity several hours a week in the music room where she accompanied him to prepare for his lessons with Rose. The foul smell had arisen out of the blue after she spotted the grey hair.

A few days later, Evelyn broke down when she and Sam retired. Sam held her closely:

'It's your imagination, Evelyn. Pubescent boys often smell. I haven't noticed his voice changing. What's one grey hair? Even babies can have one.'

Evelyn continued to weep, piteously rather than angrily.

'Sam, something is wrong. I know my son. We must get him medically checked.'

Sam acquiesced. A few nights later Evelyn again sobbed. Sam turned off the light and held her, wondering whether she rather than Richard was decomposing. Evelyn wrote in her diary how the memory of that night stuck with her, the first time she realized the morass awaiting them.

A week later Dr Herman Zide, the family internist, escorted Evelyn into his office while the nurse helped Richard put his clothes back on.

'It's puzzling, Evelyn, I don't know what to make of it. It's probably coincidental that the body smell you detect has appeared simultaneously with the grey hair.'

Zide spoke slowly, cautiously, with the gravity of decades of experience. His symmetrical profile and blue polka-dot bowtie conferring the gravitas he projected. Evelyn and Sam had been his patients ever since they moved to Forest Hills.

'The change in his voice, the pitch you notice, may be temporary and hormonally generated. I suggest we monitor it.'

They told Richard the office visit was a routine check-up. That night Evelyn and Sam assessed every shred of Dr Zide's advice before going to sleep. Sam judged it sensible but Evelyn demurred. 'Suppose it's more serious than that – the quicker we find out the better. We'd be starting early.' Sam gathered her drift and calmed her.

Another grey hair formed, then others. His nose also seemed to alter: its slope drooping as if the nose were shrivelling, its skin growing rough and pale. Richard's voice remained constant, but the stench intensified: a type of foul stink arising from sweating armpits never washed, as if he were a workman toiling in boiling heat. Leonard Rose, who also came into close proximity with Richard, remained silent, tactfully said nothing, but Rabbi Ellmann, who was coaching Richard for his Bar Mitzvah, commented on the voice shift.

In seven months Richard would turn thirteen, the age at which Jewish boys are presented to the Torah in this symbolic ritual commemorating the attainment of manhood. Rabbi Ellmann wrote a note to Evelyn inquiring whether she noticed Richard's voice getting higher. Evelyn replied, putting him in the picture, and said they might need to amend the Bar Mitzvah arrangements.

Dr Zide knew more than he said, was too tactful to alarm them. He witnessed Evelyn's fragility years earlier when she was a new patient and saw her recovering after the debut debacle, nor was her maternity entirely smooth. Evelyn withheld information then about her past and Zide wondered whether she also did now. When she returned with Richard a few weeks later, she asked him to examine Richard's skin, his hands and arms. Evelyn noticed a change in colour, a roughness not present earlier which she never saw while accompanying him.

Richard wondered why his mother kept taking him to bespectacled Dr Zide, who looked, touched, felt, measured the palm with a ruler, and then called Evelyn into his office and spoke softly while Richard remained outside with the nurse.

'Evelyn, it isn't normal, you're right, but I don't know what it is. I think we should refer Richard to a specialist.'

'What *kind* of specialist?'

'A dermatologist.'

'A *dermatologist* for the voice change and grey hair and body odour?'

'You're right, Evelyn, I don't know what to make of the smell.'

'Nor do I. The first time it stank like rancid fish!'

'It's strange but these features could be related to his skin texture.'

'He isn't schizophrenic, is he?' She pronounced the dreaded s-word as if about to swoon.

Evelyn sank into the leather chair, now as if drowning, her heart pounding. Racing through Zide's mind was a rare condition he had once heard about whose medical name he could not remember: *the premature aging of children.* He had attended a lecture in medical school decades ago where it was mentioned as a newly discovered condition. It was so rare only a few doctors ever saw a case during their working lives. In three decades he had never again seen, or heard, a reference to it. Richard's symptoms might, of course, lead elsewhere but a specialist should examine his skin.

'I think we should tell Richard something,' he said.

'What?' Evelyn asked without snapping.

'Let's tell him he may have a skin condition that could interfere with his practicing the cello. And let's say we're seeking a specialist consultant's advice.'

Evelyn and Sam agreed this was the best way forward. They sat Richard down and told him what Dr Zide advised. An appointment was made with the dermatologist for the following week.

Richard was unfazed. He noticed no grey hairs or smells, had other things on his mind, like the Bar Mitzvah lessons, school, his cello, to which he was deeply attached, and satisfying Leonard Rose at their lessons. He had grown to admire Rose and wanted to please him. By now he was tackling several cello sonatas requiring lots of practice. His mother's fixation on a few grey hairs was excessive, he thought; he was amused rather than horrified, as if they conferred a certain gravitas and maturity on him.

The consultant's day came. Both parents and son travelled to the clinic. Dr Newcomer seemed more excitable than Dr Zide. He was a tallish man of about sixty flanked by three of four assistants and two nurses. He stalked about, one eye half closed as if it had been damaged in some casualty. Every few moments he opened it, where it remained, in partial proof he was in charge of its movements.

Dr Newcomer took Richard into his office. Evelyn and Sam waited outside. When his nurse called them in Newcomer asked Richard to remain. He sat down at his large desk and invited his parents to sit down too, as if he had something momentous to announce.

'We're going to watch Richard very closely. It may not be anything to get too worried about but from today we're watching this boy, especially his vision.'

'His vision?' Evelyn blurted.

'His eyesight will hold the clue.'

'What do you mean, his eyesight?' Evelyn asked again, thoroughly baffled this time.

Sam remained silent despite wondering what Newcomer meant.

'It's part of the picture with the grey hairs and rough skin.'

Neither parent had ever heard of such a conjunction of symptoms in a young adolescent but Dr Newcomer pulled no punches. The half-shut eye flapped several times as he spoke: 'There is a condition of premature aging in children that presents with these symptoms. It's so rare Richard probably does not have it. These symptoms will turn out to be something else. But we must consider the possibility.'

'What's it called?' Sam asked shyly, as bewildered as his wife.

'Progeria', Newcomer said, 'it means premature old age'.

'How is it treated?' Evelyn asked.

'It isn't; there's no treatment.'

Evelyn sank, Sam blanked. No treatment, incurable, final, each thought in their idiosyncratic way.

Newcomer continued, watching the desperate stare of their faces.

'Don't get yourselves worked up. Progeria afflicts one in a million children. It's so rare that none of us has ever seen a case. I never have. I knew someone who had. Dr John Cooke at Children's Hospital in Boston has diagnosed several cases but no one in Queens. Most doctors won't even consider the possibility. I don't think this will turn out to be progeria but it is my ethical duty to tell you it is *possible*.'[8]

---

[8] My memoir recreates characters, places, frames of mind, as well as states of knowledge as they existed in their time; the picture of progeria presented in *Rachmaninoff's Cape* reflects thinking about it during the 1950s, not today, when it has made great strides despite the lack of pharmacological or other therapy. Progeria was first identified in 1886 by Jonathan Hutchinson (1828-1913) and was later independently described in 1897 by Hastings Gilford (1861-1941), both English surgeons. After World War One the condition was named Hutchinson-Gilford Progeria Syndrome (HGPS), sometimes called 'Progeria Syndrome', but was not yet recognized as an extremely rare genetic disease wherein symptoms resembling aspects of ageing are manifested at a very early age. Popular discussion about progeria during the 1920s stimulated author F. Scott Fitzgerald to write a short story, *The Curious Case of Benjamin Button*, released as a film in 2008 starring Brad Pitt and Cate Blanchett, whose main character, Benjamin Button, is born as a seventy-year-old man and ages backward. Although the generic term progeria applies to all diseases characterized by premature aging symptoms, and is often used as such, it is more commonly applied in reference to Hutchinson-Gilford Progeria Syndrome (HGPS). Its embryonic genetic basis had been suspected but not yet proved when Richard was diagnosed in 1954. The word progeria derives from the Greek words 'pro' (πρό), meaning 'before' or 'premature', and 'gēras' (γηρας), meaning "old age". During the 1950s it was unclear how rare HGPS is; since then it has been statistically established that the disorder occurs in only 1 per 8 million live births. Those born with progeria typically live from their early teens to early twenties but no such knowledge existed in Richard's day. Neither the Amsters nor their doctors knew that progeria is a genetic abnormality that occurs as a new mutation and is rarely inherited. However, by the 1990s several families, especially in Asia and Europe, had been located wherein it was passed down from generation to generation and, less typically, afflicted all siblings within particular family clusters.

They took a taxi to Dr Newcomer's office in Jamaica and returned to Forest Hills by taxi. Silence prevailed. Sam was relieved he had not driven; now he was too shaken to drive back. To imagine his only son, he said to Evelyn, stricken down with this unpronounceable thing, this death sentence, this terrifying acceleration of aging as if Richard were pushing himself into the ground overnight. Sam was now more wound up than Evelyn and more frightened. He could not bring himself to articulate the P word, but he remembered it. 'Progeria,' he said over and over inside his head. How could a gifted and decent son like his have 'progeria'? The Amsters had been healthy, no cancer, no rare diseases, all died of heart attacks in old age.

Evelyn's interpretation was more nuanced but she gave Mihaela and Cezar only a mini-version of the truth. It was the way she could probe the medical history of her grandparents and great-grandparents in Romania without arousing suspicion. She kept pushing for information: did they remember anyone in Barlat who had rare diseases? Who aged prematurely? Whose hair prematurely turned grey? Mihaela reported no one. Why was her Evelyn on to this weird tack?

Evelyn made coffee when they returned and put out the small brownie cupcakes she had baked the night before. Sam retired to their bedroom. The clock struck noon when she peered directly at Richard and stared at him as he picked at his lunch. Could he detect the excruciating anguish collecting in her eyes? She felt her own hair turn grey.

As Evelyn stared she saw before her the visage of an old sour man, not her son; someone aging as you watch him, not over years or days but hours, like the gruesome flowers breaking up through the earth in time-lapse films. She sniffed the stink and gazed at his senescent expression: an old man tired of life. In shock and horror she understood what Newcomer meant. Their son had a disease that *turned you prematurely old*. By the time of Richard's scheduled Bar

---

Today scientists are particularly interested in progeria because it may reveal clues about the normal process of aging.

Mitzvah in November 1955 he'd look twenty or thirty or ... be entirely grey and then have no hair at all next year. How long did he have?

Dr Newcomer's weekly appointments rolled around quickly enough. Evelyn herself took Richard while Sam worked: Monday afternoons at 4PM. She wrote to Leonard Rose, asking to 'talk to him personally, in confidence,' and when she did, a few days later, he was baffled. Rose had never heard of this medical monstrosity: a young boy suddenly grows prematurely old? Rose assured Evelyn that Richard's cello hands were as strong as ever, his bowing more proficient every day – how could he be aging so quickly if his motor control was improving?

Every Monday Newcomer's team measured, touched, felt, and took notes. After four visits Newcomer requested an ophthalmologic colleague in Manhattan to check Richard's eyes. Evelyn took Richard to Sloane Kettering and was told he was slowly developing symptoms of premature cataract. The specialist would send a report to Newcomer, who would in turn study it and report further on the way forward.

Two weeks later Newcomer requested both parents to come in to the 4PM appointment. Sam left work early and they drove.

'I think it's *progeria* but it's not the end of the road.'

Sam asked what Dr Newcomer meant by 'the end of the road'.

'We may be able to slow it down.'

'Are you certain,' Evelyn countered, 'it *is progeria*? It was one of the first times she had pronounced the dreaded word to anyone other than Sam. Her heart was breaking open in half.

Newcomer sat stony-faced, looking down at the brown carpet rather than the despairing parents he was trying to advise.

'We *must* tell Richard he may have a serious illness', he said, 'even if the diagnosis proves to be wrong.'

Both parents disagreed, simultaneously interrupting with pleas not to. How they imprecated. How do you tell a Bar Mitzvah boy his life is over? A boy destined to become a great concert cellist? How tell him he'll look fifty in a year and never grow up?

Newcomer was silent. Though savvy he had never broken news to a patient's family about progeria.

Medical ethics is dicey business in America and rarely consistent. Even in the 1950s a view had arisen that patients must be informed of their conditions, whether old or young, whether or not incapable of understanding the diagnosis – they must be told something. Families could subvert the process, as Richard's parents now hoped to do, but Newcomer's approach had always been direct: with a child you level with the parents. Progeria treatment was non-existent, but he had been on the cutting edge of many dermatological genetic conditions involving chronic dry skin (such as *keratolysis exfoliativa*) and knew how to explain it to his patients. Newcomer believed transparency helped families deal with catastrophic illness.

He would follow Richard for a few weeks, then refer him to Children's Hospital in Boston. His mind switched gears: the Amsters have money, Richard their only son, Richard's talent as a cellist makes him special; they will do everything to save the boy. Evelyn had recently told Newcomer about Chotzinoff, Leonard Rose, Juilliard, everything, and despite Newcomer's habit of announcing diagnoses aloofly he now felt a special urge to save this young man – to go the extra mile.

Children's Hospital on Longwood Avenue in Boston was an old institution by the time Sam and Evelyn took Richard there in September 1955. It had profited from years of association with Boston's great teaching hospitals, especially the Harvard Medical School. Some of progeria's earliest cases had been diagnosed there between the two wars, and its paediatricians would not be confounded by one more case. The autumn began to appear bleak to Evelyn: Richard would be thirteen on November 22, his Bar Mitzvah was slated a day later, on Saturday November 23 at the Jewish Reformed Temple Sinai on 112th Street in Forest Hills, but increasingly her thoughts turned to Boston rather than Queens.

Dr Enders was the Hospital's Chief of Paediatrics, accustomed to telling parents their children might die. He himself had not treated progeria cases but supervised the attending physicians who did and monitored their relations with parents. Official diagnosis was left to

Dr Walter Schmidt, a German paediatrician who had diagnosed several cases. He was educated in Heidelberg and migrated to Harvard only two years earlier, then brought to Children's Hospital to continue his research into genetically determined illnesses such as progeria.

Schmidt retained Richard for three days of tests. Sam and Evelyn accommodated in the hospital motel on the other side of Longwood Avenue but could not sleep. They were fidgety and restless during the daytime, and compounded their already nervous state by drinking hourly coffees and pretending to read newspapers in the hospital canteen. On the third day Schmidt's assistant summoned them. They remembered his words despite being strung out.

Evelyn wrote in her diary that years later she could still conjure Dr Schmidt's visage. Her mind's eye still visualized this distinguished European physician immaculately decked out in white coat extending beyond his knees, black leather notebook in hand, wearing bifocals he let slip well down beyond his nose's bridge. She still heard his soft mellifluous voice speaking slowly in a thick German accent.

The Amsters were not surprised. They asked Dr Schmidt to explain the medical terms. Evelyn recorded from memory, she said, the words he spoke but his formal diagnosis letter was not in the trunk:

> 'We think Richard has progeria or a version thereof. We cannot be sure but we are ninety per cent certain. There is no treatment or cure for progeria. Later today we will bring Richard to this office and all of us, the whole team, will tell him together – in this room. You, in your role as parents, should then take him home and give him the best quality of life for whatever time he has left. He will age quickly. There will be more grey hair and then it will fall out. His skin will grow rougher than it is now. The body odour can modulate again. His personality will probably also change. Eventually he will be unable to play the cello. With luck he could live to twenty or even thirty; it is

impossible to predict how long or with what quality of life. But he will disintegrate and cannot be cured. Medicine has nothing to stop the course of progeria. Proceed with the Bar Mitzvah if you like. It will mean much to Richard. He probably will not alter much in eight weeks. Try to enjoy yourselves.'

DR SCHMIDT'S ASSESSMENT OBSESSED THEM on their return journey to Forest Hills. Richard, when apprized in half-truths, received the news with composure, uncertain whether it was good or bad. He seemed foggy, said little, suddenly seemed scared, as if a stricken deer who has been stunned rather than shot through with a dart. He said he wanted to go home after three days in 'that hospital'. He nagged his mother, yanked on her blouse sleeve. 'Can we go home!'

The Amster's response began irenically but swelled, within hours, into combat. What could a *version of progeria*' be? Mother and father were determined to find out; 'version' might be the key to whether their son lived or died. Dr Schmidt had been so spare with his words and precise in his usage that he must have meant something specific. Were there *types* of progeria? Were some types graver than others? Suppose it were one of the lesser 'versions'; then Richard might have more time than the Amsters were given to think or not even develop all the symptoms.

This lamentable focus on 'versions' produced further despair: what support would there be for them? Dr Schmidt never suggested they should return to Boston, instead intimated Dr Newcomer would monitor Richard's condition: 'Newcomer', he had vigorously stated, 'is a superb doctor perfectly competent to deal with Richard's case'. Even if invited to return to Boston, nothing would be different because no treatment existed. Their son would be left to die. Dr Schmidt said the attending physician would deal with each episode as it occurred: skin, eyes, hair, even stench if necessary.

Evelyn was so crushed that stoic resignation was the furthest response she imagined: '*something* must exist, *some* experimental drug, *some* therapy, *some* expert doctor somewhere.' Cancer at least elicited compassion, even if it was often fatal, but progeria ... if the leading expert in Boston, who had diagnosed so many cases, could not diagnose the correct 'version', what likelihood was there that in Forest Hills the local hospital would, or even some other more specialist facility in Manhattan?

Sam was more restrained and practical. He concurred about getting the right diagnosis and affirmed he would spare no cost or effort in penetrating to the root cause of Richard's illness even if he had to sell off the company and trek from coast to coast. He talked profusely about nursing care, medical insurance and specialist's fees, as if all were realities on the morning's horizon.

Richard fared better. He continued to attend school and practice the cello but his parents noticed he was practicing less each week, as if too tired, missing classes and becoming more isolated. Was he in fact more tired or were the boys shunning him? His appetite seemed undiminished but he wasn't growing, became increasingly irritable – feisty and tetchy in the way the very elderly can be. He hadn't grown in the last three years and still was the height of a ten-year old.

The Bar Mitzvah was only a few weeks away. Richard's parents decided to proceed with it as if normalcy ruled. All four grandparents had been kept in varying states of bewilderment about their grandson's condition, but now uncertainty altered to scepticism and distrust, and nothing could assuage them except constant assurances that the Bar Mitzvah was still going forward on November 23.

'How serious can it be,' Sam's mother inquired, 'if he can memorize all that Hebrew and recite?'

'Is he still going to play?' Sam's father asked on the phone.

The Amsters assured her it *was* serious, that they decided he would not play, but simultaneously that things were not as drastic as they were given to believe in Boston. When your son may be dying you have nothing to hold your world together except the cement of hope.

The day came, Richard enunciated the Hebrew words well but slowly, so slowly the listeners must have wondered; his mind held up, but he did not respond to the congratulations and showers of kisses at the reception. He was distant and cold; seemed to want to repel people. Anyone watching closely could tell he had physically altered despite his parents' best efforts to make him look, and smell, exactly like the Richard they knew.

That morning Evelyn stared at Richard as he had fixed his tie at breakfast and recognized in silent disbelief what her son had become – the spectre of a thirteen-year old boy going through the charade of a Bar Mitzvah. How much longer would he be able? Could they keep up the pretence, even the grandparents might, but how much longer could others?

Meanwhile the parent's approach, especially Evelyn's, on 'progeria's versions' was progressing through the medical establishment. Evelyn's letters to research doctors at the Mayo Clinic and Johns Hopkins Medical School brought encouraging replies: they wanted to examine Richard and persuaded his parents to present his 'case'. 'Travel as soon as you can in December after the Bar Mitzvah', was their wording. The consultants of both hospitals stressed that progeria was a cluster of conditions rather than a single disease. Depending on which part of the cluster Richard displayed the prognosis might be different.

Father, mother, and patient boarded a train from New York to Baltimore and then to Rochester Minnesota in the weeks before Christmas. At the Johns Hopkins University Hospital, in Baltimore, panels of doctors rather than a single physician evaluated Richard, as had been the case in Boston. A gentle medical administrator named 'Jenn' coordinated their assessments and communicated daily with the Amsters. By day three she revealed the preliminary collective view as a condition called 'Werner's Syndrome' rather than the more general progeria.

The new diagnosis puzzled them. What was it, they wondered. After the consultation in Boston Evelyn had visited the New York

Public Library and Columbia University Physicians and Surgeons Library to look up progeria in their medical dictionaries. She discovered that two English physicians, Jonathan Hutchinson and Hastings Gilford, originally named it at the end of the nineteenth century, and also noticed the name 'Dr Otto Werner' cropping up in the same dictionaries. When Jenn diagnosed Richard's condition as 'Werner's Syndrome', a bell struck in Evelyn's mind.

Jenn was more explicit. She explained to the Amsters that Otto Werner (1879-1936) was a German expert on progeria, dead for two decades, one of the few doctors in the world who had actually treated a few cases. If her colleagues' diagnosis was correct, based on the symptoms he was displaying Richard could well live into his twenties. All depended on how they monitored and managed his secondary symptoms: skin conditions, cataracts in the eyes, and especially the complications of cardiac arrest. The progeria itself would probably not prove fatal as most deaths from progeria came from these other causes.

Their jaunt to Minnesota occurred in freezing cold, just days before Christmas, although the great winter snows had not yet begun. The train was heated but Richard was proving tetchier than usual, quarrelling with his parents and refusing to cooperate in anything. Mayo was already decked out in Christmas trees and holly boughs, their staff beginning to leave for the holidays. The Amsters found them less attentive than the group in Baltimore but immensely courteous and avid to help out. One doctor, whose role was as note-taker for the group, was especially attentive and admitted he had never seen a case of progeria – this would be an education for him, which hardly instilled confidence in the Amsters.

The Mayo team confirmed Werner's Syndrome and provided further reasons why this could not be classic Huntingdon-Gilford Progeria Syndrome. But their advice was identical to the Hopkins group: take your boy home, provide the best daily care possible, watch over him, talk to him about the reality of what has happened to him, encourage him, let him dictate his pace and rhythm, mention death – and prepare yourselves for the long haul. They were as explicit as they needed to be, but never said anything in such stark language as to be unbearable. Neither group said anything tantamount to Dr Schmidt's early diagnosis that split open their hearts.

They returned to Forest Hills as the last Chanukah candles were being blown out, having missed it, as the American world began to shut down for two weeks. On the long-distance train back they discussed 'Werner's Syndrome' with Richard; tactfully relating some of what they had learned; between themselves, when Richard was dozing, they rehashed, over and again, a layman's sense of the differences with classical Huntingdon-Gilford Progeria Syndrome. To him they stressed what a lucky boy he was: he had by far the less lethal of the two conditions. They tried to impress on him that he must help them keep the secondary complications at bay by taking no chances. He must tell them at once as soon as he noticed any symptom.

These conversations continued over the 1955 Christmas holidays. Any neutral observer would have reported that Richard was doing his best to comply, but he was a fourteen year old boy with a death sentence hanging over him, who had suffered a colossal loss whose magnitude he could not comprehend, let alone articulate: not merely loss of a future healthy life but as a concert cellist, the one life idea that meant something to him.

He had played the cello best around a year ago, in the autumn of 1954, just before he had started to enter competitions. He won all three he entered, his prize a concert for each. His identity as a performer was beginning to form but since then he was getting tired and practicing less. The irritability he displayed masked his almost complete inability to express his loss at this base root of his developing musical identity.

The Amsters were rising to the challenge, however knocked out by the harsh reality. They, especially Evelyn, intuited Richard's current inner life, this radical puncture of every expectation he had held; yet they kept assuring each other he might still be able to enjoy a limited musical career. Leonard Rose never lost hope. But it was proving insurmountable for Evelyn – while Sam worked – to hold the strands of Richard's much curtailed life in balance: new diet, altered sleep, fierce mood swings, changed cello practice, the tutor they had hired to give him private lessons at home, occasional visits to school, including Chatham Square, the lack of friends and impossibility of his making any new ones now, the elder Abramses and Amsters clamouring for news.[9]

I kept minimally in touch with Richard during those years, 1954-56, but only saw him when his parents brought him to Chatham Square and on a few occasions in Flushing; we were friends but Richard was fast declining and his absences became more frequent. Sam drove me a couple of times from Brooklyn to their Flushing house for the weekend to play duets with him, and I still recall the shock each time. I imagine I did everything possible to dissemble, both to my decaying young friend and his distraught parents, but this time the catastrophe was not a cello that had been dropped.

Richard was now in the eighth grade; if he had had a normal academic development he would enter high school the following September 1956. The Amsters hoped he would attend Performing Arts but it was eliminated after the visit to Boston, and now they were becoming convinced he could not attend any high school. Long-term plans were shattered – they lived a week at a time. From 1955 forward they took no holidays and saw no friends. Any spare day – a Sunday in the sun – was given over to Richard, with their awareness that Monday would bring some new hazard.

It came in January 1956 when Richard developed a conjunctivitis that would not heal. Dr Newcomer, now in charge, alerted Evelyn it might not repair itself, that Richard might require hospitalization. The

---

[9] There is no reverse medical condition of progeria in which the creature ages downward and grows backward. In the less literal realm 'Benjamin Button' is a literary character hewn from science fantasy rather than medical realism (see n. 8), and F. Scott Fitzgerald's source for Benjamin Button, perhaps Samuel Butler, author of *Erewhon*, was an imagination steeped in science fantasy rather than medical science. No medical malady had been identified by the 1950s claiming to be the reverse of progeria, nor has it in the intervening six decades to the present time.

Amsters did their best for two weeks, but when it was clear that the skin around his eyes was so inflamed Richard could barely open them or see, they took him to Queens Hospital.

It was the first of many visits that year, mostly for eye-related problems, but also when Richard himself caused an infection that gave him raging fever for scratching the skin on his leg so fiercely it bled. Not too many new grey hairs appeared, but the body odour became more fetid and he was having trouble running. He said his legs hurt him, which knocked out playing ball with Sam. No cologne or body spray Evelyn could find disguised the smell: as soon as applied it seemed to evaporate into his own compromised stench.

By summertime it was plain Richard would never attend high school: his first reckoning of what toll this illness was taking. Loss of a possible musical career is one thing to a thirteen-year old, the disappearance of normal growing up another. Evelyn often heard him crying in his room. He ate less, and wasn't sleeping. Evelyn told Dr Newcomer, who recommended a child psychiatrist, to whom Richard was taken, but he was adamant he would not return a second time. The prospect of not being able to grow up took the wind out of him. He was dying.

Richard's downward slope was gradual: each week brought some new impediment but was always lessened in Evelyn's loving hands. Richard was receiving the best care domestically and medically available. The right diagnosis had been made. He was the only child of parents who doted on him and gave him their full and undivided attention. Yet Sam and Evelyn were realistic enough to know what fate held in store.

That September, as high schools reopened, when Richard would have entered one had he not acquired this debilitating disease, he developed crustaceous red boils on his feet. The skin became rough and inflamed. He hurt too much to walk. The Amsters wondered why the feet. He had still not developed manly hair on his face to need to start shaving, and his arms and torso were clear of the boils. But his feet were swollen and oozing a foul substance. After brief inspection Dr Newcomer asked the Amsters to return Richard to Queens.

This time he remained for two weeks, the longest stay so far. When Evelyn visited him each day she noticed further alterations to his personality: a new sadness, as if he were a melancholic old man. Sam and Evelyn conferred and thought it must be related to the opening of high school and Richard's first awareness of the finality of his predicament. They contemplated bringing the child psychiatrist to the hospital for another try, but Richard cried when they suggested it. He turned his head away from them, clutched his hands, and banged on the table by his bed.

Evelyn's diary is silent on the number of times mother and father went back and forth: driving down Queens Boulevard to 164th Street; home to hospital, hospital to home; short visits, long visits, missed visits, confused visits. But the diary draws attention to their fatigue. Sam was taking sleeping pills almost every night, and Evelyn lying awake in bed thinking about the bleak future. They were losing their son and becoming financially ruined to boot. It was as large a task to keep four grandparents at bay. Eventually they too visited Richard in hospital, and when they came all they did was moan. They tried to behave normally but could not hold back the tears in the presence of a fourteen-year older looking fifty. Their sobs wound up Richard, who told his mother and father he did not want to see them anymore. He worked out for himself how they were unable to cheer him up and were intensifying his depression.

The following November 1957 Richard would turn fifteen. In June 1957 he stopped playing the cello. His parents judged this decline more rapid than the doctors at Hopkins and Mayo gave them to believe was the customary pathway for Werner's Syndrome. 'He can live to thirty or even forty', they had encouragingly said, but Richard was barely fifteen and had already been in hospital six times: always in a private room, often in the same private room on the fifth floor.

This time Richard developed an early winter cold, which gave him fever and turned to pleurisy. Dr Newcomer placed him on antibiotics, which worked and cleared up his nasal cavity and lungs. He stayed in bed at home. But Richard said he could not breathe, which the Amsters understood as the cold's residue. Dr Newcomer agreed and sent him back to Queens Hospital.

Hospital tests there diagnosed cardiac complication. They showed pleurisy, which the antibiotics were slowly attacking; but also detected an irregularity in his heart potentially more serious than the pleurisy and they would not release Richard until its source was located. The Amsters asked lots of questions but were only offered doubt: no one knew what, if anything, was wrong with his heart.

Richard turned fifteen on 22 November 1957, a Tuesday. He had been at Queens for five days without mention of release. He told his mother he did not wish to die. He said the words in a weak voice, slowly, securely, as if afraid but perhaps aware of what lay in store.

The ongoing tests produced no answers. Every Wednesday before Thanksgiving is one of America's busiest days of the year: workers leave their offices early to travel significant distances, to faraway cities and states, for this most family oriented of holidays. July Fourth and New Year, more predictably riotous holidays than Thanksgiving, intrinsically differ from it, and to this day and however much commercialized it remains an epitome of the American family's curious way of life.

That Wednesday morning, a day after his fifteenth birthday, Evelyn visited Richard in hospital while Sam went to work just for a half day to close the place down for the five-day holiday. Richard seemed grumpy but plausibly himself. Evelyn spent most of the time with the attending house physician inquiring whether she could bring Richard home to Forest Hills for Thanksgiving. He never said 'no', just kept emphasizing that the tests on his heart were inconclusive; at any time he might require oxygen and if he were home might have to be rushed back. The doctor's best advice was to leave him at Queens.

Evelyn relayed the advice to Sam by telephone, and he was as disappointed as Evelyn. He drove from his office in Astoria to Queens Hospital and had a second go with the house physician – to no avail. The Amsters conferred what to do in the waiting room. Perhaps the doctors were right: to what avail to bring Richard home if they'd have to summon an ambulance on Thanksgiving Day to rush him back? A better plan was to bring a home-cooked turkey to Richard and set up a festive family gathering in his private room. They should also bring all his grandparents.

Husband and wife reluctantly agreed. Evelyn spoke to Richard in a bright voice, with the cheeriest face she could muster, exclaiming 'this could be fun': his very *own* Thanksgiving in his 'other' room. She left Queens well before four to shop for the turkey and components; Sam was already home when she returned. She cooked until seven, they had a bite, and then stared at each other. They knew why the house seemed more hollow than usual: it was the night before Thanksgiving when all families assemble. Evelyn tried to play a Chopin nocturne – the rueful opus 55, number 1, in E flat major – but the music would not flow. She shut the lid in the middle of a phrase. They retired early in anticipation of the next day's arrangements. It would be no usual Thanksgiving, with four grandparents nervously assembled in a hospital room.

Around 10AM on Thanksgiving morning the phone rang. Evelyn answered. It was a different house physician this time from the male they consulted with on Wednesday. Her voice was calm: she said Richard's situation had deteriorated during the night and they should immediately come down.

Evelyn inquired how it worsened. She reported Richard having trouble breathing. Evelyn gulped; her brain working overtime to reflect how prescient yesterday's house physician was: he predicted this possibility when imploring the Amsters not to take Richard home.

Evelyn put down the receiver. She and Sam abandoned the notion of a 'festive day around Richard's bed', left their turkey cooking in Forest Hills, and rushed back to Queens Hospital. The roads were deserted, as always on Thanksgiving Day morning when the whole American world basks in the smells and sights of the coming banquet. They said nothing to each, just stared ahead at the empty road.

Twenty minutes later they were seated in a white-walled room alone with this house physician; a young woman of about thirty, low-keyed, and genuinely sincere.

'I'm so sorry but Richard is *gone*.'

'*Gone*,' Evelyn blurted out, 'what do you mean *gone*?'

'He died at eight-thirty this morning.'

'How?' Sam came to her instant aid. They were not expecting this news.

'His heart was compromised and we think he walked to the window gasping for air.'

'You mean all that oxygen could not keep a healthy fifteen-year old going?' was Sam's emphatic reminder that there must have been some negligence.

'It isn't so simple, Mr Amster,' she calmly volunteered.

'Simple?' Evelyn tagged on.

The doctor spoke slowly, almost counting the words.

'He may have jumped out of the window. He had difficulty breathing all night. The nurses thought he would need to be moved to the ICU as soon as possible. I wrote the orders to move him at 8 AM. The attending nurse on his floor entered his room to prepare him very soon afterwards. But he was not there.'

Sam and Evelyn looked at each other in dismay, still speechless and bewildered.

'He could not be found'.

'Was he wandering around the hospital then?' Sam inquired.

'No, he left his bed, and probably opened the window gasping for air. While inhaling for air and gasping he may have lost his balance and fallen out.'

Then haze permeated everything, invaded all space and time and consciousness. Nothing was discrete, borders ceased to exist, and colours combined. During the first few days after Richard's death Sam and Evelyn never acknowledged that their son plunged to his death or threw himself out the window. The solace they gave each other was of a softer, more idyllic variety: 'lovely, sweet-scented Richard, so talented and gifted, desperately gasping for breath, trying to find oxygen in the close night air, his lungs heaving, *accidentally falling* out of the window. If only they had been there to bring him oxygen.' This was how they coped.

Their Richard would not jump to his death; their boy would not kill himself. This was an accident, an unspeakable accident, no matter where it occurred. Even the hospital agreed with them. It became the official version for the police who required no inquest.

Richard's funeral took place on Monday 27 November 1957, five days after his fifteenth birthday. Jews bury swiftly but not on the Sabbath. Having died on Thursday, Richard would ordinarily have been buried within forty-eight hours on Saturday, but as the Sabbath was outlawed in Jewish religion the Amsters awaited the Monday.

A raw East wind blew, chilling them to the bone as they entered the front door of the Jewish chapel in Forest Hills. Four desolate grandparents side by side in one row, their intractable faces starched in white pallor, while Evelyn and Sam were concealed behind a curtain that shielded devastated parents. A few dozen friends and former classmates attended, as well as cousins who knew Richard was declining, several of the medical staff in Boston, and Leonard Rose. Evelyn's diary estimated it at fifty people.

The rabbi spoke eloquently, saying God alone knew why bad things happen to good people and enumerating Richard's achievement as a cello prodigy. His theme was the unknowability of God's ways. No mention was made of progeria or the hospital's fifth floor. The implication was that Richard died in hospital of a rare illness, the immediate cause of death cardiac failure. The death certificate read as much. If you did not know before arriving at the Jewish funeral chapel that Richard had plunged five floors to his death, whether accidentally or intentionally, you'd never have found out at the funeral.

Sam and Evelyn wore black. Evelyn insisted on wearing the same black belt she had worn years earlier in Town Hall – the belt that held together the debut velvet gown; a new half-length black coat complemented it. Evelyn was too distraught to reflect on her decision to wear it, just reported it 'as worn' in her diary. After the service finished the immediate family walked to the graveside. Then the Amsters returned home where caterers prepared tables for the bitter Jewish wake.

They were reformed Jews and did not follow ancient customs, sitting shiva, turning their mirrors, leaving a bowl of water at the front door for mourners to wash their hands. Mihaela and Cezar were devastated but still capable of bringing hard-boiled eggs and bagels on the second and third day. They chanted a prayer of condolence – Sam could not determine whether it was in Hebrew or Romanian – the Seudat Hawra'ah. Mihaela never took her eye away from Evelyn.

PERHAPS THE STRANGEST ASPECT OF THE VANISHING ACT is that spatial and temporal death can differ so acutely. All the dead leave souvenirs of some type – archival, artefactual, material, mental – and these objects and memories fuse with the passage of time; this is why it is so easy over the years to forget the exact day when a beloved died. But the spatial component is more serrated and jagged and remains more engraved in the toothstone of memory: physically here one minute, gone the next, with the imagination mired in searches for answers to the perennial question 'gone where'? The mind conceptualizes the possibility of abstract disappearance, of course, but can never bring closure to it as it can with memories fixed in time and place because memories linger almost indefinitely. The imagination remembers the 'time' of the deceased: that Richard did this last year, went there as a young child; that his birthday was only a few weeks ago, what his appearance seemed to be the other day. But sudden spatial absence is stupefying and essentially amorphous, not even clarified in cemeteries where the dead lie in bounded plots.

The more Sam and Evelyn tried to accustom themselves to their house apart from Richard, the less they could. Their memories of him remained vivid but not the spaces. Their home was a space for three. How could it be reduced in the flick of an eye to a space for only two? Cause and effect ceased to operate from the moment they were informed how he had plunged from the fifth floor.

They had no strategy for the future because Richard's death unforgivingly shocked them. They had mastered what they could of

Werner's Syndrome over several months, expecting that Richard would slowly decline, but with loving care would live on into his twenties. They were prepared to make any sacrifice for him to soldier on; indeed could not imagine not making it. But falling out of a fifth-floor window (they never said suicide) completely deranged their expectation coming so soon after the definitive diagnosis. By the New Year (1958) they were still thrashing the probabilities without mentioning the 's word'. They wondered whether Richard had had enough. Was this his way of checking out early? He was a smart young man, even in degeneration, and must have intuited what lay in store for him.

Back and forth wife and husband evaluated every motive: it was an accident, it was not suicide; no matter how discouraged, depressed with the frequent hospital visits and the lack of a cure. Richard – they concurred – would not throw himself out of that window. Still, the endless thrashing changed nothing and paradoxically drove them apart. Their only offspring was dead, leaving them with the sense of their having 'lost their lives' as well.

Dr Zide placed both on medication the day after Richard's death, which they remained on for four weeks, but Sam could not extricate himself from it and fared worse than Evelyn. He was becoming uncharacteristically combative. Arguments provoked him to rise to the challenge. Afterwards he often retracted but lost his appetite in the process and slept even worse than when Richard lived.

'If we had not pushed the cello so much he might be alive,' he suddenly yelled one evening.

'He lived for music, Sam,' Evelyn countered.

'That's not what I mean; Richard was cheated of an ordinary boyhood.'

'He died of a rare genetic illness that has nothing to do with cellos.'

'Of course, but I'm talking about the window; maybe he didn't fall, maybe wanted to throw himself out,' he rattled at her.

Evelyn persuaded herself that Richard's death was an accident. Down deep she knew Sam also believed this – his bullying her was just his way of challenging her. Their conversations, she reflected, were about *them*, not about their dead son.

'You wanted a Richard who was a carbon copy of yourself,' he started all over again a few hours later.

'How can you say that, when I did everything possible to ...'

On they bickered, Sam interrupting her, changing tack in midstream, chortling, gesturing at the piano as if about to assault the instrument, endlessly picking fights despite her not rising to the bait.

Evelyn's *bête-noire* was each endless, empty day, not the arguments with Sam whose motives she sussed out and defused. Their days grew purposeless and identical, Mondays no different from Fridays. She sat in a chair unable to be motivated for any activity and obsessed about Richard: the shrinking, grey-haired, old man at fifteen, rotting in stench, going blind, scratching away at his rough skin. The decaying man-child, biology's rarest and most incongruous living creature who prematurely ages.[10]

Her *idee fixe* ran away with itself, always down the same path, impossible to obstruct. She'd sit alone in the same chair in the living room for hours, staring into space, hallucinating about grotesque children in the bodies of old men, greying, shrivelled, dying, prematurely aging into replicas of adult nostalgic types – as she thought she might become. How, she wondered, could a healthy little boy age overnight into a premature version of the man he would never become? Silently she wept.

---

[10] Sometime in the 1970s Evelyn told me it was during these months that she realized why Rachmaninoff's music had struck such a chord in her own nervous system as an adolescent. She said he knew 'exactly what it felt like to be utterly broken, down at the bottom; not just low and flat but on the wheel's lowest spoke.' I wondered when she told me whether this was *Rachmaninoff in retrospect* when your young son is decaying before your own eyes but did not want to rekindle delicate memories. Evelyn expanded: it was not merely Rachmaninoff's lyricism, she said, his poignant imagination and melody but this awareness of being down at the bottom. I think I added that his Romantic forebears – Chopin, Schumann, Fauré – had little of this intuition, and suggested that only Tchaikovsky may have owing to his own sexual tragedy which existed without any exit except death.

Evelyn lost interest in the house. Wife and husband began to eat out most nights, two adults mute at a table. They knew they could not continue this way indefinitely; some change would occur and when it came, it would carry away everything with it, a tidal wave sweeping everything out to sea.

Cezar died suddenly that summer in Atlantic City. Collapsed listening to his favourite talk show. Mihaela called it a 'blissful farewell' at sixty-five. 'Your father did not suffer for one minute,' she boasted, as if she had preordained Fate to do it. Then Lola, Sam's older sister in Santa Barbara, whom they had seen little of over the years, announced she was getting divorced; she had been separated for about a year and was moving with her three children down to Los Angeles. However, it was strangely Evelyn's return to the piano that brought in the tide.

Lola tried to get them both into a family psychotherapy group for bereaved parents. Dr Zide alerted her about the newly forming group and recommended it. They met in sub-groups for consolation: three, four, five, sometimes larger gatherings, to make life bearable when it seemed impossible to carry on. Sam flatly refused, said he did not feel comfortable: his loss was private to him and he did not wish to share it with 'the world'.

'How, Sam, in any fairness can you call them the *world*? They're in an identical situation to …'

Sam interrupted, shifting the conversation to accusations that Evelyn had moulded Richard into a clone of herself, which left *his* son so vulnerable that the prospect of losing a concert career caused Richard to jump. He said Evelyn was *sick*, a *sick self*, that she was longing for her own lost childhood without any remorse at having stolen it from *his* son. Who cared, he yelled, whether Richard became a concert cellist?

'Of course he jumped,' he continued, 'you fool. Jumped no less than you froze up on the concert stage. Richard wasn't gasping for oxygen. He didn't jump because he could not bear the thought of becoming a patient. He jumped because he lost his identity, which you stole. Lost himself, lost his father, lost everything. You are to blame for that', and Sam broke down into hysterical sobs.

An absurd claim but Sam's preposterous notion had a beneficial counter-effect on Evelyn: elicited a suppressed redemption in her and caused her to desire to retrieve what she herself had lost. Not Town Hall and the stage fright and the lost career, but her piano itself and its physicality: the fingers' nervous interaction with the keyboard; its dexterity, activity, motion. She stopped fixating and staring into space. Her fingers were suffering – she came to believe – and she grew determined to counter their deprivation.

As soon as Sam left for work, she began to practice: two, three, four hours a day. This 'readjustment', as her diary for 1958 calls it, was not sudden. It occurred over many months and assuaged her unspeakable loss. Evelyn never played in the evening after Sam returned. For a long time he was even unaware she was practicing again.

Evelyn's diary contains this passage:

> You may think it strange I withheld this return to playing from Sam but my silence was perfectly normal to me. It was my new life, all I had left after Richard's death, and Sam had little part in it. By playing again I realized I had loved Sam in a limited way; he had been the father of our son, of course, and was a good father, but he never understood what it meant to have 'music in your blood'.

The diary continues this way at the point she is barely recovering from grief:

> I told Sam everything about freezing up in my Town Hall debut while we were courting – he said he understood. At that time, in 1941, before Richard was born, the hesitation was mine: I was still too close to the nightmare to confront it and could not present it dispassionately to a fiancé. There would have been no point trying to explain

the concert programme – especially the Rachmaninoff Sonata – that had caused such conflict with Adele. Sam would not have understood. Only a musician can appreciate the point about defective technique, or know what the challenge of playing Rachmaninoff's piano music is.

EVELYN FADED FROM MY PRESSING CONCERNS OVER THE NEXT DECADE. I cannot even recall exactly when I became aware of Richard's death. It must have been in 1958, during the winter or spring after he died, while I was still hanging around Chatham Square on Saturdays. That year I was a senior student at Performing Arts High School preparing myself to play Rachmaninoff's Second Piano Concerto. I had won the music students' concerto competition, whose prize was a debut concert in Town Hall with a professional symphony orchestra conducted by Julius Grossman.[11] I was over the moon at having won. Deaths, even poor Richard's death, appeared in my mind as interloping predators to be removed.

Another, more recent, pursuit called for attention: the allure of reading, the atmosphere of books, acquired knowledge, and unrelenting curiosity about the world beyond my Brooklyn origins. My parents were second cousins whose parents – my grandparents – prearranged their marriage. My mother was uneducated but wept when she heard classical and ethnic music; my father would have completed his Ph. D. in Romance Philology at Columbia University if the Great American Depression had not hurled him, instead, into Orchard Street with his pushcart filled with fancy ten-cent apples. Theirs' had been an arranged marriage that ought never to have been

---

[11] Julius Grossman (1912-2002) was the Head of Music at Performing Arts High School and a conductor who led free music concerts for half a century in metropolitan New York.

made – so different were their mindsets and emotional orbits except for their similar genetic makeup and identical immigrant backgrounds.

My mother wanted me to become a rabbi but would have settled for a high-school principal, and she constantly encouraged me to excel on the piano in the belief it would lead to one of these two professions – how I do not know. My father, almost deranged by the poverty the Great American Depression heaped on his side of the family, and indicated for him personally, hoped I would choose a more secure profession, medicine above all: 'You'll never suffer as a doctor'. He was an atheist, my mother a believer, especially in the rituals of Jewish orthodoxy. Unable to agree about religious upbringing they permitted me and my only sibling, a sister Linda, to go our own ways. In my case this meant I could play the piano, which I did for many hours each day, until an African-American high-school teacher, Celia Drewry, who later became a Dean at Princeton, instilled in me the bug of learning in a big way – so magisterially it temporarily deposed the piano.

Once bitten by the new curiosity – learning, reading – I persuaded myself that no matter how much I wanted to play the piano, and pursue some musical career, I must attend university. In 1957 I applied to America's great institutions of higher education: Amherst, Harvard, and Yale – and was told I had a good chance of admission. The great pianist Rudolf Serkin had heard me play when my Chatham Square teacher, Mme. Anka Berstajn Landau, sent me to him; he took me on for a few lessons in preparation for a concerto concert.[12] I had also won a place in the WQXR Radio Station Young Artists competition, which gave winners a chance to play on their nationally

---

[12] Polish born Anka Landau (1879-1976) enjoyed a celebrated career as a piano pedagogue at the Vienna Conservatory of Music, where she was Richard Robert's main assistant, and later in Manhattan at Chatham Square Music School. Chotzi eventually assigned me to her. Richard Robert had taught Rudolf Serkin and George Szell, both of whom became instrumental in rescuing Landau from the Nazis in the late 1930s and bringing her to New York; see Juilliard School of Music Archives for Landau's letters appealing to Serkin to abort her fate in the death camps. While still in Vienna Landau became the friend of Pablo Casals with whom she had a lifelong correspondence. I learned most of what I know about piano playing from her.

known radio programme, and on that basis Serkin offered to supply a reference for my college dossier. Amherst and Harvard accepted me with full scholarships; Yale did not. I fell in love so swiftly with Amherst's bucolic atmosphere that the campus became irresistible in my treeless Brooklyn sidewalk imagination. When Dean Eugene Wilson admitted me as a Merrill Scholar I swiftly accepted.[13] Harvard was America's greatest university but could not compete in this adolescent's mind with Amherst's rustic setting. And I had not yet seen its burnished maple trees basking in paradisiacal autumn sunlight. All these activities – Rachmaninoff concerto in Town Hall, WQXR, college applications and visits, the decision where to attend college – occurred within five months of Richard's death, so it was unsurprising he would then recede in my rushed on-the-make mind.

After graduating from Amherst I attended graduate school at Princeton, and after gaining a Ph. D. there I was offered my first academic post in the Harvard English Department – so I ended up at Harvard anyway despite not attending its famed undergraduate college. After several angst-filled years at Harvard I moved to a professorship at UCLA, where I remained for twenty-six years, and it was while still working there that I reconnected with Evelyn.

My intellectual interests changed over these decades. At Princeton and Harvard I concentrated on 'catching up' as an academic student, having been left so far behind my fellow students by years of piano practice. My doctoral dissertation at Princeton recreated the role of medicine in the eighteenth-century novel and in its wake all things

---

[13] Charles Merrill (1885-1956) spent time at Amherst College but did not graduate; after he made millions at Merrill Lynch, the American stockbrokers, he endowed a scholarship at Amherst for academic excellence. Our family was poor and it would have been impossible for me to attend Amherst without this annual scholarship. My father astutely took a night job as a filing clerk so his son could compete for the Merrill Scholarship sending just one boy (Amherst was not yet coeducational) to Amherst. Dean Eugene Wilson was then one of America's most innovative deans of admission and willing to admit students, like me, whose academic credentials fell below the norm. I never would have been admitted without my proficiency on the piano and testimonials from Anka Landau and Rudolf Serkin.

medical began to assume grand proportions only equal to my former life at the piano (was I a frustrated doctor?). By the time I started to teach at Harvard in 1966 I was construing myself as a 'specialist' in the relations of literature and medicine, and attending classes at Harvard's Medical School to learn about medicine from the inside.

The *longue durée* of one overlap especially intrigued me: the growth of nostalgia, or 'longing for the home' in Western civilization. My curiosity about nostalgia awakened long before Evelyn's death; in any case, I did not discuss the subject with her until it became apparent that her quest 'for Rachmaninoff' was not entirely dissimilar from my own, admittedly far more academic, developing concern. But we spoke different languages of nostalgia: hers' was intuitive, disconnected from her life in any systematic way, and certainly unhistorical. My interest in nostalgia had probably awakened during my transition from music to the pursuit of an academic career, when I began to recognize that 'mindsets' were also types of 'homes' – *mental homes* – no less than those constructed from bricks and mortar. My curiosity about nostalgia's past was doubtlessly shaped as well, if not more consciously so, by the glaring facts of my biographical multi-outsiderdom – child of immigrant Sephardic-Jewish parents; like Evelyn, aspiring concert pianist; unlike Evelyn, intellectual and homosexual – and further consolidated during the 1970s by dissatisfaction with American life and my decision, made much later in 1993, to migrate abroad. When Evelyn died four years earlier, in 1989, my disaffection was peaking.[14]

---

[14] The reader many well wonder what I mean by disaffected. I was a professor at the University of California, having lived throughout the 1970s and 1980s, as it were with my colleagues, under the regime of our actor-conservative icon and State Governor, and then President of the USA, Ronald Reagan. The mood of the University during those two decades became increasingly demoralized, our budgets repeatedly cut; and because our State Governor, now national President, had risen to fame and then public election from the ranks of second-rate actors in Hollywood, the tone of life in LA seemed to grow ever-more tilted towards the entertainment industry and away from academia despite its world-class university. But indubitably the larger cause of disaffection was cultural and historical: my interests were in areas usually designated as 'high culture' whereas LA life cultivated 'popular culture', and the 'past' was relegated almost to yesterday; so much so that

Nostalgia's historical trajectory and my predicament about it dovetailed in oblique ways. An Alsatian military doctor had coined the word *nostalgia* at the end of the seventeenth century.[15] By 1980 its story had still not been told, particularly the *medical* and *non*medical

---

advertisements for houses, for example, would read 'Old Norman chateau, antique, high ceilings …' for a modern edifice on the Sunset Strip built in 1949. As a cultural historian I was living in a place without the history that interested me (of course it possessed a superabundance of its own local history), nor could I imagine there would ever be any, and I even began to write a book provisionally entitled *Written Out of History*.

[15] Johannes Hofer (fl. 1680s) described his ailing soldiers in a landmark treatise entitled *Dissertatio Medica de nostalgia* (Basel, 1688). An English translation by Caroline Anspach is given in the *Bulletin for the History of Medicine*, 2 (1934). During the Enlightenment, medical doctors sought to locate the organs most affected by nostalgic longing, and concentrated on the midriff region as its chief site, especially the heart, stomach, spleen, and liver. Their medical theory converged with an earlier Renaissance melancholy whose anatomy also focused on that somatic region; thus the condition, in English, known 'the spleen', vapours, low spirits, or, more recently, our broad generalized depression. But this long medical tradition from Hofer forward should never obscure the *other* nostalgia: the universal condition of longing lodged in memory rather than in particular organs of the midriff. The memory of history, the past, and the collective emotional heritage accrued by nations. This *other* nostalgia, this non-symptomatic variety stored in memory, is not merely an individual sickness but a malady of collective memory and trauma. It is the one Freud labeled 'uncanny', or 'unheimlich', in his famous essay of that name, and pronounced as a fundamental structure of human life inherently related to the death instinct. In this sense Freud's psychoanalysis itself entailed a return to 'home' through the reification and subsequent analysis of childhood traumas. Freud further transformed individual nostalgia from longing for physical home to searching for one's childhood as the likeliest antidote to the maladjustments of adult life. But his vocabulary and paradigm of nostalgia has proved elusive since the partial disparagement of psychoanalysis in the mid twentieth century. And if Freud and his psychiatric brethren privatized and internalized this *other*, non-symptomatic nostalgia, others since then have removed its site to a different sphere altogether, located in the interstice between individual and collective memory, especially among vast numbers of immigrant populations. It is, finally, this *other* far more elusive nostalgia, in both its original Freudian and post-Freudian versions, which spoke so forcefully to the collective Russian imagination as the search for mother country and 'homeland'. Nothing less than these complex contexts can explain how a late Romantic figure, such as Rachmaninoff was, could become so enmeshed in its slippery net. See also n. 16.

overlaps, the extraordinary ways in which great imaginative literature from the time of Homer's *Odyssey* described this malaise of longing for the home – the Greeks called it yearning for the *oikos*, the home – to the moment in early modern civilization when military doctors like Hofer first embedded its symptoms in their medical works.

The more I learned about nostalgia's past the more convinced I became of the impossibility of amassing a sweeping panopticon of its heritage. It sprawled too wide, encompassed too many alterations over centuries; would resist a single model to combine its multicultural traditions – European, Asian, African, American. I came to believe that only a microhistory – a miniscule case history exquisitely narrated down to the minutest detail – would permit me to demonstrate how its various medical and *non*medical strands combined.

I remember myself during the 1980s as forever in search of a suitable figure for this microhistory but every candidate I proposed to myself was eliminated. A was too-well known or her nostalgia already too well documented; B insufficiently nostalgic or inadequately capable of biographical documentation; C was an anomaly; D such a minor figure no one would be interested, etc. An historical incident or episode might satisfy the criterion of 'microhistory' but it proved even more treacherous to identify than a single historical figure. How could one 'incident' in someone's life illuminate a whole biography?

Nostalgia's trajectory since Hofer first named it 'nostalgia' intrigued a cadre of medical historians, especially for the way it manifested itself among Nelson's sailors and during the American Civil War. But literary scholars at the end of the last century were still preoccupied with situating its appearances in particular epochs: Romanticism, among the Victorians, in Modernism, in Russian cinema, in Joyce's and Nabokov's exile, in the poems of homesick Russian poet Josef Brodsky.[16] But no *single figure* cried out to be

---

[16] Svetlana Boym's *The Future of Nostalgia* (New York: Basic Books, 2001) remains the most thorough treatment of the cultural history of nostalgia for all things Russian; she is silent only about Russian music. Boym curiously omits Russian film maker Andrei Tarkovsky (1932-86) whose film *Nostalghia* makes for a

identified as 'nostalgic' to the degree that reclassification would alter our whole sense of the person; and the figures that did – Nabokov – had already been studied.

Evelyn's jottings, like a poet's rainwater, seeped into my consciousness and began to haunt me. Rachmaninoff had to be that figure. The revelation shook me, not for its novelty but the long time it took me to recognize the obvious. I asked myself how I, whose Performing Arts prize had been a celebrity performance of Rachmaninoff's Second Piano Concerto; I who had been reading about composers for decades since that Town Hall debut concert in 1958; how I could not have recognized *this* Rachmaninoff earlier? Music was my most native cognitive domain – I knew about music before I learned anything about language or literature and long before I knew anything about medicine; surely I ought to have recognized that one of the great composers would fit the bill. But who? The great Romantic composers were permeated with melancholy and nostalgia – Chopin, Schubert, Schumann, Brahms, just as the Romantic poets were: 'Ah, knight at arms, alone and palely loitering, what ails thee?' in Keats's coinage. But their biographers said everything that could be said. No debate existed about the status of their Romantic nostalgia, and reports of a nostalgic Byron or Shelley would hardly be news in the 1990s. Besides, the Romantic Movement itself had been the medium for nostalgia, and to write, for example, about Chopin-the-nostalgic or Schumann-the-nostalgic, or the nostalgia of the great Romantic symbolic painters, would reinvent the wheel. Flashing

---

brilliant example of the type of longing for Russia some of Rachmaninoff's displaced contemporaries experienced. In the film, protagonist writer Andrei Gorchakov yearns to return to Russia after residing in Italy to research the life of eighteenth-century Russian composer Pavel Sosnovsky. Another of Tarkovsky's films, however, *Andrei Rublov*, even more exquisitely captures the type of nostalgia Rachmaninoff experienced for the old Russia: replete with icons, church bells (a huge bronze bell is cast in the ground), birch trees, pagan celebrations in the forest, a boy drinking well water out of his mother's pail, traditional Russian log houses, scents of tar, turpentine and linen seed oil, and dandelion seeds floating through the air. The scenes in *Andrei Rublov* are either set outdoors in meadows near lakes, or in buildings where the viewer peers through gaps to see the rain pouring in.

forward a century, once Modernism set in – the aesthetic of abjuring the past while simultaneously and paradoxically longing for it – changed all this. Prokofiev, Stravinsky, Shostakovich – to consider only Russian Modernist composers – spurned all nostalgic traces in their music, yet vivid residues remain while being transformed into ironic and parodic musical forms appearing as anything but nostalgic.

Likewise the great 'Russian Five' composers, in Russian 'the Mighty Handful' – Balakirev, Borodin, Mussorgsky, Rimsky-Korsakov, and César Cui[17] – whose music evolved from other sources, thriving on nostalgic threads while emphasizing its Russian roots above all others. Tchaikovsky and Scriabin were too original to be included: the first indulging all these characteristics while defining his own childlike voice in idiosyncratic ways, the other, Scriabin, too allegorical and mystical to be comfortably classified among them.

Where did this Russian musical taxonomy leave Rachmaninoff? A misfit: a late Romantic, derivative composer, unable to break out of his all-consuming sentimental mould, constrained as a composer by dint of becoming one of the era's most distinguished – perhaps the most superlative – virtuoso pianists.[18] Yet composers and performers have been configured differently for generations. The twenty-first century preoccupation with a dead *composer's* personal relationships appears as a leftover from the nineteenth century's investment in the artist as a deviant psychological type. Critical moments in that life are constantly becoming imperilled by the artist's small irritations and

---

[17] Besides, the 'Mighty Handful' met in St Petersburg and Rachmaninoff was associated with Moscow. Cui, their spokesman, attacked Rachmaninoff as a Romantic throwback to a bygone era and wrote dispraisingly about Rachmaninoff's second piano concerto.

[18] Chopin, Schumann and Brahms were also pianists but not in Rachmaninoff's league nor professionalized and managed by the American Charles Foley in the slick way he was. They were composers *first*, pianists second who often performed only to introduce their compositions to the world. If Beethoven had never composed as he did – an absurd *as if* position – he would not be remembered as the greatest virtuoso pianist of his generation, nor would Chopin, but Rachmaninoff undeniably was *sans pareil*, rivalled only in his era by Josef Hofmann. If one wants to compare Rachmaninoff with the greatest pianists of bygone eras it is Clara Schumann, not Robert, who should be invoked.

great distractions, reversals in financial and amorous affairs, health, and luck.

More to the point, Rachmaninoff's biographers had recognized his intense yearning for a past shattered by the revolutionaries in late tsarist Russia and, after 1917 by the Bolsheviks, but had not provided the details. The contexts were missing: social, economic, political, even symbolic and apocalyptic. Most had written as if Rachmaninoff lived in a Platonic Cave where neither life nor culture enters, as if he were neither flesh nor blood. Yet even forgotten Evelyn, who was no scholar, knew there was something paltry about the way Rachmaninoff had been understood. Her identification with him exceeded rational understanding, although she learned to possess the facts of his life and play the notes of his music. She sympathized with him to the point of inhabiting his personality and locating her symbolic home in him.

My pre-1990 sense of Rachmaninoff was jagged. I was uneasy about his received profile but could not articulate which aspects required recalibration. During the years I spent immersed in her jottings, light gradually broke about my own mad quest for Nostalgia's (with an upper-case N) century-long curve. Two figures crystallized: Rachmaninoff and Evelyn, both racked with nostalgia despite their different time and place, both ruined and energized by nostalgia, both parasitically feeding off its psychic nutriment while fettered to its chains and prisonhouse.

But patience was giving out. I had received several national research grants to write *'nostalgia's history'* yet felt imprisoned myself until I could locate the 'right' figure. I had discarded dozens of candidates, as one does shoes and trousers in department stores, yet the right figure with just the perfect 'nostalgic feel' did not come forward. Books about collective memory and trauma permeated the early 1990s but it was the work of a Harvard Slavicist, Professor Svetlana Boym, which brought the 'right figure' into sharp relief.[19] Rachmaninoff was the omitted figure in Boym's *Future of Nostalgia*: an artist caught between high Romanticism, the so-called 'Silver Age' of

---

[19]See n. 16.

Russian culture at the end of the nineteenth century, and the new Modernism in music and literature – a misfit tragically captured by dint of historical circumstance and his own inability to innovate.

I PINCHED MYSELF AND FORESAW the coming malaise. Was Rachmaninoff *really* the 'right' figure? Was Evelyn *really* obsessed with the 'right' (right for me) biographical nostalgic during the decades I had somewhat lost track of her? More pressingly, the connection between Evelyn's story and Rachmaninoff's. I was persuaded beyond all reasonable doubt that I had needed Evelyn's prior tragedy to understand Rachmaninoff's, but others might not see it this way. A great biographer might persuade readers about Rachmaninoff's plight without ever having heard of Evelyn Amster.

This, in nutshell, was the dilemma, and it raised multiple questions about 'stories' I could not answer. Questions such as what happens when stories are shared between figures of the same generation, or figures who lived in different generations? How does one story enable profound understanding of another? Evelyn and Rachmaninoff inhabited different mental universes; does my ability to hold them simultaneously in mind as parallel universes make a significant difference to either story? Why not write two books? Besides, who owns a story? This is the story of both Evelyn *and* Rachmaninoff, not of one without the other, and both were real, biographical, historical figures; or the reverse: they may have been real biographical subjects, but as constructed in my mind they amount to fictional figures. Not the real Rachmaninoff who composed all the music but some imaginary psychological configuration.

So I agonized and procrastinated and wrote nothing. When the despair intensified to breaking point I swung to an opposite position, wondering how I could have been so *lucky* to know the one person in the world capable of clinching the deal for me. 'No Evelyn, no Rachmaninoff', I would caution myself. In more sanguine moments, 'who cares if *Rachmaninoff's Cape* never existed? The world has too many books already'.

One development overtook all others: the idea about parallel universes: Rachmaninoff's *and* Evelyn's, constantly back and forth between the two figures, both dead; figures who had never met, wondering what each would have said to the other… the secretive composer captured by nostalgia for Russia, and my friend whose son was destined to become a great cellist. The philosophers and historians had written a great deal about the validity of the idea of parallel universes. Why should I discard it so blithely?

The few people I confided in were puzzled. 'What a story' was the typical refrain, capped by wonder if this were the *same* Rachmaninoff they knew. Everyone assumes Rachmaninoff's Hollywood celebrity status automatically reflects a sane body in sane mind but nothing could be further from the reality. Some knew he was very tall, others that he had abnormally large hands.[20] A few, to whom I told the story, were more fascinated by Richard's progeria. They had never heard of this medical condition … 'how awful it must have been for poor Evelyn', they said, so would I please 'focus on the patient-son'. I listened to these responses for years, wondering how I could avoid succumbing to the fate I most feared: to write *two* books – one about Rachmaninoff, another about Evelyn – or write one book entitled *Rachmaninoff's Cape* (for Evelyn's sense of his performative stage shield and my more psychoanalytical reconstruction of his nostalgic defences) and to be told the two parts, the two parallel universes, did not hang together.

No need existed for a new *factual* biography of Rachmaninoff: Sergei Bertensson published it in 1956, an accurate account of the great composer's life.[21] Enticing me now was a taste of what a new *cultural* biography of Rachmaninoff might resemble – its feel, scope, boundaries – one sketching the contours of his overarching nostalgia and explaining the toll it took on both his lived life and musical

---

[20] Although they were probably not attributable to Marfan's Syndrome, which usually displays large limbs, especially very large hands.

[21] For Bertensson and other biographers of Rachmaninoff, see p. 23.

compositions. If Rachmaninoff's music is what counts now, then all lovers of his music – and classical music lovers more generally – need to understand why he composed the works the way he did; why *all* the great works we love him for were written *before* he departed Russia in 1917, and why his creative imagination so precipitously shrivelled after he emigrated.[22]

I TOLD MY FRIEND HELEN about my predicament, especially the quandary about writing *two* books. Helen worked in Brooklyn as a journalist and wrote for top newspapers; single, mid-forties, a couple of years younger than me, Yale Ph. D. in Comparative Literature, one of those persons who read everything in those days when reading still necessitated long hours in libraries, spoke a half-dozen languages, enjoyed a rare neuroplasticity of mind capable of connecting everything to everything else – and published nothing except her short columns.

Helen said take a plane from LAX and come to my summer place. 'I'm editing, we can talk in the interstices.' She used words like interstice in ordinary phone conversation. This is how I recall our visit during the summer of 1992.

I closed my laptop, packed a small case, flew to JFK, rented a car, and drove out to Helen's secluded cabin in the Catskills.

'I can't go on. It's no good.'

'What do you mean, no good?' Helen sweetly asked.

'Too highbrow. Literary memoirs for the literate few. Publishers will fluff it off as another humdrum biography of Rachmaninoff. They won't

---

[22] This imagined biography is all the more pressing insofar as the leading scholars of Russian music have 'written Rachmaninoff out', even in sprawling histories of Russian music, no one more influentially than distinguished American musicologist Professor Richard Taruskin of the University of California at Berkeley.

notice the difference, the parallel universes. Or they'll recommend discarding Rachmaninoff and telling Evelyn's story alone.'

'But Rachmaninoff is a big, big fish,' Helen offered, 'if this story had involved Mozart or Beethoven they'd pounce on it.'

I knew the fish's size but persuading the masses was something else. Most people are captivated by Rachmaninoff's music but could not tell you two facts about him other than that he was Russian.

Helen poured me a stiff gin and tonic. The air was close and the windows open. You could smell the pinecones infiltrating her patio. We drank in the green oasis she had created there overlooking huge, dark pines.

'Well, my dear, then how else can you write it?'

'I cannot imagine it as two books.'

Helen was a savvy and well-tested writer who had been through a lot. But she was not the most patient creature who ever lived and unimpressed by moaning. She pierced to the bottom of my quandary: 'Why not?'

'Because it's not two books, it's one book; it's the story of a woman fixated on Sergei Rachmaninoff, and her friend George who has been searching for a nostalgic figure like Rachmaninoff to write about, and would never have found it had it not been for Evelyn.'

'Wow, that's a mouthful!'

'Yes, and this is what I need to bring off in the writing. I have to persuade the reader that you cannot have one story without the other.'

'So, you mean the memoir is about you*?'*

'No, it's not about me*, but I'm the axis in the middle of the two parallel universes'.*

Helen grasped the theory behind the point, and spelled it out for me without the geometry: 'So, it's two parallel universes, Evelyn's and Rachmaninoff's, and your presentation of a new type of life is the third?'

'You could say so, yes.'

She looked puzzled: 'Two of the universes embrace two different worlds, but isn't your point that they converge into identity?'

I resisted: 'Are they ultimately really the same?'

She grimaced: 'either way, honey, this is a lot to bring off.'

'My new imagined biography of Rachmaninoff is not a third parallel universe, it's the result of a quest I've been on for years'.

Helen flashed to make the connections: 'Yes, to show he was the ultimate Romantic nostalgic, and that's why the memoir is yours — your very own'.

'Yes, the memoir is mine, the nostalgia is Rachmaninoff's'.

'And where does this leave Evelyn?'

'Do you mean her psychology?'

'Well yes, if you want to call it that'.

Helen's caveat implying mild censure stymied me. Over the years it was difficult for me to criticize Evelyn in the light of her triple tragedy — how do you dissect a woman who has lost her only child in adolescence? I plunged in nevertheless:

'Her psychology was wrapped in loss and failure,' I pleaded, 'first her career, then Richard's death, then Sam's, and the final blow of all, people thinking she was nuts because so fixated on Rachmaninoff.'

Helen pushed on: 'then why was she so fixated? Did she think she'd meet the great man revived from the dead in Beverly Hills?'

'No, Helen, she wasn't stalking him, but you know damn well how fixations play out. Rachmaninoff was the connective tissue among the different parts of her troubled psyche. She buried him there with her failed career together with Richard and Sam. Then, when she finally broke loose and was brave enough to leave New York, her unconscious self pushed her to come to terms with this burial ground engulfing her, this cemetery of her dreams.'

'I can see that,' Helen rejoined now much less stridently than before, her tone of voice modulating into a purr. 'But you run the risk of destabilizing readers who may think you're inviting them to revisit their own psychic burial grounds.'

'OK, I concede the constant peril, but I want readers to feel compassion for Evelyn, not become stirred up by her.'

'Sure you do, but Evelyn chased an imaginary ideal object long since dead. It sounds like stalking to me — besides, it's extreme narcissism, the *sense that she was the only person in the world entitled to follow in his footsteps after his death. Her narcissism was no milder than his nostalgia.'*

Helen's last words stopped me in my tracks: she saw all, the two protagonists' parallel universes even more lucidly than parallels between narcissism and nostalgia. I wondered whether she was suggesting that everyone – every reader – is eventually forced to deal with their own narcissism, reluctant though they might be.

I took another big sip to disguise my momentary destabilization, but before I could swallow more than two sips Helen pushed even harder:

'Besides, whose story is this, yours' or hers'?

I did not need to think.

'Rachmaninoff's Cape is my story, although Evelyn imagined it too. Don't you see – there's a big difference between a story and a memoir, Helen, even if both organically fit together into sequence? I would never have become Evelyn's friend if I had not broken Richard's cello. Evelyn led me to Rachmaninoff. Her facilitation enabled me to imagine him as the focus of my nostalgia research. I know it's crazy but it's true. It's a big cock-and-bull tale that happens to you once in a lifetime and then you spend years trying to figure it out what it means'.

Helen cut in: 'provided you can weave the various strands together the right way'.

'You mean they'll think it's too high brow?'

Helen squirmed. She knew the ropes of publishing: 'They're not idiots. You'll have to write brilliantly to make it work'.

'The structure is right, and in my own voice'.

My friend was a grub-street fighter: 'You've got to try'.

'Yes,' I said in ultimate resignation.

Helen pursed her lips; as I looked her in the face she seemed to be a cat. Clearly she had gone out on a limb but was I hallucinating?

'Maybe I should quit now?' I continued, my pitch slightly raised.

'Don't be ridiculous, George.'

I'm sure I'm right: Rachmaninoff dried up because he was suffering, not because he couldn't wait to bank the next five-thousand dollars and become a millionaire.'

'Then what exactly was he suffering from?'

'Helen, we've been through all this before. You know what it was. He was yearning for Russia, pining for the lakes, for his boyhood. He was sick with nostalgia ...'

She cut in before the 'gia' in my 'algia' tripped out.

'Lots of people crave their childhoods. All the Romantics. Half the Modernists. Most exile literature and film. What was so different about your Sergei?'

I could have eviscerated her. I had spent a small fortune in long-distance phone calls to her dissecting Rachmaninoff's situation for two years; had persuaded her that the Russian variety was different. Russian nostalgia was a different beast.

'But Helen he was Russian. Not French or German but a morbid, late, Russian Romantic and the Russians are different. Don't you understand?'

'How are they different?'

'They're unbelievably and eternally gloomy and think everything is fated.'

Helen knew about Russian gloom — bless her, she knew about everything — but thought she could extract clarity from me by taking me through the steps all over again.

I capitulated and restarted: 'I know it was that. The Rachmaninoff we all love creatively dies in 1917 when he flees Russia. After that, he cannot compose. What he produces is no good. Something in him collapsed. Forever.'

'So what was it, sex, a miserable wife, mistresses?'

'No,' I insisted, 'something deeper, something difficult to explain without resorting to biography, psychoanalysis, Russian history.'

I was getting in deeper and knew it but not too intricate for warrior Helen.

'*So Richard Strauss would have said Rachmaninoff lost his "shade?"*'

'*No, Helen, it wasn't his symbolic shade.*' *She would have been offended if I proceeded to lecture her about* Die Frau ohne Schatten *who does lose her sexual potency, but this wasn't Rachmaninoff's problem.*

'*So why is it so important to demonstrate this creative death through nostalgia, George*'?

'*Because,*' *I snapped back well aware of her strategy of groping for the steps, 'because he was one of the greatest talents Russia ever produced and the biographers have it f---ed up. We don't need to understand every pianist who dazzled audiences but canonical composers – they're creators, magicians, gods…*'

Helen interrupted again: 'isn't it sufficient to locate the nostalgia in his music? I mean the way the musicologists do it, in melody and harmony and rhythm?'

'*No! We also have to understand it psychologically and historically. Otherwise we can never know why the Russian Rachmaninoff composes so brilliantly and the American Rachmaninoff so indifferently.*'

'*Indifferently, come on, who can resist Filthy Lucre!*'

'*Yes, indifferently, pathetically, derivatively, a shadow of his Russian self. Only Stravinsky and his Boswell, Robert Craft, the music critic, were willing to call his card, and a few other musicologists like Richard Taruskin. Everyone else, especially Rachmaninoff's biographers, are compliant hagiographers. They're too frightened.*'

'*Even the scholars?*'

'*Even them. Worshipping in his temple of virtuosity because he can fill auditoriums. Imagine how they will trash my memoir.*'

Helen's witty streak was naughty: 'I suppose the Rachmafia will be the reviewers approached.'

'*Yes, the wrong reviewers for this book.*'

'*Well, dearie, you can't chose your reviewers.*'

'*Of course not, but I have principles too.*'

Helen was coming to the end of her tether. She liked classical music but was ultimately indifferent to Rachmaninoff-the-man and nothing I had said on the phone over two years could persuade her otherwise. She routinely listened to his piano concertos, as so many music lovers do, but never before realized that everything she liked had been composed before he left Russia.

I carried on: 'Every detail in the life of Mozart, Beethoven, Chopin, the lot, has been blown up. The Schumann story with Clara has been told a hundred times — how he threw himself into the Rhine, and Clara the great love of his life. And Clara the key to Brahms too. Bla, bla, bla. But Rachmaninoff remains shrouded in mystery, an enigma, he's been written out, and no one will speak.'

'George, calm down, you're ranting,' Helen noted matter-of-factly while elegantly refilling my gin.

'What do you expect — you're getting me plastered.'

Helen raised her eyebrows as if to shirk off herself as agent.

'Helen, you're right, there IS a Rachmafia out there, in Europe and the US. I could defy the Rachmafia police, by extolling or trashing him, but I don't want to do either. I want another kind of life altogether.'

'You mean it's that black and white'?

'Almost, worship him as the traditional biographers do, or trash him as some musicologists have done.'

'But you don't seem to want to do either,' Helen acquiesced.

'No,' I acquiesced with a whimper.

'Then what kind of biography of him do you want to write'?

'I don't want to write a biography at all. I want to sketch out what a genuinely new biography could look like but not write it. I want to write a nostalgia memoir.'

I did not elaborate. I had only mentioned Evelyn in passing and did not want to recount her long, sad, complicated tale again. Helen knew well enough what parallel universes were and had accepted them as Rachmaninoff's and mine, these two without Evelyn. But she perked up: 'a nostalgia memoir sounds enticing. I'd grab one for review if sent to me. Don't think I've ever heard of one, let alone seen one, come to think of it.'

'That's just it – but I also want to tell the truth about what happened to him, neutrally, honestly, as impartially as I can. And to do it I need to construct several parallel universes in a blended genre.'

Helen recognized something was missing: 'what will the truth hang on?'

'His nostalgia,' I replied, 'but his nostalgia is enigmatic. Homesickness is the clue to his creative urge, in both halves of his life. Nostalgia creatively drives the first half and then undoes him in the second. The problem is that nostalgia is a non-starter.'

'And how, my dear,' slightly condescending, 'are you gonna present this metaphysical nostálgia to the world?', lingering on the 'ta' in nostalgia to display her scepticism about my enterprise.

'Helen, you've never liked nostalgia!'

'Well it's not some guy I might date.'

'You know what I mean, you've never granted that nostalgia's a valid psychological state of mind that can debilitate as well as energize, as corrosively as depression or hysteria or …'

'Then why don't we take Nostzac to calm it?'

'We will some day; nostalgia was once recognized in medical classification as the condition of people who emigrate and become sick in the new country. Like all the Eastern Europeans in America.'

'Well, I review books and I've never seen a history of it.'

'There aren't any: it once had a huge profile, especially during periods of war, among soldiers, but it's dropped out.'

Helen now listened more attentively to her inebriated friend.

'That mother-fucker Freud wrote it out. If only he had built it into his psychoanalysis, raising it to equal status with hysteria, you'd know what I was talking about.'

'OK, you've persuaded me,' and she turned away to sniff her pots of gardenias and stare out at the pines.

But I was in full swing and could not desist, like a top that has begun to spin and must finish its cycle.

'Karl Jaspers, the philosopher, tried to persuade Freud but he would not listen. He turned deaf to the N word.'

So did Helen, who meant well and really cared for me, especially before we had broken up a million years ago. She used to say back then I was the love of her life but resigned herself to what she called 'sexual realism'. She could not really understand why I was making such a fuss over these parallel universes but made this concession:

'You're a good writer, George, you'll bring it off.'

Suddenly I sat silently, more quiescent than earlier. Somehow Helen's points had hurt. She knew I had collected masses of material for a 'cultural history of nostalgia' but on this gardenia-fragrant night was describing a memoir called Rachmaninoff's Cape.

OUR 'CATSKILL CONVERSATIONS', as I afterward referred to them, were more edifying for me than for Helen. I flew back to the West Coast as an *anti-narrative convert*; or, at least, with an invigorated sense I was trying to fit the mould of Rachmaninoff's life, from start to finish, into a coherent model of a man racked by nostalgic longing for the Russia he lost. I had assumed, for as long as I could remember, that *all* lives consisted of unified stories rarely surrendered by their owners until the moment of death. The possessor only foregoes the fiction of its presumptive organic unity under duress at the very end of life: in terminal illness, as the boat sinks, on the deathbed – even then rarely. Otherwise, if surrendering much earlier, if conceding that lives can unfold incoherently or randomly in discrete units, as isolated stories, we inexorably hand ourselves over to Death as his ineluctable Tragic Victim. Imagine the pain of acknowledging a life, especially at its end, which is now perceived as disjointed and unintelligible. Only the muddled, the confused, or the seriously disturbed, dare do that.

In our subsequent days together Helen and I exercised our wits on the virtues and defects of the *anti-narrative* stance, each of us attacking and defending it in turn. The narrative-unity model is less tragic than its opposite: who can deny its advantages? Most people implore art, especially fiction and drama, to supplement their lives with further meaning by permitting incoherent narratives of themselves to vie with the closed-end theories they read about in history, philosophy, theology – all the so-called sciences-of-life; where lives are presented as if they were of a piece from day one. But imagine if *real* lives – lived lives – unfolded incoherently, in bits and bobs, as isolated moments without connection? Or, similarly, evolved as if so intrinsically connected to the lives of *others* that it would be a further fiction to construe individual lives as if *discrete* or *dis*connected?

I was advancing on the belief that Rachmaninoff's life, like most life-stories we tell ourselves, was coherent and unified, even if jagged at the edges; that I could bring form to this story – his *biography* – if I could discover the 'truth' about his inner mental universe and what drove it. All along I hoped to bring flexibility to my imagined sense of his selfhood without surrendering the basic premise of narrative unity. The 'Catskill Conversations' helped me realize that Rachmaninoff may have been 'many selves' and that his basic biographical self may have been less nostalgic than I imagined; that I might need to enlist, as well, the *non*-nostalgic aspects of his experience. The result might be a less unified narrative about the man – a looser *Rachmaninoff's Cape*, so to speak – yet a fuller and richer likeness. Or, at least, a truer sense of Rachmaninoff-the-man, even if framed in a less unified narrative.

This was why Evelyn's departing gift – her trunk – was such a blessing. Her mission was to rescue herself through the composer who had both enchanted and vexed her: a mad pursuit permeated with the possibility of insight and vision. Rachmaninoff's biographers – especially Bertensson, whom she had read, as we will see – erred both in the direction of coherence *and* incoherence: producing a protagonist without a central pulse (what I am calling 'narrative unity') who nevertheless evolved within chronological time and experienced a coherent beginning, middle and end to his life. Evelyn's jottings opened another window to nostalgia's riddles. In her versions of the nostalgic life, which she experienced first hand, human beings suffer from, or alternatively exalt in, nostalgia; they tap into its protective fortresses, defensive masks, and illusory shields, not just the cultural consequences from epoch to epoch but from nostalgic person to nostalgic person. If Evelyn can hypothetically be imagined as Rachmaninoff's biographer (which, of course, she never was), then Evelyn-as-nostalgic was writing the life of her kinsman. This extreme form of sympathy elicited in her many more anti-narrative gestures than unified types. Her jottings, notes, fragments, dreams, jokes, doodles. The non-conventional life suggested by her notebooks, thrives on a broader and more flexible sense of the-man-Rachmaninoff, although perhaps just as tragic, as the one put forward by the radical unifiers.

Even Evelyn's pre-California jottings teem with revealing morsels:

1961: why is the C-sharp minor Prelude so beloved – this kitsch piece of fakery that has so mesmerized the masses?

1962: reading Bertensson for the first time, awful, dry, factual. He hoovers up facts and dumps them in but has no sense about R.

1963: the gap between loving to play R's piano music and knowing anything about the real man is great.

1963: would I like to sit next to R at a luncheon? – you bet.

1964: the Russian soul is sown into Russian music, the only question is how it gets implanted: the R way or the Prokofiev way.

1964: I return to Bertensson most weeks, but he hasn't a clue about R's main lines, just sweeps up the facts.

1965: I wish I could meet someone who knew R.

1965: Have just heard Dvorak's New World Symphony on the radio – seems to me all about homesickness (for Bohemia?). How many other composers (Mahler?) or writers (Dickens?) were terrifically homesick while in America? R was different: his homesickness was a lifelong pursuit.

1966: I am not crazy in my pursuit, I am a sane person.

1966: What does it means to love your country more than you love your own child? I didn't but R did. He dearly loved his two daughters but Russia more. I've never read good books about nostalgia.

1967: My youthful attraction to R's music was justified but I would never have dared to play for him in person.

1968: Another revolution in Paris this May … like the ones R experienced.

1969: August beach days, new to me, watching the hunks on Venice boardwalk. I clipped the review of a young Russian pianist playing Rachmaninoff's first piano concerto at the Hollywood Bowl. The radio interview was hysterical, the pianist's English incomprehensible. Savvy interviewer: 'would you have liked to meet Rachmaninoff? Russian pianist: 'Yes, of course.' 'Why?' Pianist: 'He was so enig-mah-tic'. Interviewer: 'what was enigmatic about him?' Russian: 'I want to ask him what it was like to compose this concerto – he was only seventeen at the time; to ask him what went through his mind as he composed'. Interviewer: 'But we usually think of Rachmaninoff as old: this six-and-a-half foot giant in his black suit and crew-cut, even dressed this way in the heat'. Pianist leaning on the word Russian: 'it

was Russian black suit, Russian half cape, half
pants, he was not old, no dina-sauer.'

Evelyn's notes also record her reading on specified dates:
*September 10 1972, scorching heat, sitting by the window all day soaking up any
sea breeze, Bertensson in hand, he's no better than the last time. January 5 1973,
rains still teaming since the New Year started, can't go out, at my little desk
dipping back into Victor Seroff's biography – at least he didn't clutter his book
with all Bertensson's trivia. May 10 1975, meeting Daisy Bernheim on Elm
Drive fired me up to read about R again, so back in Bertensson who doesn't use
the word nostalgia or understand what it is. Didn't Bertensson himself suffer from
it when he migrated to America?*

Evelyn's intuitive sense of her ideal portrait – what she wished to
find in Bertensson but never did – can be reconstructed from the
notes she took on her reading. Remarkably, she wrote she wanted *'a
cape'*, her shorthand symbol for her spectral profile of the Russian, and
perhaps something of a shroud encasing his life. Her jottings suggest
how she pictured the protective cape, as well as imagined an
unwritten book entitled *Rachmaninoff's Cape*, her fable of parallel
universes tied together by three tragedies: hers', Richard's, and
Rachmaninoff's. The 'black cape' was her symbol for a buffer against
the ruins nostalgia creates, as well as her mental image of the
perpetually performing Rachmaninoff, a puppet incapable of ceasing,
captured in the legendary portrait of him wearing it.

Did Rachmaninoff wear his black cape on the two occasions
Evelyn heard him play in New York? Her diary is silent, but she
makes plain she could never imagine him playing a concert without
his black, Russian, button-up coat.

I also wondered whether Evelyn knew that musicologists were
among the worst obstacles to her imagined life. Most noted that
Rachmaninoff's creative spirit dried up after he departed Russia and
left the matter there: *two* Rachmaninoff's, or maybe *three*, an unstable
biographical subject, as if he had been bifurcated or trifurcated, and
dismissed the sources of his creative urge, his loves and sexual flings,
his hypochondria and emotional collapse, his secretiveness, his loss of
Russia and émigré status – all irrelevant. A new, flushed out life would

explain how the loss built up over six decades and, before then, what force within him died when he forfeited Russia. Otherwise, another derivative biography would reinvent the wheel, repeating that Rachmaninoff's compositional ability was too minimal to enable him to innovate:[23]

But all this is *Evelyn's* imagined *Cape*, not mine. *My Cape* includes *her* story, which hers, of course, did not. Evelyn never thought of herself as a subject. The parallel universes I developed after emerging from her papers was *another* type of Cape, a *different* Cape altogether; the weird double-story of her infatuation with Rachmaninoff and of Rachmaninoff's with Russia – as if they were *dopplegangers*.

Historically Rachmaninoff was a late – very late – Romantic imagination, steeped in nostalgia for the Russia he and his generation of aristocrats had lost. It diminishes his nostalgia to reduce it to a mindset based on the disappearance of hierarchy and patriarchy, an awareness driven by gut feeling over other considerations, no matter how genuine the losses of land, family, country, and national affiliation. When late Romantics became expatriates (the widespread band from Henry James to James Joyce and the German-Austrian exiles in America), they mourned the mother country far more poignantly than their early Romantic counterparts (the Shelley-Byron circle, William Beckford) so desperate to forge ahead. The possibility that their overriding nostalgia was a sign of degeneration, the sense that they could not move on with the times, concerned them less than the razor-sharp experience of their losses.

The biographical Rachmaninoff never imagined his pining for Russian things as a sign of degeneration. The music he composed while still in Russia is suffused with this nostalgia to a greater degree than that of fellow late-Romantics Gustav Mahler and Richard Strauss. Besides, both innovated in musical form far more than he did. After 1918, now having fled Russia, Rachmaninoff's

---

[23] Michael Scott's biography *Rachmaninoff* (Stroud: History Press, 2008) is an example but there are several others.

compositions took a stylistic turn, as musicologists have shown.[24] And when formal similarity prevailed Rachmaninoff relied on ingrained habits – fixed stylistic patterns from which he could not divest himself – carried over from pre-Bolshevik days.

My imagined biography would vivify the *man* behind these magisterial losses and explicate the toll they took on the composer. So I hungered for a life integrating approximately a dozen categories, and Evelyn's diaries persuaded me, even more than I believed could have been the case before reading them, that no *new* appraisal of Rachmaninoff could be significant without the dozen.

As the months flew I imagined a book divided into fourteen chapters containing abundant sources and endnotes. A group of scholars, not one superhuman biographer capable of mastering all these fields, would write it. The team would consist of experts in Russian history and literature, the history of medicine and psychoanalysis, music history and theory, the sociology of aesthetics, piano pedagogy, theory of musical performance, and an imaginary historian of nostalgia: this last the in-progress category, so formative for the human element of Rachmaninoff's story, still searching for its master-builder. I would write the chapter on hypochondria, hypochondria of the heart rather than physical organs. No such team exists, of course; the group is imaginary, and no such book has ever been written. A full-length version would be much longer than the following skeleton.[25]

---

[24] See David Cannata's important book *Rachmaninoff and the Symphony.* (Innsbruck and Lucca: Studien Verlag: LIM Editrice, 1999).

[25] All dates in the biography of Rachmaninoff proposed here follow the Old Style Julian calendar until the end of 1917, and then revert in 1918 to the New Style Western Gregorian calendar. The difference becomes essential during the events of 1917-18 when the Rachmaninoffs were in flight from Russia.

Part 2: Rachmaninoff's Cape

'It is always interesting and sometimes even important to have intimate knowledge of a composer's life …'
(Daniel Barenboim, 'Beethoven and the Quality of Courage'[26])

'Rachmaninoff – well, I'd rather say nothing about him. The truth is that we hated each other.'
(Sergei Prokofiev in an interview about the development of Russian music with British music critic Alexander Werth[27])

'… the tragedy of [Rachmaninoff's] being torn away from his country is still gnawing at his being. Curious is this silence of the tomb, literally sepulchral, which has overtaken the creative genius of the composer since the moment of his departure [from Russia in 1917]. True, he has composed the Fourth Piano Concerto. But still a period of eight years of silence is an enormous span for a composer. As if something had snapped in him at the time he parted with his native soil, his genius, rooted by mysterious ties in his fatherland, has no longer been able to issue a single sprout.'
(Leonid Leonidovich Sabaneev, *Modern Russian Composers*, Freeport, N.Y: Books for Libraries Press, 1971, p. 117)

'… to reconcile [all] with the ridiculously small number of seasons that had gone to form the inexplicably nostalgic image of home …'
(Vladimir Nabokov, *Speak, Memory*, London: Penguin, 1977, p. 51)

---

[26] *New York Review of Books* (4 April 2013), p. 21.
[27] Alexander Werth, *Musical Uproar in Moscow* (London: Turnstile, 1949), p. 83; also recorded in his *The year of Stalingrad: an historical record and a study of Russian mentality, methods and policies* (London: Hamish Hamilton, 1946).

AGE-OLD WISDOM ABOUT THE CREATIVE URGE is that it lodges within all of us – this desire to produce something different, to make something out of nothing, to change our environment, to create an enduring work of art. But in 1900, when Sergei Vasilyevich Rachmaninoff was caught up in his emotional collapse, you practically had to create something yourself if you wanted to be entertained by the arts, that is, unless you lived in St Petersburg or Moscow. A few years later Picasso, the Spanish painter, quipped that 'every child is an artist,' and there is much truth in the aphorism, but Picasso continued to admonish that 'the problem is how to remain an artist.' He meant that the creative urge – the desire to make art – exists in nearly all children but dies by adolescence in most, leading to adults who are mere consumers, rather than makers, of art. Around the same time psychoanalysis was coming into its own: Freud and Melanie Klein, the preeminent European psychoanalysts then, extricated from children this creative urge to make things (playthings), and relocated it as part of the tendency toward survival, propagation, sex, and other life-producing drives; Freud affirming that it existed to counter the overwhelming death drive and Klein contending, more explicitly, that it arose both in children and adults as a result of 'the sublimation of the depressive position.'[28]

Klein's analysis of infantile depression can be applied, with reservations, to the known facts of Rachmaninoff's early life. Time would show that the young Rachmaninoff was a genius, but he would not have soared so quickly without his mother Lyubov's incessant pushing, her constant nagging, and her driving him to achieve rather than blithely create, all of which depressed him.

This was Lyubov Petrovna Butakova, a wealthy general's daughter, and Sergei's mother who brought a huge dowry to augment husband Vassily's five estates. But nothing worked out and Lyubov

---

[28] Melanie Klein, *Contributions to psychoanalysis, 1921-1945 with an introduction by Ernest Jones* (London: Hogarth Press, 1948), chap. 7. Klein was specific in her analysis, maintaining that this creative urge especially arose in depressive types. That is, a normative depressive position results when an infant develops the capacity to experience complete objects rather than split fragments.

Petrovna ejected her husband – Rachmaninoff's father – for drink, dissipation, and the depletion of their funds, which further depressed her son. It was also mother Lyubov who took her young pianist son to cousin Siloti, Lyubov who arranged for Siloti to place him in a communal piano school, Lyubov who engineered everything and was inflexible in her expectations.[29] Lyubov, who held him in her lap, telling him he was her favourite child, would become a great pianist some day, exceeding all other greats. By day and by night she filled his head with these fantasies. By the time he was ten his illusions about himself had swollen to proportions that could accommodate Lyubov's delusions.

(As I reconstructed Lyubov's relation to the young Sergei I could not help but imagine Evelyn's relation to her child Richard: an ardent mother's prating to her infant baby, their interconnectedness, holding his hands over his first cello, Evelyn's dreams for him as a virtuoso. Sam's imagined accusations, after Richard plunged to his death, also reverberate in my ears, and the sense that other types of death exist than the cessation of the pulse and the very last breath.)

Rachmaninoff's early outpouring – all those beauties he composed before he was twenty – would not have occurred without her coaching and coaxing of a son craving, more than anything, for his absent father. Lyubov was the tyrant who damaged him in extraordinarily subtle ways. Rachmaninoff's relation to women for the rest of his life can be traced to her menacing ways from his earliest days.

---

[29] Cousin Alexander Siloti (1863-1945) was Vassily's nephew, a brilliant pianist, tall, lithe, a decade older than Sergei, who had studied with Liszt in Weimar and was becoming one of Russia's most notable young virtuosos. He had graduated from the Conservatory in St Petersburg, which would change its name three times during Rachmaninoff's lifetime. Siloti was Zverev's prize student (as we shall see), as he had been Liszt's, and Tchaikovsky's favourite young pianist in Russia. He dazzled everyone who ever heard him play and married well; the daughter of wealthy and well-connected art collectors who sold to millionaire industrialists. He too fled Russia around the time his nephew Rachmaninoff did, and migrated to New York where he became a professor of piano at the Juilliard School until his death at eighty-two. Adele Marcus knew him after she began to teach there part-time in 1936.

Adolescent Sergei also knew that his love of music did not descend from her, even if she had been his first piano teacher. In reality Lyubov Petrovna disliked music. She walked away when the Cossack band played marches at Oneg, the family estate near Novgorod where Rachmaninoff spent his childhood, and she encouraged Sergei to practice only because it was *hard work* – he may as well have been laying bricks or digging ditches. Her rule was the torture of formidable routine. Sergei's musical penchant, especially the attraction to the keyboard, derived from Vassily and grandfather Arkady Alexandrovich, who had been a talented pianist and composer.

Riddles about the creative urge, of course, extend far beyond psychoanalytical moorings. Each creative artist should also be considered in context, within his time and place, the whole of his cultural milieu. Would Rachmaninoff have turned out as he did – only half his compositional genius attained – if he had been born in 1810 or 1910? Would he then have become a second-class Robert Schumann or Samuel Barber? The question is thorny and pierces to the heart of historical analysis far more than Romantic aesthetics. Romantic composers given over to excessive sentiment and melancholy have existed over many centuries; the matter is how they transform their emotional stance – their voice, their affect – into musical forms. This is a technical matter others have considered, even if they often do so without addressing the composer's biographical circumstances. In Rachmaninoff's case I believe that Lyubov exerted greater sway over her son's compositional methods than has been credited. The masters who taught Rachmaninoff also did, especially Taneyev and Tchaikovsky – but there were also solid psychological reasons why Rachmaninoff could not break free from the old Romantic mould.[30]

---

[30] Igor Stravinsky (1882-1971), barely ten years younger than Rachmaninoff, dispraised Rachmaninoff's music from the first time he heard it and remained ill disposed to it well after Rachmaninoff's death. In this sense his view paralleled Prokovief's, who loathed it. Stravinsky's first teacher was Rimsky-Korsakov, who also had great doubts about Rachmaninoff music. Rimsky-Korsakov was critical of Rachmaninoff's compositions despite his sleekly polite manner toward the younger

In maturity Rachmaninoff's creativity responded to erotic stimulation with women. This was especially evident when he reached his twenties while still unmarried. By his thirties, when he married his first cousin, Natalia Satina, all this changed; he wrote some of his very best work during this decade (1903-13) but he was, in a sense, recovering lost time after his emotional collapse and it is impossible to conjecture what his compositional path would have been had he not become seriously depressed in his late twenties and unable to compose.

During his first two decades Rachmaninoff moved house – by my count – over two dozen times. Each occasion was traumatic, and even those where he voluntarily moved left him pining for another place. Worst were the migrations from home to home during his early youth: from the lakes and forests of Oneg, near Novgorod, to sophisticated St Petersburg and competitive Moscow; from Zverev's basement practice rooms to the room with a view at the top of his house; then to his cousins' houses in city and country. Forever moving, never grounded. He moved numerous times as a student, and even more as an adult. His 'incarceration' in Zverev's 'harem' was painful, as we shall see, but much less so than when he became a fugitive in flight from Zverev. On several occasions when still a student, illness hounded him, so he moved vagabond-like from one abode to another, sometimes taken in by a wealthy student who took

---

man; and Rachmaninoff, for his part, came to realize by the time he left Russia that his compositions might have been different if he had studied with Stravinsky's teacher rather than Taneyev. The latter was a skilled concert pianist and breath-capturing polymath, if also tactless curmudgeon, but his students in Moscow did not turn out well; only Medtner and Scriabin composed lasting works and Scriabin broke away from Taneyev's theory of composition as swiftly as he could. Tchaikovsky admired his taste in musical composition but also feared him and privately recognized how imaginatively limited Taneyev's works were. Stravinsky was also intimately familiar with music composed by Taneyev and Tchaikovsky, but slimly built on its base rather than imitated it, as Rachmaninoff did. By 1910 Stravinsky had finished *Firebird* while Rachmaninoff was still writing backward-glancing songs and programmatic pieces about bells. Only his piano works, particularly the third piano concerto (1909), could rival the innovative forms the young Stravinsky's was generating.

pity on him.[31] Small wonder creative rush especially flowed during periods, such as the first years of marriage in 1902-04, when he was *not* in search of a permanent home. The great irony of his life was that even after taking up residence in America, after fleeing revolutionary Russia, he and his family, Natalia and the girls, continued in flight from one home to another, usually crossing continents and oceans to arrive. At the peak of his concert career he played more than one-hundred concerts a year, and it is no surprise he would sleep in a different bed each night. Yet the exchange of homes is hardly tantamount to a concert artist's holding up in hotel rooms provided he can return to the same bed in the same home each time. He could not.

For the oddest of reasons Rachmaninoff was both a voluntary and involuntary fugitive over six decades. Involuntary after the revolutionary uprisings when he persuaded himself after 1917 he could no longer have a double career as composer *and* concert pianist; voluntary because he was free to settle wherever he wished in the West, yet, when he did, he continued to move back and forth over continents. At first the Rachmaninoffs could not imagine themselves living in America, so they held up in Dresden, Paris, Italy, wherever they could feel themselves comfortable and Rachmaninoff stimulated, eventually building a villa on Lake Lucerne ('Senar'), but when the Nazi menace rendered travel over the Atlantic perilous they settled in Beverly Hills, California, having been attracted to its paradisiac temperatures, as well as its large expatriate Russian community. Rachmaninoff died there during the Second World War. Had he lived on, if the skies and oceans were again restored to relative calm, he would again doubtlessly have continued his peregrinations, perhaps building another 'Senar' on some other middle-European mountain lake. The point is that having 'lost Russia' no single country, it seems, could replace it or contain him. Nor did he want it to.

Rachmaninoff's number of days composing cannot be correlated to his geography – the sense that he composes, and composes well, in certain places and does not in others. The Great Divide, nevertheless, the two halves of his life punctuated by 1917, stares the student of his

---

[31] Such as the rich Yurovsky and his merchant family.

life and works in the face: once he left Russia his creative urge dried up no matter *where* he was. Whether this was because he was so intensely yearning that it drained all his psychic energy, or because he had plainly exhausted whatever creative vision he was endowed with, and now – after 1917– its spring dried up, is impossible to know.[32] But the notion that lack of time was the culprit amounts to nonsense: his Russian family's absurd alibi that he was so busy practicing and giving concerts he had no leisure to compose.[33] He himself disclosed the reason in 1933 in a public statement made to the *Daily Telegraph*: 'For seventeen years since I lost my country, I have felt unable to compose … certainly I still write music – but it does not mean the same thing to me now.' At least he was less hypocritical than his relations. If money was the villain, the Rachmaninoffs could have eaten less caviar and built fewer villas.[34]

Biographically Rachmaninoff was an early bloomer, the reason he was less easy to fathom. He was not a prodigy à la Mozart or Mendelssohn, nor, alternatively, the type of composer who slowly matures, magisterially mellows, and writes his greatest works – the late Beethoven or late Schubert – at the end of his life. The compositions most loved today and most widely associated with him, he wrote

---

[32] Concert artists are also 'creative' but in different ways from composers: virtuoso piano or violin playing requires consummate anatomical and physiological skills, as well as intelligence, memory, and profound understanding of musical scores, but not the unnamable creative springs usually labeled 'genius' for lack of a better concept of their origin. Virtuoso composers like Chopin and Liszt must have possessed both to achieve what they did in each realm, a niche to which Rachmaninoff himself of course aspired.

[33] One of his descendants has even excused him on these grounds in a documentary made for the BBC in 2010, contending he would have continued to compose concertos and sonatas equaling the great ones he wrote in Russia, if only he did not need to make piles of money to support Natalia and the girls.

[34] I cannot emphasize forcefully enough how simplistic the notion is that he stopped composing because his densely packed concert career in America left him with no time. No doubt exists of its extent and the dozens of concerts he gave each year after 1920, but the Rachmaninoffs did not have to live in the splendour they chose, continent-hopping for expensive holidays and to build successive villas in Europe. The loss of the motherland – Russia – brought in its wake a loss in creative urge, which has not usually been conceded by those pronouncing on his life.

during his twenties and thirties in Russia. He turned forty in 1913, as the clouds of European warfare widely gathered and bellicose uprisings at home intensified; indeed composed very little in this period, and almost nothing when fleeing Russia and resettling abroad during the next decade. He enjoyed a *petit renaissance* during the late 1920s, when he produced his fourth piano concerto, but by now he was in his fifties and his creative flame almost extinguished. During his sixties – his last decade – he composed almost nothing at all except the glitzy *Rhapsody on a Theme of Paganini*, which hardly elevated his niche as a composer.

Comparison with Chopin, whom he admired above all others both as composer and pianist, is revelatory.[35] Both were composer-virtuosos, both political exiles from their Eastern European country who spent roughly half their lives abroad without returning to the homeland; both thrived on refinement, luxury, good manners, and the manifest attributes of aristocratic society; both were often ill, hypochondriacal, and intensely melancholic, and both bloomed early rather than late, by twenty. Chopin voluntarily settled in Paris, Rachmaninoff in Western Europe and America. In November 1830, when revolution broke out in Warsaw and the newly created Kingdom of Poland sought to throw off the Russian yoke, the young Chopin carried on from Vienna to Paris, where he was to have gone anyway on his European tour, and demonstrated solidarity with fellow Poles by remaining there and choosing a life of exile. So too Rachmaninoff who, like so many other 'White Russians', fled Russia. Rachmaninoff was aware of his similarities with Chopin and in many ways basked in the parallels, even if he would not have enumerated them in this categorical way. And by the time Rachmaninoff graduated 'with honours' from the Conservatory in Moscow in 1892,

---

[35] No one sanguine would want to diminish his Russian idols – the group extending from Glinka to Tchaikovsky – but Chopin existed in a class of his own so far as Rachmaninoff was concerned. Rachmaninoff's most memorable compositions, especially the sonatas, concertos, preludes, and opus 22 *Variations on a Theme of Chopin*, glance at his Polish forebear, and no other composer had a more palpable influence on his compositions for piano.

Chopin had come into his own as a musical celebrity in Russia and a Slavic idol among the Intelligentsia.[36]

But Chopin's creative urge *flourished* abroad in *Paris*, far away from Poland, whereas Rachmaninoff's *evaporated* in *America*. In geographies and urges their differences are stark. It would be naïve to claim that Chopin's nostalgia – his defined Polish '*żal*' caused by sorrow – sustained his creative spirit to his last days, writing mazurkas to the end; whereas Rachmaninoff's Russian equivalent – his *toska* – quashed his. More than monolithic determinants were at work. Their differences in the nostalgia domain pinpoint the general area of Rachmaninoff's slippage but must be flushed out. I believe Rachmaninoff's *yearning* was his dominant emotion, the one most influencing his disposition, high above all others; nevertheless it was but one of several prevailing moods and the others cannot be discounted. I think his relation to sex and love, illness and suffering; his bizarre secrecy and unshakable sense of his own fate must also be considered. The springs of the creative urge in all artists are as submerged as the root causes of yearning for the homeland in composers like Chopin and Rachmaninoff. But for extreme Romantic temperaments like Chopin's and Rachmaninoff's, 'homeland' and 'yearning' often cannot be separated. And for a very late Romantic

---

[36] Even before Rachmaninoff's birth short celebratory biographies were circulating, such as an anonymous *Kratkaia biografiia F. Shopena* [A Short Biography of F. Chopin] (St Petersburg: F. Stellovskii, 1864). Liszt's full-length tribute, originally published in French in Paris in 1852, three years after Chopin's death, appeared in a Russian translation before Rachmaninoff graduated from the Conservatory in 1891; see Franz Lizst, *F. Shopen* (St Petersburg: tipografiia 'Peterburgskaia gazeta', 1887). Short, popular biographies published in later years included Lidiia Karlovna Tugan-Baranovskaia, *Fr. Shopen, ego zhizn' i muzykal'naia deiatel'nost'* [F. Chopin: His Life and Musical Works] (St Petersburg: tipografiia S. N. Khudekova, 1892). Rachmaninoff began to write his Second Piano Concerto in 1899 when the 50th anniversary of Chopin's death was widely celebrated in Russia's two major cities. Besides articles published in general-interest periodicals of that year, at least one further popular book discussed Chopin as composer-pianist and nationalist exile: G. Timofeev, *Friderik Shopen: ocherk ego zhizni i muzykal'noi deiatel'nosti* ['Frederic Chopin: A Sketch of his Life and Musical Works'] (St Petersburg: tipografiia brat. Panteleevykh, 1899).

imagination like Rachmaninoff's, the conjunction also had other resonances enmeshed into the texture of his life.

SEX IN THE 1880'S, WHEN RACHMANINOFF WAS FORMATIVE, was far more secretive than it became after Freud and Jung perfected their hysteric treatments. Sexual relations were intensely private despite forming the source for public gossip. Sex had not yet crystallized into our lines about heterosexual and homosexual types, the sex and money syndrome, the cliché that fame and celebrity are instant routes to attain it, or – more recently – our new twenty-first century puritanism about enacting it. Sex was still licit and illicit, within and without marriage, mostly unconsummated for fear of progeny, conducted with prostitutes, disease always lurking as its backdrop, and heightened by romantic stereotypes – dalliances among aristocrats and professionals, military lovers, undiscovered *femmes fatales* waiting to be ravished. The world of Emma Bovary and Anna Karenina lurked everywhere on boulevard corners from Paris to St Petersburg. How different the whole picture from Evelyn's Jewish New York during the Great American Depression in a nation still deeply puritanical despite the Roaring Twenties.

Rachmaninoff's biography can seem to depict a man who was the least sexual of creatures. Only once during his adolescence did he rise to the bait of a dalliance, a comic one to boot: with three Skalon sisters, the youngest of whom – Vera – impressed him.[37] His attraction was as capricious as her flirtatiousness, yet nothing further developed when her parents intervened.[38] Later on, his courting of Natalia Satina, his first cousin, was based on gratitude and common sense rather than wild passion or illicit romance. When they married

---

[37] Rachmaninoff called her 'his muse' and dedicated his first work for cello and piano to her.

[38] Russian critic Tom Emel´ianov claims that Vera Skalon burned Rachmaninoff's love letters to her without giving his evidence; see 'Posledniaia liubov´ Sergeia Rakhmaninova', *Zhurnalist* (2003), No. 9 (September), p. 87.

and had two daughters, their life was ruled by order and routine above all. At a few other junctures in his young life Rachmaninoff seemed to succumb to the temptations of the flesh – as with the singer Nina Koshetz in the Crimea. But only rarely – first when he was barely pubescent, later during his early twenties, and fleetingly in America – did sex stare him in the face and put him on trial.[39] The three occasions cannot have been more different and beg to be understood.

Nikolai Zverev (1832-1893) was a mystery, especially the route he had taken to become the foremost professor of piano at the Moscow Conservatory. He claimed to have studied math and physics but had little proficiency in these subjects; just liked their symmetrical order and formulaic symbolism. As an aristocratic son who inherited millions of roubles of family money he could follow any pursuit and he did. His 'school' was *nonpareil*, and Rachmaninoff soon discovered that no other teacher would ever again carve out such a niche in his psyche.

Most acute for Rachmaninoff was Zverev's sexuality – he liked young boys. He was fortunate not to be mentioned when a scandal broke out at the Conservatory during the very late 1880s – while Rachmaninoff was studying there – alleging improper sexual relations between staff and students. Canadian historian Dan Healey has written an eloquent book explaining (among other topics) how homosocial desire was expressed and policed in late tsarist Russia: because the Imperial regime frowned on a large bureaucratic machine to administer penalties, it conveniently claimed that sodomites did not

---

[39] His friendship with the young poet Marietta Shaginyan, the 'Dear Re' of his letters, was avuncular and paternalistic, anything but erotic. One pose he struck with young women was to play the part of the indulging and loving father, almost as if he was imitating Vassily Rachmaninoff.

exist in Russia and – more consequential for daily life – that those indulging in it practice euphemism, denial, and secretiveness.[40]

The two decades before 1905 relaxed both sodomitical laws and penalties, so that elite men like Zverev, backed by huge sums, could readily have indulged his sexual proclivity by acting discreetly. Instead he chose to place his wealth in the service of young piano students, 'cubs' who lived in his house. One cub described him as '... tall, slender, with carefully combed grey hair like Liszt, and unexpectedly black bushy eyebrows over a clean-shaven face ... peace and calm seemed to radiate from his kind, fatherly countenance.'[41] Other cubs disagreed: Zverev clothed and fed them and supervised the totality of their education, but his place amounted to more than a 'school of piano' – it entailed a way of life paralleled in Moscow by only a few German or Polish equivalents.[42]

There is another clue. Zverev taught piano to the wives of absent military commanders and patrons of the arts but everything else in his life suggests he despised women. His mad vision was the opposite of an Ottoman seraglio. He craved a Wagnerian monastic order focused around the piano with himself enthroned as its Amfortas. He and his cubs could exist on bread and water in Spartan surroundings; no women, no furniture, no tenderness, no home in the proverbial sense – just a few dilapidated pianos.

Zverev was bowled over when he first heard Rachmaninoff play at twelve. Rachmaninoff's cousin Siloti, who had also been Zverev's student, forewarned his mother Lyubov Petrovna, and her son too, about the prime piano master of Moscow but the more noteworthy

---

[40] See Dan Healey, *Homosexual Desire in Revolutionary Russia: The Regulation of Sexual and Gender Dissent* (Chicago and London: University of Chicago Press, 2001); chapter three dealing with 'Euphemism in the policing of Sodomy.'

[41] Cited in Bertensson, p. 16.

[42] Zverev's 'school' in his home was the only one of its kind then in Russia. German poet and editor Stefan Georg (1868 –1933), then well-known in Germany as homosexual, had a similar school for students of poetry in his home, and wrote love poetry to some of them, but no evidence exists that Russians knew about it.

fact is that Zverev was unprepared for what he heard – and saw: a *krepky paren*, a strapping tall lad, big for his age and possessed of enormous hands, capped by a sombre face exuding maturity and cutting a pensive shadow. Zverev had never heard Liszt's études so proficiently played by someone of this age, not even by his prize-pupil Siloti whom he had sent to study with Liszt himself. Zverev instantly guaranteed Sergei a place in his 'school' and, later on, in the Moscow Conservatory. Lyubov was relieved after the grade-card debacle when Rachmaninoff practically failed his academic subjects. Her son would get somewhere: she kissed Siloti for his kindness and crossed herself thrice. Sergei would become a great pianist, like Chopin or Liszt. This is what she wanted more than anything.

Mothers throughout history have expiated their own guilt in the sacrifices they make for their children. Those mothers who internalize their failure as celebrities, especially in music, often harbour dreams of ambition for their sons. Lyubov had no callings to greatness in Imperial Russia in the 1870s, but – like so many Russian mothers – imagined a musical career for at least one of her children.

Seven boys, eleven to sixteen years old, accommodated in Zverev's house. They compulsively practiced and followed Zverev's routines that demanded rigor and responsibility. Zverev taught the boys harmony and solfeggio but no arithmetic, history, geography or even music history, to the young Rachmaninoff's relief. A strict timetable was *de rigueur*: rise and sleep at exact, inflexible times, awaken earlier than normally on the day of their lesson so that they could practice an extra three hours, and – most of all – agree to practice with Zverev sitting beside them two hours each day. Rachmaninoff succumbed but wondered how Zverev had rigged such an intricate timetable.

Sitting beside Zverev every day bothered Rachmaninoff, not his physical proximity but Zverev's continual contact with his hands, wrists, arms – lowering their angle from the keyboard or moving his wrists in certain directions. He often seemed to want to edge closer. Zverev had no wife; his '*cubs*' were his life. He was the prime piano master of Moscow – Rachmaninoff conceded that; and the very young Rachmaninoff would have endured Zverev's intimate physical proximity if Zverev allowed him time to compose, for he was already composing little pieces – nocturnes, preludes, fragments for piano – musical representations of his reverie and former solitary states with father Vassily and *babushka* Butakova.

How well he remembered them. Often at their childhood estate, Oneg, Vassily pushed the boys in. *'Esli vy ne nauchites lushche plavat, to mozhete utonut.'* You'll drown if you don't learn to swim better, he lovingly cautioned. Vassily pinched them, made them laugh, gave them a few pennies to listen to the hurdy-gurdy man's songs, and changed their wet swim trunks. He was everything the stern, reproaching Lyubov was not.

Child composers cannot coherently articulate why they compose but upon occasion they do so both naturally and because prompted. For Rachmaninoff solitary composition differed from mechanical piano practice: the already blissful state of being alone and unfettered with his imagination – except for Zverev who kept intruding.[43]

The boys slept together in a large dormitory on the top floor of Zverev's house. They practiced in small rooms containing pianos, roughly half the time alone, the other half with Zverev at their side. Rachmaninoff followed the rules for three years but crisis flared when Rachmaninoff requested his own room to compose in. He told

---

[43] Piano practice in late nineteenth-century conservatories, and especially in private schools like Zverev's, was not a solitary activity: students practiced en masse, often with several pianos in a single room despite the din and cacophony, their teachers often sat with them playing four hands on a single keyboard, two seats before the keyboard, as did Zverev, and directing their hands, and even when the students were on their own they heard the others in nearby rooms. One of these was Matvey Presman, a Rachmaninoff fellow student in Zverev's *pensionnat* and so preoccupied with the *krepky paren*, the strapping tall lad, that he left many recollections of him at this time. His notes, still in the original Russian and now collected by Z. A. Apetian in *Vospominaniia o Rakhmaninove* (Moscow, 1988), are lucid about the manic way in which the fourteen-year old composed. 'He became very pensive, even gloomy, seeking solitude, pacing about with his head hung low, his gaze straining towards some point in space. Moreover, he would utter things under his breath, waving his hands as if he were conducting. This state of mind lasted a few days…' The contrast between young Rachmaninoff's solitary states and communal practice could not be starker.

Zverev he needed silence and privacy, pleading his case as forcefully as he could. Zverev denied it, their relation deteriorated, and each accused the other of 'lapses'. Eventually the young man decided to leave. He would have run away had he not feared Lyubov Petrovna's reprisal and cousin Siloti's admonition. No one less prestigious than Tchaikovsky acknowledged Zverev's niche as Russia's greatest piano teacher; no one fled, Tchaikovsky said, Zverev's hand-selected 'cubs' who included Scriabin, whom Zverev dressed up as a military cadet. Imagine, Rachmaninoff reflected around this time, what Lyubov Petrovna's retribution would be — fate far worse than his grade-card debacle and more annoying than Zverev's knee brushing against his.

How these arrangements differed from Evelyn's weekly lessons with Adele Marcus; one-hour encounters free of emotional propinquity, let alone bedroom intimacy presided over by the venerated master surrounded by his young cubs. Imagine if the young Sergei challenged Zverev in the way Evelyn did Adele over the inclusion of Rachmaninoff's piano music at her debut concert.

Yet this is precisely what the young man did. He was now almost sixteen and assessed the consequences of flight. Where would he go? He had no money. Lyubov Petrovna, *babushka* Butakova, cousins Siloti and Skalon, aunts and uncles in St Petersburg and Moscow — not one had contributed a single rouble to Zverev because he accommodated his 'cubs for free'. Funding was not the issue in Rachmaninoff's mind but something else.

Where would he go? Always this dilemma about *home*: first Oneg disappeared, then their flats in St Petersburg (even if mother Lyubov remained in the city and moved in with relations). Now he might be fleeing Zverev's prison house too: always men were the culprits, like his profligate father Vassily (no matter how much Sergei loved him), while the women kept his homes intact (as wife Natalia later would). It isn't necessary to be a cultural anthropologist to assess why Rachmaninoff was so heavily invested in homes and would be to his dying day: he learned from his earliest years that homes were symbolic places intrinsically related to the creative urge. In the right home, with conducive atmosphere, creativity could flourish. Remove home, replace Oneg, and creativity disappears. Yet home, he intuitively knew, need not be physical; could be psychological, temporal, spatial, yearning for 'an absent place'. Papa Vassily represented home too, and he had been ejected by the formidable Lyubov.[44]

The practical matter was pressing: Rachmaninoff had to leave but had no money for accommodation. He hung on for a while in 1889, only sixteen, but when composition seemed more urgent to him than practicing scales and études, he again appealed to Zverev. Tempers flared, the taskmaster sought to strike him. Rachmaninoff was shocked his teacher might assault him. Enraged Zverev wrote to Lyubov Petrovna to inform her that her son was ruining his career. Matriarch-manager Lyubov Petrovna summoned both teacher and student to a family interview, having already decided that son Rachmaninoff must return to Zverev's clutches because he must have a career and Zverev was the surest path forward.

Cousin Siloti initiated it, even if Lyubov presided. He appealed to aunt Varvara Satina, Vassily's sister, apprizing her of the situation and

---

[44] Without becoming overly psychoanalytical it is probable she was the castrating mother who ruled the household regardless of the degree to which all three children doted on their father. In addition, the very young Rachmaninoff moved from the solitary spaciousness of a large country estate into an urban and crowded homoerotic dormitory shared by other 'cubs' in Zverev's piano school, a tense transition that would have jolted the sturdiest adolescents, which the young, narcissistic, and already somewhat depressive pianist-composer was not. Compounding these psychological and physical dislocations was Lyubov's overbearing interference in all domestic matters: she threatened her husband with fierce ultimatums, evicted him when he did not comply, decided what to do about retaining their estates in sight of financial and political threats to them (they owned more than one estate), planned where she would take her two sons (Rachmaninoff was the younger), and hyper-managed her pianist son's early musical career. Nor did the death of her daughter Yelena (seven years older than Rachmaninoff) to anaemia dent her determination or will power. Lyubov died in Russia in 1929 at 93, only fourteen years before Rachmaninoff. Crucial also in his father's absence was the further psychological splitting, in Rachmaninoff's mind, of his two main mentors in youth, into mother and Zverev: each a castrating threat in their own way. Then, in the charged environment in Zverev's school, the young Rachmaninoff tried to become a 'great pianist', while dissociating (this is the operative psychoanalytical concept) himself both from his mother, with whom his Oedipal ties were strong, and from his hero-teacher who turned out to be fatally flawed and mired in sexual frailty.

begged her not to permit Lyubov to prevail even if she did anyway. Determined that her son must do whatever was required to become a great pianist, Lyubov travelled from St Petersburg to rescue him, and at the 'summit' everyone sided with her: Rachmaninoff must return to Zverev's school or come back to St Petersburg. Only aunt Varvara took his side. Her solution at the 'summit' was free accommodation in Moscow and a room of his own in her house in which to compose. He would be treated like one of her own sons. The summit had produced a satisfactory solution to the young man, but the troubled matter of homes arose yet again and took a huge emotional strain on him.[45]

L'affaire Zverevienne did not end here. Aunt Varvara Satina was no fool: she had had her own demons to tame and had sought the help of 'nervous doctors' after marrying and bearing her husband four children. After each birth she became stuck in some type of post-natal depression, which – when combined with her hypnosis treatments – provided her with extra-sensory intuition about herself. This heightened sensitivity alerted her to her nephew's extraordinary musical gifts. Moreover, the word about Zverev and his 'cubs' was out in private circles. Ever since her nephew began to study with 'the dreaded Zverev' four years earlier, in 1885, and accommodate in his monkish *pensionnat*, she suspected Zverev's spartan discipline as surrogate for something else.

---

[45] It was, in fact, one of the most momentous shifts in Rachmaninoff's early life. Aunt Varvara was a Rachmaninoff who had married a prosperous Moscow merchant named Alexander Alexandrovich Satin. When Rachmaninoff moved into their house in 1889 he was treated like a son, a fifth child. Yet one of their younger daughters, Natalia, would become Rachmaninoff's wife. Psychologically understood, an older brother marries a younger sister: biologically his first cousin but psychologically his half-sister. The implications reverberate, especially when viewed in perspective: within the space of a few weeks Rachmaninoff moves home, leaves his teacher of four years to whom he never spoke again, replaces piano practice with composition lessons that give new urgency to his sense of himself as a composer, is adopted by a new surrogate family (his aunt's) who will give him her daughter to be his future wife and with whom he now interacts on a daily basis. Rachmaninoff's was not the type of courting free of family tie.

Now she saw his despotism in action, exposed in her own sitting room. She would rescue her nephew, would not allow him to reside there one day longer. After four years of hard labour in Zverev's 'harem', as Rachmaninoff's new composition teacher Taneyev waspishly referred to Zverev's setup, Rachmaninoff finally had a room of his own. It was on the top floor of their large town house and possessed a small but charming window at its front overlooking the square and spires of distant churches. If opened, the bells chiming in distant churches could be heard – memories of Oneg. Long before Proust attached such significance to sounds and smells for the rekindling of memory, Rachmaninoff intuitively did so. It may not have been musically formalized, as we shall see, in ways to enhance his niche as a composer. Nevertheless, he made bells the primary symbol of his personal religion whose mixture blended the rituals of Eastern Orthodox Christianity with childhood fantasies of permanent homes containing both mothers and fathers.

He also endured another raw experience. Having profited for five years from the Satin family's domestic benevolence and now aged twenty-one, Rachmaninoff felt ready late in the summer of 1894 to venture out on his own. Together with a few classmates he rented a small apartment in central Moscow in a house called 'America', but was not up to the challenge. His pattern of crisis followed by malady was already established, although it rarely manifested itself as life-threatening illness, and it intervened again, this time knocking him out and accompanied by raging fever.

The Satins had not only accommodated and supported him in Moscow but also took him with them to their country estate, Ivanovka, in the steppes hundreds of miles southeast of Moscow. What a contrast, Rachmaninoff thought, to the northern forests of Oneg, which he loved, or the Crimean cliffs Zverev had taken his 'cubs' to climb each summer. Perhaps it was his late adolescence that heightened his attraction to Ivanovka; or perhaps the congregation of the families – the whole microcosm of his world. The Satins, Skalons (Vera's family), Silotis: all gathered there.

During that summer of 1894, when Rachmaninoff had by now routinely been part of the Satin family in town and at Ivanovka for five years, he also crammed in a visit to his paternal grandmother, Vassily's mother, on her country estate ten hours away from Ivanovka by train. There he had a sudden creative burst. The opening theme of a Second Piano Concerto – the famous Hollywood one – came to him as he walked the forests and swam in the lake. Just before leaving her estate late in August he took a final swim, threw his clothes and musical scores into a trunk, and boarded the overnight train to Moscow.

Back in the city he began to shiver with fever and chills. Everyone was still scattered on summer holidays – no one could look after him. Slonov, a roommate in 'America', grew frantic; appealed to classmate Yuri Sakhnovsky who claimed that help must be found or their friend might die.[46] Ensemble they went to cousin Siloti, who offered to find a medical specialist and produced a 'Professor Nikolai Mitropolsky' who charged a small fortune and advised them the patient would probably die. Sakhnovsky was the son of wealthy merchants who agreed to take in their son's best friend and nurse him. This was the established pattern: temporary home, ejection for a variety of reasons, rescue, and, finally, accommodation offered to Rachmaninoff in another (usually grander) house or townhouse, followed by adoption

---

[46] Yuri Sakhnovsky's role in the formation of Rachmaninoff's early career should not be underestimated, he and his family's generosity matched only by the Satins'. Sakhnovsky himself meant well but lacked talent. He was struggling with lessons in music harmony and approached Russian teacher Richard Glier with an offer of free accommodation if Glier would provide tuition in return. Impoverished Glier quickly agreed. Sakhnovsky had an excellent sheet-music library at home with his mother in their elegant residence near Tverskaya Gate, he knew many musicians in Moscow, and often hosted gatherings of young musicians and artists, including Rachmaninoff who usually performed his own compositions. Crucially Sakhnovsky possessed orchestral scores of Wagner's operas – *Götterdämmerung, Das Rheingold, Parsifal, Siegfried* – the composer he considered 'a miracle of modern music' and whose sheet music he had obtained from Germany at a time when it was difficult to find it. Sakhnovsky provided abundant alcohol and the group, encouraged by their host, hummed Wagner's melodies and drank. Rachmaninoff withdrew from the Circle early in 1897 after his first symphony failed and his collapse began.

into the new family. The pattern had been repeated numerous times, emphatically with the Satins, whose daughter Natalia they gave to Rachmaninoff to marry, but also with others, as it did now.[47] But Rachmaninoff's severe headaches and chills continued, while the Sakhnovsky family handsomely paid Mitropolsky, who specifically diagnosed 'brain fever'. Rachmaninoff's condition worsened; he sank into a coma. When he revived a week later the diagnosis was changed to malaria, but the professor cautioned him to remain sequestered.

He was not well enough to return to the room he shared with Slonov until November, by which time his finances were again depleted. But more astonishingly Rachmaninoff told Oscar von Riemann, who recorded the information in a notebook, that 'he lost half [his] facility for composing.'[48]

He mustered strength to give piano lessons but was only relieved when the Satins – perhaps through the intervention of their youngest daughter Sophia, Natalia's younger sister – invited him, again, to return to their town house by Christmas (1894). The Satins' continuing altruism gave him a second creative lift that year.[49]

---

[47] The pattern raises valid questions about Rachmaninoff's neediness in relation to traces of narcissism, as well as issues about mother Lyubov, as she watched from afar in St Petersburg. He appeared to be developing into a narcissistic type even if his variety was mild and fortified by defences ranging from hypochondria and secretiveness, after 1900, and of an unusually protective wife expert in keeping the world at bay. Austrian-born American psychoanalyst Heinz Kohut (1913-1981), one of our sages for the modern understanding of narcissism, explains how the 'narcissistic blow' leads to hypochondriacal symptoms, hypomanic excitement, cold-imperious behaviour, secrecy and distrust of others – all of these displayed by Rachmaninoff (Kohut, *The Analysis of the Self: A Systematic Approach to the Psychoanalytic Treatment of Narcissistic Personality Disorders*, New York: International Universities Press, 1971).

[48] *Rachmaninoff's Recollections* (1934), p. 77.

[49] Sophia Satina (1879-1975) was two years younger than her sister Natalia (1877-1951) and six years younger than Rachmaninoff. She had playfully nagged her parents to invite the dashing and brooding young man back to the house. Years later she recalled as a girl of ten the 'summit with homosexual Zverev' in her family sitting room, from which meeting she was, of course, debarred. See S. A. Satina, 'Zapiska o S. V. Rakhmaninove' ['Notes about S. V. Rakhmaninov'], in the earlier mentioned (n. 43) *Vospominaniia o Rakhmaninove* ['Reminiscences about

Something else momentous also occurred that autumn of 1894 although it did not present itself, at first, as sexual. While recovering in Yuri Sakhnovsky's Moscow house, Rachmaninoff met Pyotr Lodyzhensky, a professional cellist and quondam composer in his thirties who had once taught fellow student Sakhnovsky. Rachmaninoff and Pyotr shared their interests in composition and the

---

Rakhmaninov'], *edited by Z. A. Apetian*, (1988): vol. 1, pp. 12-115. This two-volume work was first published in Moscow in 1957. In the preface editor Apetian explains that Satina's biographical sketch was a manuscript 'sent by her [Satina] from the USA to the Soviet Union in the mid-1940s' and deposited in what was then called the M. I. Glinka State Central Museum of Musical Culture, today the M. I. Glinka All-Russian Museum Complex for Musical Culture. An identical copy of the same manuscript was simultaneously deposited in the Library of Congress and became the cornerstone of the Rachmaninoff Archive located there. Biographer Bertensson used this manuscript when writing his biography published in 1956, and much of his material lifts entire passages from it, crediting his source as Satina.

Sophia herself never married and lived for almost one hundred years. After the Russian Revolution she followed Rachmaninoff and her sister Natalia, now Rachmaninoff's wife, first to Dresden where she worked in the Higher Technical School, then to America where she was employed as a scientific researcher at the Carnegie Institute (Cold Spring Harbor, N.Y., 1922-1942), and after Rachmaninoff's death worked in Northampton Massachusetts as a geneticist at Smith College, where she acquired a Ph. D. and left her papers. Three years after Rachmaninoff's death she gathered a volume of tributes from friends and admirers, mostly written in Russian, privately published it, sold copies from her apartment in Northampton, and enlisted M. B. Dobuzhinskii to edit it: see *Pamiati Rakhmaninova* (New York: S. A. Satina [publisher], 1946), 184pp. Included among the contributors are Rachmaninoff's agent Charles Foley, his future biographer (in 1956) Sergei Bertensson, pianist Josef Hofmann, Chaliapin, and writer Chekhov's nephew, Michael Chekhov, who had already developed his famous acting technique in Hollywood used by Marilyn Monroe, Clint Eastwood, and Yul Brynner (did Michael Chekov know about his uncle's great admiration for Rachmaninoff's playing?). However, the chapter of seven pages written in colloquial Russian most to be noted for our purposes was contributed by 'O. G. Mordovskaia', and describes the composer at the end of his life. This was the Russian nurse Olga Mordovskaia, born in 1881, who was one of the last persons to be with Rachmaninoff just before his death. The reasons for calling attention now to this obscure contribution in Dobuzhinskii's volume will become clear in Part 3. It remains vital for a new life of the composer that emphasizes the man as well as his music.

cello, Rachmaninoff's preferred instrument after the piano, for which he was later to write a famous sonata and other works. Pyotr brought his sister-in-law, a celebrated gypsy singer, Nadezhda Aleksandrovna, to the Sakhnovsky's Moscow town house. She flashed her sashes and scarves, and sang gypsy songs at their soirées to enraptured audiences. Such exotic people swept Rachmaninoff off his feet.[50]

Far more alluring was Lodyzhensky's gypsy wife, Anna Alexandrovna, who further contributed to his recovery. Was her exoticism the health remedy captured in flamboyant strides? In her wild animal magnetism? It cannot have been any calculated sense on Rachmaninoff's part that she would inspire him to write gypsy music, which already had a venerable pedigree in Russia by the end of the nineteenth century. All the Sakhnovskys noticed young Rachmaninoff's infatuation but no one could tell why. Plainly he was mesmerized.

To compare Anna to the giggly Skalon sisters, even deliciously attractive, young, puckish Vera (despite her heart trouble, which may have endeared her further to Rachmaninoff), or the steadier Satin girls, was foolish: Anna was mature, curvaceous, had breasts, exuded sexuality – everything the compassionate and caring Natalia was not, no matter how generous and concerned for her cousin's welfare. Anna was dark, mysterious, secretive, seductive; a ripe woman in her late thirties, allowing herself to be flirtatious with the very tall, pale young composer who also happened to be ailing now and recovering. She led him on. Twenty-one year old Rachmaninoff began to imagine flower bouquets he would bring her, songs he would write, tea he would drink from her samovar. Her coy sexuality fired him up too, her perfumes tormented his senses – his first enticement into the realm of such wild abandon. He would dedicate musical compositions to her, even if disguised by dedications to Pyotr to suit bourgeois Muscovite sentiment. And he would keep the dedication a secret. Only Anna would know.

---

[50] Biographical information about the Lodyzhenskys is scarce but her sexual entanglement with Rachmaninoff is discussed in Tom Emel'ianov (n. 38), pp. 87-90.

Now exhilarated, Rachmaninoff wanted to recover so he could pursue this mad chase, wherever it led. While recuperating in Sakhnovsky's house he began to imagine a work for Anna, a 'capriccio on gypsy themes' that would be different from anything he had composed earlier, a vivacious rhapsody capturing Anna's moods. Once installed, upstairs in seclusion in the Satins' apartment, he started to compose – except when dreaming about Anna. Here, alone at the end of 1894, in undisturbed silence, he also began and finished his first symphony, writing to his dear roommate Slonov, 'I compose ten hours a day'. It would be a sprawling work lasting fifty minutes, but Rachmaninoff did not then know the degree to which its brutal reception would shape the rest of his *fin-de-siècle* and temporarily halt his compositional career. He was thoroughly unprepared for the savage attack the critics gave it.

Meanwhile he had hardly finished with Anna whose entry to his life proved to be the wave that also capped his one-act opera *Aleko* written two years earlier (1892). Based on Pushkin's poem, *Tsygany* – 'The Gypsies' – and on a libretto Vladimir Nemirovich-Danchenko built around that work, it tells the story of Aleko, a stranger who enters a gypsy camp, and becomes Zemfira's lover, but when she tires of him and turns her romantic affection elsewhere Aleko discovers the two and kills them. The gypsies then drive out Aleko and he remains alone, forlorn on the Russian steppe. Rachmaninoff's opera had a limited success and was forgotten by the time he met Anna two years later in 1894; but not his inquisitiveness about gypsies, which had formed before he met her and was, so to speak, in the Muscovite air. His romance with Anna was heightened by memories of composing it and he even believed in the providentiality of the chosen libretto: composition teacher Arensky had assigned it, praised it, yet here Rachmaninoff was, two years later, flinging himself before a *real* gypsy singer, bringing her flowers, hot in her pursuit, and plotting how to dedicate his future works to her, even his first symphony. Was this love not ordained?

Anna was everything Lyubov was not – and more. The force feeding his ego, imagination, and mental universe. Anna encouraged him to woo her and win her away from Pyotr; simultaneously to be realistic and reach his goals in composition. Death ceased to exist when in her presence – her charisma and charm abrogated it. He could do anything if bonded to her. She was Nature itself in defiance of Eternal Night. Had he gone too far, broken too many boundaries, by courting her, indulging her fantasies of him, dedicating to her, serving up his life on a platter? Perhaps … but he could never die if she were close by. If he could just win her – he dreamed – he would be carried away at the other end of life by Valkyries soothing his imagined Wagnerian wounds.

His recent illness also invigorated his faith. He grew more pious in orthodoxy and invested in Russian Orthodox liturgy. Two opposing tensions on the tip of his imagination as he composed were his religious imagination – not merely belief system about God – and the erotic Anna, both, unsurprisingly, playing major parts in the new symphony. The first, the religious, in the repeated chants that provide the symphony with its structure; the second in the gushingly melodic portrait of his beloved female muse in the slow movement. Unabashedly he dedicated it to 'A. L.' without disguising her initials or filtering them through Pyotr. Did he consult the Satins about this move? Probably not.

It pays to stand back, as well as flash forward in time, to assess Rachmaninoff's romantic relation to women throughout his life. One facet of his attachments craved any other type of mother than the tyrannical disciplinarian Lyubov; another the young sister he lost to anaemia, this need undoubtedly surfacing in his preference for Vera among the three Skalon sisters. Anna elicited the third component – perhaps more virile and creative for his music than the other two. No one so powerfully sexual would ever again intrude in his life. He was in his early twenties and Anna enabled him to experience a Dionysian sexual urge he could transform into Apollonian creative burst. He was to learn it could crash down as quickly as it erupted.

Two decades after he had become enamoured of Anna, a further episode flared as Rachmaninoff approached mid-life in 1916, not very long before taking flight from Russia. It made a mark on his inner sense of vulnerability, even if not so momentous as his 'gypsy love' for Anna. This time it was a Russian soprano young enough to be his daughter. Nina Pavlovna Koshetz was born in the Ukraine during the year 1891 when the eighteen-year old Rachmaninoff was fantasizing about exotic women he might meet. By her mid-twenties she had acquired a reputation an as upcoming opera singer who was performing in Europe's finest opera houses. Rachmaninoff was dazzled by her looks and talent and was determined to perform concerts with her, perhaps rationalized as further boosting his own developing career then in need of none.

But context counts for much: by 1916 Rachmaninoff was one of Russia's most famous pianists, the father of two girls and husband of Natalia for almost two decades. Why did he latch on romantically to her? Did Natalia have a clue? When the duo performed in the Caucasus, segments of their audience detected a wild sexual spark between them. In Moscow, they entertained at Siloti's chamber concerts – the gossip intensified. Rachmaninoff wrote ecstatic letters to Nina – far less avuncular than the epistles he penned to other female admirers or collaborators or, much earlier, to the skittish Vera Skalon who fleetingly grabbed his fancy two decades earlier.

He also composed six songs for Nina, romances dedicated to her, which have become his much admired opus 38. This music basks in romantic intimacy, aided by selected texts of Russian Modernist poets. 'Daisies' would become one of his most prized compositions, which he soon transcribed for piano solo, and if this gesture were insufficient he set out to write Lisztian *Études Tableaux* dedicated to her even though she was not a pianist.[51] His musical contemporaries

---

[51] Tom Emel´ianov (see n. 38) further comments: 'The six romances dedicated to Nina Koshits were Rakhmaninov's swan-song, and he performed them with her, in Russia. These were the last six of his life. And in this "swan-song", Rakhmaninov bade farewell to his last love (as it turned out). And as a keepsake, he gave Nina the notebook with his sketches of the vocal part. He was also preparing to present her with another priceless gift — the exquisite "*Études-Tableaux*" for fortepiano, but then remembered the "little scandal" that was developing (our artistic *intelligentsia* do not live by bread alone, but by feeding on gossip): Rakhmaninov had so persistently shown to the public signs that he was in love with Nina Koshits, that there was, at

were, contrarily, driven by mystical fantasy (Scriabin), a Modernist rage for innovation (Stravinsky), and social horror at what Russian life had become (Prokofiev and Shostakovich), but Rachmaninoff's muse was elsewhere. In 1916 he still remained the legatee of Chopin and Schumann, inspired by his George Sands and Clara Wieckes, and – of course – by an equally romantic mentor, Tchaikovsky, who could not dedicate his own works to his young men, afflicted as he was with 'the Love that dare not speak its name'.

News of the Rachmaninoff-Koshetz performing duo met with none of the doom and gloom of Rachmaninoff's first symphony. The critics raved about their pairing, trumpeting the duo as a new facet in Rachmaninoff's profile. If his Second Piano Concerto lifted him out of the doldrums of the first symphony two decades earlier (1900), his new, intimate love songs buoyed him again (1916). But revolutionary politics intervened to disrupt their future: like the Rachmaninoffs, Nina Pavlovna also fled Russia and migrated to America. She sang in major American opera companies during the 1920s and at the Paris opera during the 1930s, her celebrated diva career interrupted only by the Nazi menace. Then she hurried back to America and – like Rachmaninoff – retired to Hollywood. In film land she played any number of bit parts, her voice having given up by 1940. Former diva Nina lived above her means in Hollywood: wrapped in fine furs and drenched in Chanel and often seen driving down its palm tree-lined boulevards in the latest deluxe Chevrolet. She died in 1965, long after Rachmaninoff, leaving her daughter Marina Schubert (1912-2001) with the task of telling the world what her mother's romance with Rachmaninoff had amounted to.[52]

---

that moment, exaggerated gossip and whispering, which has even left a trace in the diaries, letters and memoirs of a few contemporaries. Others of these so-called memoirists describe the epistolary echoes of these events as "legendary" — as if to excuse certain of "Rakhmaninov's weaknesses"'.

[52] Daughter Marina Koshetz Schubert recounts it in a book and film both identically entitled *The Last Love Song*, which suggests that mother and composer were more than family friends. Marina was almost as well known in Hollywood as her film-star mother had been, despite possessing none of her international stardom. Still, the Rachmaninoff-Koshetz collaboration remains shrouded in

Two loves – Anna Lodyzhensky and Nina Koshetz – each illicit in a different way: erotically charged flings no matter how conceptualized or explained. Only Zverev's attachment, about which Rachmaninoff's biographers have been so puritanically timid, was a crushing blow to the pubescent pianist, all the more so in light of Rachmaninoff's much-loved absent father Vassily and Zverev's symbolic replacement of him. The boy of fourteen entrusted his soul to Zverev; in return he reaped maniacal discipline and disguised lust.[53]

---

uncertainty, even if it is clear that the composer-pianist was attracted to glamorous and exotic larger-than-life women (i. e., Anna the gypsy). It seems unlikely that Nina Koshetz had rejected Rachmaninoff in the Caucasus, and even odder that no record survives of their rediscovering each other much later in Hollywood in the 1940s. The main question remains: why did Rachmaninoff compose these most romantically intimate songs for her and then give her the original handwritten manuscripts (which daughter Marina Schubert donated to the Rachmaninoff Collection in the Library of Congress)? One clue is found in the cycle's second song ('Pied Piper'), whose piper warbles about the inconstancy and fickleness of women. But true light only begins to shine when Nina and Anna the gypsy are compared.

[53] Much later in life, in the 1920s after Rachmaninoff fled the Old Russia, he had another taste of homosexuality in another key, this time when his son-in-law, Irina's husband, the Prince Wolkonsky, killed himself just before their son was born. Wolkonsky married Irina Rachmaninoff in the hope his desire for men would vanish but it did not; weeks before his first child was about to be born he could face the hypocrisy no longer. Russian historians Nikolai Bazhanov and B. S. Nitikin have confirmed the account from Russian sources; see N. V. Bazhanov, *Rachmaninov* (Moscow: Raduga, 1983), p. 272 and Nitikin, *Sergei Rakhmaninov: Dve Zhizni* (Moscow, 1989), p. 175. Neither Bazhanov nor Nitikin reveal their archival locations, which may have been oral. But their research reveals a promiscuous Prince Wolkonsky who may have become embroiled in flagrant sexual affairs or been exposed by blackmail in ways that embarrassed his pregnant wife. The effect of his promiscuity and suicide on the Rachmaninoffs has never been explored, and a half century later, in 1956, biographer Bertensson was silent in his biography. An émigré biographer, as Bertensson was, writing at the height of the MacCarthy Era in America, would not have been expected to comment at length on the Wolkonsky affair, even if it did not offend the surviving members of Rachmaninoff's family. It is possible, of course, that Bertensson knew more than he revealed in the biography; this said, even if he did, he would have been cautious not to offend Sophia and Natalia, who made all documents available to him.

RACHMANINOFF'S RELATION TO LOVE – enduring love apart from impulse, infatuation and sex – was something else. In relation to persons, he was as logical and sensible as could be, bestowing it only once; on first-cousin Natalia Satina who was doubtlessly the love of his life despite her family's generosity. I have emphasized how they took him in; calmed his fervid nostalgia already manifest; paid for much of his musical education; and – later on – funded psychological treatment when he grew clinically depressed. It is no exaggeration to contend that without the Satins his career would have taken off more slowly or perhaps not at all. Wife Natalia aggregated all her energy on managing him and his affairs. The wives of great artists were often protective and managerial in this way, notoriously Jaqueline Roque (Pablo Picasso), Wanda Toscanini Horowitz (Vladimir Horowitz), Frida Kahlo (Diego Rivera), even Alma Mahler, although Alma possessed other talents than managerial. Natalia's supervision of her husband strengthened as time marched, especially when they settled in America and Rachmaninoff's concert career rocketed, often traveling with him and ensuring all went according to plan. Rachmaninoff, for his part, rarely wandered from her side, except for his brief infatuation with Nina Koshetz, which probably never amounted to much. With Natalia he produced two daughters to whom he was fiercely loyal and retained their welfare as the crown of all his concerns.

But a love for specific persons is not the *only* love, and for ardent Romantics like Rachmaninoff it was rivaled by his 'love for places', especially when places were attached to houses in his imagination – houses in the country, houses in whose gardens and on whose lakes to compose, houses with long memories, past or present, where mind and body could indulge the senses and revel in forests and hills.[54] Here, again, a context for Rachmaninoff enhances the point: the ethic

---

[54] Attachment theory in classical psychoanalysis focuses the attachment on persons, usually a parent, and classic attachment theory à la British psychoanalyst John Bowlby fixes it on the mother, especially the mother's breast that first fed the child; but with proper adjustments it can be extended to attachment for *non-persons*, such as the places I suggest loomed so large in Rachmaninoff's subconscious mind.

of Romanticism was so debunked by Modernists after c. 1920 that its values had no hope of high-brow taste, and two wars coupled to Modernist works of art made the case for it harder, especially in Russia. Yet throughout much of the nineteenth century, its aesthetic appealed to diverse types of lovers of art, as Rachmaninoff well knew. Today a sincere defense of high Romanticism appears as a preposterous gesture to most of us, at a moment when Postmodernism and its information technologies have also challenged Modernism let alone Romanticism – and renders Romanticism so remote, excessive, and inaccessible to our contemporaries that its profile needs to be explained, almost *gradus ad parnassum*, except to academic Romantic scholars well apprized of what it had been.

Emotion is paramount in this approach to the reality of love, as is mood and atmosphere, but setting in all its forms and shapes is primary. Mind and body conspire with the senses – all five and even an imagined sixth – in its landscapes, lakes, forests, and mountains. Each sense suspects it has reached its limit or soon will, and the 'eye' takes in more than it ever thought it could. Smell and touch, of sheep and glades overflowing with cool leaves. The whole body seems electrified and feels itself existing in another, higher realm of being where memory and imagination are liberated. In the process, the charged body has become an enthralled vassal not to one, but to two, lords, memory and imagination. Separately, or in tandem, they can range over the compass of the terraqueous globe, in Rachmaninoff's case to compose.

For Rachmaninoff place and setting focused on the house within the landscape: the almost classic Romantic ethic in which the five senses are placed in the service of memory. Rachmaninoff also included a house, usually a *country* house. In this he was similar to a point to another late Romantic composer, Mahler; the latter composing in Austrian huts to which he was attached in the spectacular lake-and-mountain region of Salzkammergut, and then at Toblach (now Dobbiaco in the Alto Adige in northern Italy).

But Rachmaninoff's 'composing houses' were ones where he had lived for many years, such as Oneg and Ivanovka, or the 'Villa Senar' intended to replace the Ivanovka he had lost to war, whose extended associations inspired him to compose his finest melodies and rhythms as well as elicited his worst hypochondria. He filled his imagination within rooms inside houses for psychological reasons extending back to his earliest youth in Novgorod. Oneg, his parents' estate in the forests of Novgorod northwest of Moscow, which he forever associated with the intact family before the parental dissolution and Vassily's ejection, was primal. Then, contrarily, in succession were his shared rooms and perceived imprisonment in Zverev's 'harem' from which he fled to the freer spaces in the Satins' Moscow townhouse: a room of his own at the very top of a grand house from whose window he could see church spires and hear their bells.[55]

Next in succession was Ivanovka, the Satins' country estate in the opposite direction from Moscow of Oneg, constructing a north and south axis in Rachmaninoff's geographical imagination whose pleasures complemented each landscape, especially Ivanovka's flat steppe and rolling fields. Finally, after his flight to the West, 'Senar' on Lake Lucerne, which he tried to model into a Swiss Ivanovka, and the very different 610 Elm Drive in Beverly Hills, as my friend Evelyn would discover in 1975. Six symbolic places (more than six if residences in Dresden, Paris and New York are counted) whose significance in his creative life rivaled any attachment to people.

He learned that this absorption in houses within landscapes is a type of 'love' too; a love of place, a love based on the unfettered life of the senses in specific settings. In no way did it detract from his love for wife Natalia and their two daughters, but it begins to describe Rachmaninoff's pedigree of late Romanticism and provides some explanation for why he could never write music similar to the mystical

---

[55] Even in his very first concert tour at the age of twenty-two with the young violinist Teresina Tua (1876-1939), he abandoned her over 'rooms'. They set out for three months, a distance two-thousand miles east of Moscow, but Rachmaninoff refused to play, complaining about the beds in the inns and the furniture far more than the stench of the coaches or the condition of the roads. Here already was the *cri de coeur* about 'rooms' he would lament for the rest of his life. The disappointed agent was relieved at not having to pay them for the remaining concerts as they were losing money.

Scriabin, the innovative Stravinsky, the politically shocked survivors Prokofiev and Shostakovich.[56]

Rachmaninoff himself has described these places. Here, one of dozens of similar letters, he remembers Ivanovka decades earlier:

> I grew fond of this broad landscape and, away from it, would find myself longing for it, for Ivanovka offered the repose of surrounding that hard work requires ... There were none of the beauties of nature that are usually thought of in this term – no mountain, precipice, or winding shore. This steppe was like an infinite sea where the waters are actually boundless fields of wheat, oats, stretching from horizon to horizon. Sea air is often praised, but how much more do I love the air of the steppe, with it aroma of earth and all that grows and blossoms.[57]

A final facet of his brand of Romanticism was its pervasive melody *and* morbidity – the two, when coupled, formed a unique type of dreamy melancholia encompassing his nostalgia. But even so Rachmaninoff's melancholy was in its terminal stage; a kind of 'Russian Byronism' on its deathbed pining for the *ancien regime*. Composing under the sign of his master Tchaikovsky, Rachmaninoff extended the master's more cheerful versions of song by turning melody morbid. The view may appear strident yet we need think no

---

[56] Accounts like these will not change the minds of critics like Richard Taruskin and Alex Ross whose concern is the formal musical product, not the biographical circumstances of composers or their milieu. Francis Maes has more to say about Rachmaninoff in *A History of Russian Music: From 'Kamarinskaya' to 'Babi Yar'* (Berkeley and London: University of California press, 2002), but even his large-scale 'history' says comparatively little about Rachmaninoff for reasons unexplained. Daniel Barenboim's approach is the more balanced in 'Beethoven and the Quality of Courage,' *New York Review of Books* 4 April 2013, pp. 21-22.

[57] Cited in Bertensson, p. 25.

further than to Tchaikovsky's melodies; they can seem to be tragic blasts about Fate but capture, more typically, the enchanted and magical world children love. Not Rachmaninoff, who cultivated *adult melodiousness* (if it can be labelled this way), and whose melodies are further matured by their dark and mournful tones, anything but effervescent and lighthearted. Rachmaninoff's version of Romanticism, furthermore, was morbid rather than innovative – or ecstatic, as in Scriabin's case – and he allowed his nostalgia for the *old Russia* to dominate him, even after he migrated to the West. Always the *old Russia* that was dying away; the land, the people, the religion of *old Russia*; folk songs of yesterday; never the new Russia that was coming or could arise in the new socio-political order: this was his continuing song.

His contemporaries before the Bolshevik revolution recognized this melodic morbidity (even his former classmate Yuri Sakhnovsky, who became a leading Moscow music critic), as did César Cui when demolishing his first symphony in 1897. Cui was the most ruthless, even despicable; invoked the language of pathological illness to describe this first attempt at a symphony, and invoked phrases such as his 'sickly perverse harmonization and lack of simplicity and naturalness'. The 'pathological' was routinely summoned in turn-of-the-century Russia to describe Rachmaninoff: as someone impotent, semi-conscious, stooped in stupor, drugged, existing from mood swing to mood swing.

His brand of romantic melody also sustained musical (i. e., non-biographical) dimensions. The Russians – as Evelyn had intuitively jotted into her notebook in 1964 – sow their souls into their music; the only matter is whether of the Rachmaninoff version or the Prokofiev-Shostakovich type. Rachmaninoff's way is melodic, his successors rhythmic. He perfected sentimental melody – especially its degenerative morbidity – at the expence of rhythm. Rhythm was his weak point, forever appearing as secondary and derivative in its forms. Tchaikovsky was something *else* and perfected both melody and rhythm. What need did the Russians have for a Rachmaninoff when they already had a Tchaikovsky?[58]

FROM THE TIME OF YOUTH RACHMANINOFF'S FACIAL COMPLEXION struck his family and friends as 'pale'. It lacked the ruddy redness of youth. 'O,' as Keats had written in *La Belle Dame sans Merci*, 'what ails thee knight-at-arms, alone and palely loitering?' It was a symptom of Rachmaninoff's quasi-medical melancholy and chronic hypochondria that lingered to his dying day. He could be light and frivolous but they were not his dominant temperament, as the Renaissance doctors might have said. Having just conducted *The Isle of the Dead* and while working on his third piano concerto in 1909, he told his faithful correspondent Nikita Morozov to whom he more often than not bares his heart on his sleeve, that he has done nothing more than 'take treatments, walk, and sleep ... I realize that my health, or rather, my strength, has clearly begun to decline.'[59]

This is a man (in 1909) of *thirty-six* not seventy-six, a man so prematurely preoccupied with aging and death I could list his hypochondriacal bouts chronologically. Marietta Shaginyan, his 'Dear Re', was another much esteemed correspondent who elicited similar symptoms, as when the secretive Rachmaninoff disclosed to her not long afterwards that his 'illness hangs on to me tenaciously and with the passing years digs in ever more deeply.'[60] What illness is this? – he does not say except to suggest these are the ravages of melancholy (our depression) and that he is 'soul-sick ... and regard myself as disarmed, and aging, as well.'

---

[58] Why did the Russians need his two great successors, Prokofiev and Shostakovich, whose Russian souls are also sown into their music? Because substantial musical evolution requires innovation; without it the great tradition withers and merely repeats itself in derivative musical forms.

[59] Cited in Bertensson, p. 158.

[60] Ibid., p. 179.

His hypochondria took such a toll a few years later that a deeply worried Shaginyan wrote in her reminiscences, 'he was so obsessed with a fear of death … he asked my mother to tell his fortune with cards.'[61] Every summer, even in blissful Ivanovka, brought new worries, a pain in the right temple, a swelling in his leg, his perennial back problems. The maladies were often mysterious – incapable of diagnosis or solution and sometimes retreated on their own.

Tall as he was, with huge hands probably not owing to Marfan's Syndrome (a genetic disorder of the connective tissue manifesting itself usually in very tall persons with long limbs and fingers), Rachmaninoff was not hale and hearty, as his face and visage should have indicated to any stranger.[62] He was often sick, agonizing over something or other, and the proclivity intensified in his thirties, perhaps in synchrony with the political uprisings, yet had been apparent from youth. There is good evidence that he rarely composed when ill or even feeling unwell. Illness in other artists – the lists are long – often stimulates creativity, even their best moments, but did not for Rachmaninoff, a correlation between health and creativity he himself seems to have understood.

Rachmaninoff's early twenties were also plagued not merely by failed love for Anna the gypsy but, additionally, from his dominant *toska*: his very Russian melancholy resistant to definition without losing its native Russian differences. The failure and loss of Anna's love, for whatever reason, took a huge toll, as did his depressive symptoms propelling him to mood swings: indeed the contemporary student of his inner life distinguishes these from his more chronic hypochondria. Had he been female a diagnosis of hysteria may have been given in 1895 or 1900, for his version was almost always accompanied by perceived physical symptoms. What glares at the student of his life is his conviction that his body parts were failing.

---

[61] Ibid., p. 199.

[62] Rachmaninoff's Marfan's Syndrome has been very fully covered by former biographers and medical historians. Its significance here is Marfan's well-known cardiovascular effect, which would have accounted for the composer-pianist's persistent complaint that he did not feel hale and hearty and his pervasive sense that his body parts were failing.

His typical pattern was to consult a few doctors, usually without being able to pay them, and to remain in a kind of limbo until the next episode occurred. As he grew older he was persuaded, as he told Marietta Shaginyan, that he was trapped in an increasingly infirm body.[63]

1898 was a tumultuous year, he thought. He wrote to a few contemporaries and penned a letter to Modeste Tchaikovsky, the late composer's brother, asking him for help, but neither their replies nor his own self-therapies lifted him. What did his hypochondria amount to? A tall, handsome man of twenty-five who should have been conquering the world with his burning talent – appeared inert and dried up. When his moods swung he returned to the physicians. One sent him south in September to recover in the warm strand along the Crimean coast. He was permitted to give a few concerts but cautioned to rest most of the time and take the waters.

At one concert in Yalta, Anton Chekhov, already tubercular and unexpectedly to die just a few years later, in 1904 at forty-four, was in the audience. Chekhov had heard much about the young virtuoso pianist and came to see what the fuss was over – we know this from his letters. Rachmaninoff, who had never been a dedicated reader but had read several of Chekhov's short stories and fell in with the then prevailing view that Chekhov and Tolstoy were the two greatest living authors, was thrilled. He knew Chekhov was also a doctor, a doctor-artist who could heal. Chekhov's medical experience is so prominent in his stories any reader would. The dual achievement – doctor and great writer – heightened Rachmaninoff's admiration and the wish to meet Chekhov.

That night Chekhov rode in a carriage from the gardens at the villa he had recently built on Yalta's outskirts. At the concert's close enthusiastic members of the audience – including host Chekhov himself – filed into the self-styled artist's room. Chekhov's biographers have recounted how the physician-writer paced up to Rachmaninoff,

---

[63] Contemporary psychotherapy and psychoanalysis would seize this non-payment as crucial and relate it to a pervasive narcissistic strand of his character: i. e., the patient's belief that he was too important to pay and that others should pay for him. His cousins, the Satins, usually did, even after his marriage to their daughter.

his dapper spectacles quivering on his sleek face, his neatly trimmed beard pointing downward, and, in concentrated gaze fixed on the pianist, prophesied: 'All this time I have been looking at you, young man. You have a wonderful face – you will be a great man.'

What chord struck Chekhov about that sombre melancholic face? Did Chekhov, the doctor-as-physiognomist, already glimpse the sadness, the loss of Anna perceived by Rachmaninoff as a failure in St Petersburg? Did the countenance reveal a future exile's yearning for imagined, sunnier places? Always for Rachmaninoff a late Romantic version of '*Kennst du das Land?*' – do you know that place I remember, with the beautiful country house in its estate, to which I might return? Or was the truth the other way round: Chekhov penetrating the pianist's interior face, piercing beyond the black suit to the quintessential Russian fatalist performing that night? Gazing at the black cape that would become Rachmaninoff's insignia?

Chekhov was on to something. No other piano immortal has ever performed more aloofly – as Siloti noticed years before this, when Rachmaninoff had performed as a boy – as if the establishment of any connection with the audience lay beyond his ken. Tonight Rachmaninoff walked on stage, almost dismissed the audience, held back as usual, and performed as if they were not present. The black suit he wore, doubled as artistic shield, like Achilles' andabatarian armour. His black suit and black piano were bulwarks. He never performed without either because they concealed, *ne plus ultra*, his psychodrama inside.

One year later, during the summer of 1899, Chaliapin provides a taste of this blackness. He reminisced that Rachmaninoff spent most of it on the Kreutzer's country estate.[64] They were minor aristocrats

---

[64] Opera-singer Chaliapin is not an entirely reliable source for Rachmaninoff's psychology or personality. Born in the same year as his friend – 1873 – and doubtlessly kind to the desperate and ailing Rachmaninoff in this fin-de-siècle, Chaliapin did not realize to what degree Rachmaninoff relied on him. Chaliapin was open-jawed and fun-loving; a transparent performer forever wearing his heart on his sleeve, and everything the gloomy Rachmaninoff was not. When Chaliapin wrote his autobiographical memoirs in Paris early in the 1930s, one of them later published as *Pages from my Life*, he barely mentioned the composer who doubtlessly

with no relation to Tolstoy's novella *The Kreutzer Sonata*, and Rachmaninoff hoped 'Nature' would restore him; the morning dew and cowbells fire him up. Spring and summer were always his preferred seasons. However, during the prior spring he felt no impulse to compose, nor could the cowbells rustle him. Writer's block had obstructed his projected opera based on *Francesca da Rimini* and he could not write even one measure of his Second Piano Concerto, and now – at the Kreutzer's – he also had chills and headaches.

These creative blocks were often accompanied by physical symptoms, and even if Rachmaninoff was not genuinely ill he imagined himself to be. It was a powerful defence in times both good and bad for a composer stylistically out of sync with his generation – he would more easily have composed in his late Romantic style if born a generation earlier. (When mysterious illness struck, as it did in a cottage the Rachmaninoffs rented for the spring-summer of 1906 at Marina di Pisa on the Mediterranean Sea to the west of Pisa, in Italy, he coped well despite any clue to its identification. Both mother and eldest daughter, Natalia and Irina, also fell sick, Italian doctors were summoned, and both eventually cleared.) These occurrences stand in counterpoint to the composer's more pervasive hypochondriacal symptoms and his fear that he was – somehow – aging before his time. This was no psychological progeria à la Evelyn's Richard, but his sense that some creative flame within him was being extinguished.

TWO MENTORS – I CALL THEM THE TWO T'S, TCHAIKOVSKY AND TOLSTOY, to underscore their combined effect during these years – fell off the radar of Rachmaninoff's visibility by the turn of the century, Tchaikovsky to death (1893), Tolstoy out of offence (1900), although Tolstoy died ten years later. Taken together, they accentuate the point about the fragility of Rachmaninoff's emotional universe as the *fin-de-siècle* drew to a close

---

had taught him much about music. Was their former friendship nothing he could remember after the Revolution?

and enhance understanding of his hypochondria. Even without his monumental losses – a flopped first symphony, scathing reviews, the loss of Anna – Rachmaninoff may have broken down.

Zverev's homosexuality had clearly ruffled Rachmaninoff, especially on the occasion when teacher struck, or tried to strike, pupil. (Despite rumours about Adele's combativeness, as I recounted above, Evelyn never once alluded to such behaviour to me.) But Tchaikovsky's homosexuality was of no concern, even if Rachmaninoff was aware of its existence. Rachmaninoff's devotion to this master existed on various planes: teacher-student, mentor-mentee, model composer, repository of the type of Romanticism he himself was trying to express. Rachmaninoff must have heard accounts of Tchaikovsky's ties to the pederasts – how could he not? – and read newspaper reports about his frequenting of St Petersburg's Chaumont Restaurant, haunt of sodomites.[65] But Tchaikovsky was no Zverev: abusive and tyrannical closet-case versus kindly mentor who may have succumbed (so far as Rachmaninoff was concerned) to this slight human failing if indiscretion it was. No, Tchaikovsky was the very model of discretion and euphemism, a further reason why Rachmaninoff and his fellow students so piteously mourned his death at only fifty-three from 'suspicious reasons'. Did he intentionally drink the contaminated water at Leiners in the Nevsky Prospekt that November day in 1893, or was his death suicide?[66] Rachmaninoff left no record of his view – accident versus suicide – yet the larger matter was his reverence and sense of loss.

The full extent of the young Rachmaninoff's loss must be comprehended to understand his later collapse. He was conflicted to say the least between love for Tchaikovsky-the master musician and the vice he represented – torn between anguish and exhortation. Love

---

[65] Dan Healey (see n. 40), p. 95, systematically provides the newspaper sources.

[66] The cause of Tchaikovsky's death continues to be contested, and was exacerbated after 1979 when the theory gained ground that a sentence of suicide had been imposed by Tchaikovsky's fellow alumni of the Imperial School of Jurisprudence as a censure for his homosexuality. Even so, Tchaikovsky's contemporary biographers, especially Alexandra Orlova, Alexander Poznansky and David Brown, do not agree.

between men was anathema in the Eastern Orthodox church; practically a curse on the families on whom it descended. Years later, Rachmaninoff on his deathbed recalled what a blow it had been to him at only twenty, and remembered how he had retreated to compose an elegiac trio in his memory. He also recalled how the newspapers had speculated about Tchaikovsky's motives.

The impact of Tchaikovsky's death for Rachmaninoff extended further than this according to Emanuel E. Garcia, M. D., an American psychoanalyst who has served as a consultant to the Curtis School of Music in Philadelphia and is *au fait* with music history in Rachmaninoff's era. Dr. Garcia published a series of articles about the psychological profiles of composers active c. 1900, especially studies of Rachmaninoff, Scriabin, and Mahler.[67] His account of Rachmaninoff's 'Emotional Collapse' focuses on the brutal reception of Rachmaninoff's first symphony and the specific biographical circumstances of the mid-1890s leading up to it. Chief among these (in descending order of their significance) were Tchaikovsky's death; failed or unrequited love with gypsy Anna (I must emphasize the uncertainties that surround their affair and the meaning of its loss for Rachmaninoff); an unstable daily routine interrupted by damaged psyche at this most vulnerable period during his mid-twenties; and two disastrous interviews with Tolstoy. All four events impinged on an emotionally fragile temperament – Rachmaninoff's – that readily succumbed to the accumulated wreckage these events could produce.

Dr. Garcia begins with the premise that Rachmaninoff was a 'genius' whose productivity would have been far greater had he not be stricken by these four events. 'Rachmaninoff the genius' is a given for Garcia. By this he means creative genius capable of composing enduring works of art no less than Mozart, Beethoven, or Chopin. He does not extend the 'genius' component to Rachmaninoff's piano playing, but Garcia would presumably not disagree that few pianists

---

[67] See especially E. E. Garcia, MD, 'Rachmaninoff's First Symphony: Emotional Crisis and Genius Interred', *Journal of the Conductor's Guild* 23: 1-2 (2002): 17-29.

of the last two centuries have succeeded so brilliantly at the keyboard anywhere on the globe.[68]

Dr. Garcia's view of Tchaikovsky's death is more symbolic than literal and takes its main toll in Rachmaninoff's unconscious. It is the view that Rachmaninoff was actually trying to break away from the 'master' and achieved his desired rupture in the iconoclastic first symphony; but that its failed reception in turn placed the breaks on Rachmaninoff's sense that he could launch out on his own. Garcia's sums up the position this way:

Before the composition of the First Symphony Rachmaninoff's idol, Tchaikovsky, had died, leaving him without a patron and mentor. After the death of a loved one, an internal revolt often occurs. Unconscious hatred towards the loved object (Tchaikovsky) is released and the subject (Rachmaninoff) experiences an exhilarating freedom that can be characterized by a manic release; this process generally begins after the process of acute mourning is finished. I must emphasize that the ambivalent nature of the relationship to the deceased is kept *unconscious*.[69]

Such interpretation is legitimate, especially what is withheld from Rachmaninoff's conscious mind, provided it supplies a context for the loss; that is, how it relates to Rachmaninoff's *other* simultaneous losses with Tolstoy and Anna. The unconscious revolt Garcia depicts may not be universal, in all creative artists, but a reasonable likelihood exists that the young Rachmaninoff participated in its unconscious dynamic mechanisms. The debacles with Tolstoy are another matter because several accounts from different sources endure, and by amalgamating them a consensus begins to form.

---

[68] It is easy to forget to what degree Rachmaninoff was received in America as a legendary pianist rivalled only by Liszt and a few Europeans, including Josef Hofmann, Moritz Rosenthal, Vladimir Horowitz and Artur Rubenstein. Not an inconsiderable part of his success was owing to the mood of American audiences in the 1920s-30s, then poised to be dazzled by Russian technical virtuosity coupled to a six-foot-plus, car-loving expatriate who sat motionless at the piano as if he were a god dwelling in Valhalla. Such positioning earned him a fortune but could not restore the urge to compose.

[69] Garcia (n. 67), p. 24.

Garcia observes that Rachmaninoff visited the great writer in 1897, already senescent and – of course – venerable, seeking advice and compassion about his creative block. What could Tolstoy say that would lift his depression?

This sketch of their first interview accommodates the facts as recounted by Alfred Swan (discussed below), but Garcia overlooks what *actually occurred* – not once but twice, on two separate occasions. The first time the glamorous Princess Alexandra Lieven came to his rescue. Her pedigree was sterling, her beauty legendary in Russia, her grandmother Tzar Nicholas' representative to the court of St James in London, and she herself would later marry an English aristocrat. Lieven had a reputation for being able to sway the most powerful of men to yield to her will.

Rachmaninoff routinely performed at her soirées, and she was so impressed she took him as a confidant, though not, as Anna, a lover. Without revealing anything to her young prodigy, she wrote to her friend Tolstoy and entreated him to talk to the young depressed composer. She described him as a 'young man who had lost his faith in his own powers'. An apt description, even if the reasons were suppressed. Tolstoy summoned Rachmaninoff to his home in the Khamovniki district, near the Novodevichy Convent and memorial cemetery in Moscow's Golden Mile, containing the most beautiful palaces. A literary account of their interview might resemble this:

Rachmaninoff went alone. Desperate to alleviate his psychological state of mind he wearily climbed the wooden staircase of this ancient house. It opened into a library built of thick wood filled with leather-bound books. Tolstoy's wife, Sophia Andreyevna, and her two sons, welcomed him and invited him to join the Count in the drawing room. Alexander Goldenweiser, equally young and another brilliant Zverev piano pupil, was already present and waiting to hear the virtuoso. He was studying piano at the Moscow Conservatory, where he was later to become a professor of piano, and would write further reminiscences of that meeting with Tolstoy.

A servant brought the large samovar of tea but Rachmaninoff was too despondent to take any. Then Tolstoy entered the room and filled it with his *dignitas* – the bearded avatar appeared even more godlike than in the well-known photographs. Here, in person, a few yards from the young composer, Tolstoy seemed untouchable.

The customary Russian amenities were exchanged, tea drunk by everyone except Rachmaninoff. Princess Alexandra had briefed Tolstoy, and he could see for himself something was profoundly amok in the nervous man before him, as he clutched his black suit-jacket closer and closer to his chest and kept resisting tea.

Tolstoy motioned that the company should leave them alone. They filed out in a row. Then Tolstoy beckoned to Rachmaninoff to sit beside him. The words he spoke came out almost as if rehearsed.

The older man took the lead. 'Do you imagine that everything in my life goes smoothly? Do you suppose I have no troubles, no hesitations, that I do not lose all confidence in myself?'

He continued in this vein, patronizing and almost chiding Rachmaninoff. Rachmaninoff's knees quivered and trembled. Then, when Tolstoy finished his set speech he fell into a silence for a minute or two – and began to rub Rachmaninoff's knees. Up and down, his right hand stroked both knees in an upward motion from the calves almost into Rachmaninoff's thighs, pressing his hands deeper and deeper into the flesh, as if massaging an ailing patient. Silence prevailed for a few minutes as Rachmaninoff lay speechless, too startled to say anything.

The young man stiffened; Tolstoy noticed how nervous he was and relented.

What was this, the young composer wondered. Some ancient Russian ritual unknown to him? Competing explanations flashed within his head, even doleful memories of the early days inside Zverev's 'harem'. He had expected anything from the avatar of Russian wisdom except this physical assault on his already nervous body. Only Tolstoy could have conferred this ritual on a fellow traveler through the untouchable realms of creative imagination.

Rachmaninoff also wondered, during those moments, whether the Princess apprized Tolstoy about Anna. 'Of course the Princess *knew*', he reassured himself. He himself told Princess Lieven about her before the ball when he brought Chaliapin to perform with him at her party.

Was this Tolstoy's tacit acknowledgment, Rachmaninoff wondered, that he was aware of Anna's existence? Then, while still imprisoned in his chair, the logic of Tolstoy's kneading dashed through Rachmaninoff's mind. Perhaps the strokes concealed Tolstoy's message: if he would just succumb to Bacchus and Venus, with Anna, his creative power would be rekindled. Its effectiveness was plausible, Rachmaninoff wished. After Tolstoy let up on the knees the old man counseled him to continue composing even if the compositions he produced were defective. Our young composer was confused.

Mine is a literary version of their first 'interview', and it is not irrelevant that Alfred Swan (1890-1970) is the source for the details of this first visit. Swan was the remarkable son of an English family who had been resident for generations in St Petersburg. He and his wife Katherine knew the Rachmaninoffs and were in frequent contact with them during the 1930s. The Swans would never have invented such a melodramatic account if Rachmaninoff had not described it. Its outlandish details nevertheless remain, especially the older man's physical stroking and verbal abuse.

The second meeting, mentioned by Garcia, occurred almost three years later, on 9 January 1900, after Rachmaninoff plummeted to an emotional nadir, felt he could not go on, as he confided to Princess Lieven. She joined up with matriarch Varvara Satina, and the two persuaded Tolstoy to 'counsel' their prodigy *again*. This time Rachmaninoff went with his friend Chaliapin, our source for the second visit. Chaliapin recounts that Rachmaninoff feared he would be asked to play again but could not: his fingers were too cold. They drank tea, sang Rachmaninoff's song 'Fate', and Tolstoy did not feel him up or rub his knees. Instead Tolstoy railed against the 'modern music' they regaled him with, adding that Beethoven and Pushkin were inferior creators (did Tolstoy know that just four years earlier, in 1896, Henry James spoke for many when proclaiming that Tolstoy himself 'was a monster harnassed to his great subject – all human life! – as an elephant might be harnassed, not to a carriage, but to a coach-house.') Tolstoy's wife begged the young men to take no notice, and they departed in disappointment that the day ended this way. According to Chaliapin, absconded in such flight that Rachmaninoff never again returned to Tolstoy's house, not even when Sophia Andreyevna invited him to be their guest at Yasnaya Polyana, their country estate, where he could compose in the utmost solitude. Rachmaninoff never saw Tolstoy again.

The dominant mood of Rachmaninoff's music offers a further clue: it is the least happy of the Russian composers of this era, suffused in a wide-ranging melancholia embracing unhappiness, misery, and all things Parisian his artistic milieu had assimilated from the *belle époque* French Romantics: *malaise, ennui, anomie, désespoir, morosité*, and – of course – *mélancolie*. It enjoys little of Tchaikovsky's nutcracker-fairy-tale festivity, none of its trusting simplicity.[70]

More needs to be made of Rachmaninoff's versions of melancholia: their transformations of an older Romantic *tristesse*, their relation to other art forms in his time, especially Russian painting, literature, and film around 1900. Rachmaninoff's sense of himself as the 'Russian Chopin', even during the time of his collapse and subsequent hypnotism, ought to have provided a clue. Like Chopin's, his melancholia was infused with nostalgia grounded in ambivalence about national and cultural loss: loss of the gentry and its land, loss of old Russian values and their spiritual potency, loss of self and identity through these larger cultural ruptures. Much more needs to be understood about our 'Russian Chopin' composing and breaking down in a Slavic social milieu seven decades removed from the 'Polish nostalgic of Paris', as one of Chopin's contemporaries called

---

[70] The difference profoundly touches on Rachmaninoff's version of nostalgia, which fundamentally differed from his mentor's – Tchaikovsky's – melancholy. Rachmaninoff's nostalgia sprung from a deep sense of loss of home and homeland in the *past*: the childhood he could never return to. Tchaikovsky, on the other hand, lamented unattainable and forbidden love: a *future* state associated with adulthood rather than childhood. His genius lay in transforming his adult desires into juvenescent musical narratives as found in his ballets and operas.

him, who wrote the preludes and nocturnes Rachmaninoff transformed into his own Slavic melancholic *métier*. This line of inquiry reveals an hypochondriacal as well as narcissistic Rachmaninoff whose creativity is simultaneously being derailed and energized by these traits. Dr. Garcia is cogent when calling attention to gypsy Anna, and when suggesting that the lovers culminated their adulterous affair. Why else would Rachmaninoff have dedicated so many works to her? And further when implying that when Anna withdrew (if she did withdraw), Rachmaninoff collapsed so forcefully he could create nothing, compose nothing, think nothing. His melancholy, pessimism and mild narcissism combined to bring him down, as well as invent monumental piano concertos.

MOST CONTEMPORARY DEVOTEES OF CLASSICAL MUSIC know something about Rachmaninoff's creative block as the new century turned, described in every concert programme featuring his music. His subsequent breakdown is usually framed as 'writer's block' or 'creative cramp' but few details are included.

His collapse had long tentacles extending back into the 1890s. Propelled by lust for gypsy Anna, and newly driven by Eros as his Muse, he composed tirelessly throughout 1895. His dream of becoming famous attached itself to this reinvigorated drive. Eros as Muse had temped many late Romantic composers; he was hardly unique here. But he had abandoned himself to the erotic impulse and the beloved's expected kiss: Anna as temptress and redemptress, and the creative rush she produced exhilarated him, turned him manic, persuaded him that with her as stanchion he could accomplish anything.[71]

---

[71] Musicologist Stephen Downes has argued the case for *The Muse as Eros: Music, Erotic Fantasy, and Male Creativity in the Romantic and Modern Imagination* (Aldershot: Ashgate, 2006). Rachmaninoff is not included, perhaps because the

He finished his first symphony by the end of the summer of 1895, having spent it at Ivanovka, and also practiced for a concert tour arranged to repair his financial condition. The tour failed to materialize, but he remained firebrand over the new symphony's prospects. He would not desist until it was finished; until he could see the printed title page with his Anna as dedicatee and hear it performed. Perhaps her husband Pyotr would head the cello section on opening night. The Programme Notes would stipulate: 'dedicated to A. L.' Anna herself would be seated in the stalls, dark eyes flashing, fiery expression charged. She would understand why he dedicated this work to her.

This was the fantasy but its execution did not work out according to plan. During 1896 a nervous Rachmaninoff became obsessed about the public performance of his symphony. He was overjoyed when the Orchestra Committee in St Petersburg approved its performance for their new series. Their decision tempered negative comments various teachers and mentors had made along the way about its form and structure. Yet even loyal Taneyev, who found much to criticize, promoted it.

The catastrophe of its first performance on 15 March 1897 has been far more often retold than the repercussions of its aftermath on Rachmaninoff's state of mind: how the critics rubbished it; how Rimsky-Korsakov, who ought to have been well disposed, deemed it 'disagreeable', to put a genial spin on his caveats; how César Cui, a harpy-mouthed music critic also influential as a St Petersburg composer, ranted and raved against 'this modernist trash' from Moscow, with its 'poverty of themes, [and its] sick perversity of harmony.'

Whether Anna and Pyotr attended cannot be documented. But it would seem odd that Anna should not be present at this musical happening whose *pièce-de-résistance* was dedicated to her if she was aware of the dedication, which she may not have been. Rachmaninoff

standard biographies have omitted Anna, but he is a perfect candidate for Downes's lineage of affected composers and would have strengthened an already strong hypothesis.

himself could not believe what he heard emanate from the orchestra. The performance was so sub-standard he thought he would vomit. Conductor-composer Alexander Glazunov, it was said, conducted like a swine – was he drunk or out to ruin Rachmaninoff? – and the players were also careless. After Rachmaninoff's death, sister-in-law Sophia remembered that night so fateful for his health and career this way:

> He told us that during the performance he could not bring himself to enter the auditorium, but hid on the stairs of the corridor that led to the balcony. … from time to time he pressed his fists against his ears to stop the sounds that were torturing him. At the end he ran out on to the street, where he walked about trying to find the explanation for his mistake, and trying to calm down sufficiently to attend the supper that was being given later that night by Belayev [an influential music patron and publisher], in Rachmaninoff's honor.

Where was Anna's exoticism now or subsequent comfort, if she gave any? She who had been his muse and inspiration, into whose body and soul he poured his imagination in the form of this first symphony – only to end in this debacle from which the young composer whinged that he would never recover.

Rachmaninoff rescued himself in the nick of time, if reclamation it can be called, by taking flight to *babushka* Butakova's country estate outside Novgorod, as he often had done in the past, and remaining there alone. From here he wrote long letters outpouring his heart's anguish to the Skalon sisters – especially charming Vera – and other friends too. But the damage was done, a knife thrust into his heart. Glazunov was the villain but he too must take responsibility for the symphony's poor orchestration, and as sacrifice, he thought, he would give up composition altogether.

(My friend Evelyn, whose diary notes that she read Bertensson's biography in the 1960s, deeply sympathized with his catastrophe, which reminded her of her own 'deep freeze' – her phrase – in Town Hall. Rachmaninoff's despair enlarged his being in her imagination and drew her closer to him. This sympathy may have played a part eight years later, in 1968, in her decision to migrate to his final 'home' in Beverly Hills.)

Rachmaninoff decided not to revise the symphony. Years later, he told Boris Vladimirovich Asafiev, a musical editor, just before he was leaving Russia in December 1917, that he 'felt like a man who had suffered a stroke and for a long time had lost the use of his head and hands'. Privately he ruminated that 15 March 1897 was the worst day of his life. Even more poignantly he told his nurse, who sat at his side at the very end of his life, that he could not have foreseen his death on this same unlucky day, 28 March 1943, forty-six years later.[72]

Rachmaninoff's collapse was not – in our terms – psychotic: he could still eat and sleep and perform life's daily functions. But he was mentally and emotionally shattered and could compose nothing. For a man who measured his entire well-being by the degree, not to which he could perform a concert but compose, this reduction was life-threatening. It amounted to loss of identity in one blow. He had been intimately attached to Anna for two years: she became the sum and orbit of his emotional and creative universe. Now, with the strike of a baton, his future was occluded, his smile gone, his shadow downcast.

For Anna he had written many of his songs of those two years, especially the poignant one that began 'Oh, no, I beg you, don't forsake me'. It was the song her sister Nadezhda Aleksandrovna sang so beautifully at the Sakhnovskys. For Anna and Pyotr he had composed the *Capriccio on Gypsy Themes* for orchestra, which became his opus 12 and which he arranged for two pianos himself. Perhaps Anna was blind to the extent of his attraction – the truth can never be known. What is certain is that the experience, coupled to the debacle of the symphony's debut, deranged him. The episode was of another order to any calamity he faced earlier – even his second sister's death – whose memory he would never forget. Recovery would occupy years, not weeks or months.

---

[72] Old style 15 March became 28 March in the new style Russian calendar commencing in 1918, so the two dates were identical in Rachmaninoff's mind: the worse day of his life and the day when he would die.

Is it any wonder, then, that contemporary music lovers today associate Rachmaninoff's music with inner suffering and personal yearning? His piano music's virtuosity dazzles them; but its dominant emotions (gloom, foreboding, annihilation, an ambivalence between the pleasures of melancholia and the virtues of strength and stamina) seem on balance monolithically pessimistic. Not merely sentimentally pining for an abstract as well as literal Russian homeland, which endures in much of his music, but the creator's musical representations of his psyche crushed under the weight of despair. This is Rachmaninoff-the-unlucky-genius who has fallen to the bottom ring of the great wheel of fortune. After he hit rock bottom and eventually recovered, his experience in purgatory enabled him to create some of his greatest works composed in the first decade of the twentieth century.

BUT NOT BEFORE HYPNOTISM COULD REVIVE HIM. The angelic Satins, especially Sophia, intervened again with the help of matriarch Varvara. By now the gloomy Rachmaninoff was firmly entrenched as a family member and perhaps already selected to be their daughter Natalia's husband.

Sophia – 'Sonechka' to Rachmaninoff – watched him sink during that summer of 1899 at Ivanovka before he went to the staid and wealthy Kreutzer's country estate; lurking around, producing nothing, and now, as the new century approached and his spirits should have been optimistic, his mood grew bleaker by the day. Aunt Varvara also pondered what to do. However matriarchal she was, she harbored her own demons for which she had sought the then fashionable psychiatric-hypnotic cure; and was treated by the very same doctor (as we shall see) she would secure for her ailing nephew. Varvara took advice and told her influential friends about her predicament. She consulted the Princess Lieven and discussed Sergei's collapse with Sophia.

In Europe the century turned forward to 1900, as did the clocks. At home the snow in Moscow that January was massive, reaching windowsills early in the month. Soon after the disastrous visit to Tolstoy on 9 January, Rachmaninoff moaned to Natalia and Sophia that he was lost, useless, a dead soul wandering amidst the living, could compose nothing. Sophia, whose psyche was anything but romantic and who later became a botanical taxonomist, confided to her diary that Rachmaninoff barely ate; his complexion started to change. She instigated a secret family meeting and persuaded them, including Varvara, it was time to consult their family friend, Grigory Grauerman – the Moscow physician – for advice.

Grauerman recommended Nikolai Dal (1860–1939), a well-connected Moscow society-hypnotist. Dal himself was an amateur violist who hosted frequent soirées in his home. If anyone could tease Rachmaninoff out of the depressive doldrums in which he had lingered for three years it was Dal. He had treated musicians, actors, artists, all types of bohemians willing to submit themselves. Rachmaninoff's troubled classmate Scriabin (whose music Rachmaninoff loathed) had offered himself to Dal, as did Mikhail Vrubel, a Symbolist painter. Vasilii Ivanovich Kachalov (1875-1948), an actor who appeared in the first productions of Chekhov's *Three Sisters* in 1901, was a patient when Rachmaninoff started his hypnosis. Dal revived Kachalov who went on to become one of Moscow's most celebrated Chekhovian stars. Dal was also rumoured to be hypnotizing Constantin Stanislavski, not yet famous but who would eventually be for developing a new system of acting constructed on the emotional realism of Pushkin and Gogol (the Stanislavsky Method). No one could have known it that winter but Dal would also hypnotize Rachmaninoff's best friend Chaliapin after the hypnotist-doctor moved to Petrograd in the 1920s.

Dal was a decade older than Rachmaninoff and had recently qualified as a medical doctor. Yet in 1899, when he moved, he had already attracted a large clientele and occupied a detached house at 14 Spiridonevsky Alley, the fashionable residential area close to Patriarch's Ponds, best known to Westerners as a central location in Bulgakov's novel *The Master and Margarita*. Here he built a dedicated music room filled with the old string instruments he collected, and paid young musicians from the Conservatory a few roubles to play chamber music in his dimly-lit nocturnal gatherings. Word circulated that he could heal any musician's impediments with his new 'suggestion cure': trigger fingers, stiff joints and shoulders, as well as stage fright. You could say he was promoting through hypnosis his own Alexander Technique before there was one in Russia.[73]

Rachmaninoff did not resist treatment and Sophia assured him he would like Dal. Dr Grauerman had filled her ears with superlatives about Dal's credentials: how he studied at the Salpêtrière under Charcot – where Dal met Freud – and at the Medical School in Nancy, France, under Ambroise-Auguste Liébeault, founder of the suggestion hypnosis. How he read Vladimir Mikhailovich Bekhterev (1857-1927), known throughout Russia as the 'discoverer' of suggestion techniques. All this boded well but the crucial matter is why Rachmaninoff responded as well as he did.

Bekhterev was a clinician who had observed dozens of patients during experiments conducted under hypnosis, his main form of psychotherapy. Hypnosis, more accurately *hypnotic suggestion*, was his specialty and his adherence to it embraced all forms of pathology. Hypnosis even inspired him to construct a medical model of same-sex relations for tsarist Russia. This was a paradigm in which upper-class elite males, already 'degenerating', capitulated to excessive physiological reflexes and stresses in their environment. Non-degenerating males (those considered to be heterosexual in Rachmaninoff's time) had stronger nerves and muscle fibres capable of resisting the tendency. Everything reduced to the state of nervous physiology among different types of evolving males (females were omitted from these forms of sexual degeneration, their nerves uniformly weak). In framing these theories of perverse sexual drives in the road to rehabilitation among his patients, Bekhterev drew upon the most up-to-date European ideas of degeneration and hysteria.

---

[73] The Alexander Technique was being developed at this very time in Australia by Frederick Matthias Alexander (1869-1955) and was then completely unknown in Russia.

Dal did not lag far behind Bekhterev, according to Dr. Grauerman, even if he was not yet so famous. He had received the most advanced medical education possible in Paris and was already publishing scientific research about the new therapy in the *Revue de l'hypnotisme expérimental et thérapeutique*. In the surgery located in his house on Spiridonevsky Alley he administered no drugs, just engaged in suggestive hypnosis. Rachmaninoff's body, he claimed, would not be altered one jot, just his mind. His creative block would be lifted, his depression vanish.

When Dal returned to Russia from France, around 1889, he had no competitor in Moscow and built up a thriving practice developing the new techniques. The gossip among fashionable Muscovites was that he was on the cutting edge of mental science, which helped him earn a small fortune hypnotizing the good and the great. His familiarity with chamber music and string players attracted him, especially, to professional musicians in need of help.

Looking further ahead than his treatment of the depressed Rachmaninoff Dal remained in Moscow throughout the revolutionary years (1905-17), then removed himself – for unknown reasons – to Leningrad early in the 1920s where he continued to practice hypnosis. In 1925, aged sixty-five, he immigrated to Beirut, recently partitioned and devolved to France, where he lived quietly and died there in 1939, soon after the German invasion of Poland, at almost eighty. Four decades later, during the Lebanese civil war in the summer of 1983, Dal's family archive was ransacked, especially his medical notes, and his house burnt down.[74]

---

[74] No vestige of his medical notes has ever been found, in Russia or Beirut, and certainly nothing pertaining to Rachmaninoff; therefore the dated accounts of the hypnosis sessions that follow are entirely imaginary. It is no small wonder that a single irate letter to Hitler survived the fire. Dal sent it late in the 1930s, a few years before the Führer's death, appealing to the Nazi leader 'to come to his senses'. Whether or not Hitler received it is unknown. Dal's reason for leaving Russia probably had nothing to do with Lenin's death in 1924 or the political instability that would ensue after Lenin's demise. He had already endured a surfeit of instability during the Civil War years (1918 to 1921). What pushed him was pressure on the psychiatric profession to conform to principles of 'Marxist psychology',

Suggestion was the buzzword of the 1880s in Continental psychological circles, especially in France and Russia, and it also filtered down to the masses. The 1880s were, more broadly, the decade of psychology – Rachmaninoff's formative adolescent years – and suggestion through hypnosis was promoted as the surest way of exerting influence over another person. The 'suggestion cure', the doctors claimed, could enter a person's psychic realm without opposition, even without the affected person's awareness that suggestion had been made. The range of possibilities it opened, especially for imaginative creativity, appeared limitless.

Masters of suggestion such as Charcot, Liébeault, Bernheim and Bekhterev, taught their students that most mysterious maladies – mental and physical – could be improved by its techniques. Hysteria, hypochondria, insomnia, anxiety, panic, generalized malaises with as yet uncharted pathologies: all responded to the 'suggestion cure', especially blocked-up creative artists to hypnotic therapy. Therapy for a farmer or sailor was fraught, but educated and elite types reputedly responded well to hypnosis as a treatment for '*period tvorcheskogo zastoia,*' a period of creative standstill, as the Satins sweetly described it to Dal.

So they swiftly engaged him after Grauerman's exaltations. They would pay the requisite fee for daily sessions; if necessary Siloti and *babushka* Butakova could cough up the balance.[75]

12 January 1900. '*Odin, dva, tri, chetyre, pyat,*' up to ten, '*dyesyat,*' Doctor Dal counts. One, two, three, four. The patient sits in a deep maroon-coloured armchair. He is fully awake, asks to walk around the dark, book-lined room. Air barely streaming in. Doctor sits in an armchair beside the hypnotic sofa. He points with his finger – he says little.

---

which began in 1923, intensified and rendered hypnosis as he had practiced it impossible. Two years later he, like his former patient Rachmaninoff, quit Russia.

[75] Bertensson claims (p. 90) without evidence that Dal treated Rachmaninoff for free. It is possible he did, in recognition that he was hypnotizing an already known composer, but the Satins may also have forked out the sums.

Patient walked over, sat down, breathed heavily, sighed.

'Odin, dva, tri, chetyre, pyat.

Odin, dva, tri, chetyre, pyat.

Odin, dva, tri, chetyre, pyat.'

14 January 1900. Notes: 'The patient is Sergei Vasilyevich Rachmaninoff. Twenty-six, thin, gaunt, very tall, moody, huge hands, withdrawn, member of the declassified gentry, struggling, no title, cousins adore him. Says he has lost his creative urge; claims to be a shadow. Composes nothing. His sleep is diametrical: either fractured or without end. Moves oddly, says little. Wore the same black jacket again. Remedy: *daily hypnotic suggestion.* The patient must be put to sleep and spoken to. Referral made by Satin cousins, through Grauerman. Payment to come from another cousin, none other than the faithful Siloti who taught him piano. Fees: a quarter of the usual.'

16 January 1900. 'The patient appears to be sleeping, utters little. '*Odin, dva, tri, chetyre, pyat.*' I have caught him in the twilight zone, I hum the opening melody of Rachmaninoff's elegiac trio dedicated to the memory of Tchaikovsky. He flicks his eyelids. 'You will compose for him, the dead man who loved you so.'

19 January 1900. I have hypnotized him into a deep sleep. Rachmaninoff dreams. Groans. I enter the dream, Rachmaninoff the dreamer speaks. 'Two vampires are preying on a lamb in the meadow. The lamb is fair and tender; expression of fear and trembling on its face. The elder vampire swoops down on the lamb and digs its claws into her.' I whisper the name *skalon: 'skalon, skalon, skalon'*, as if warning the lamb to beware. The patient recounts his torment with three sisters years ago: the older two the vampires, the third, the youngest, the lamb he so loved. The hypnotized patient suddenly cries out as if stabbed; moans in decrescendo, then falls asleep.

21 January 1900. I bring my violin and strum it. I put the patient to sleep and then whisper: the orchestra is tuning up, the great ebony concert piano rolled out. I make the sounds. The flute tuning, the oboe, the violins. The concerto will soon start. The patient lugs down in partial slumber. I keep strumming. 'You will compose your great concerto. You will compose eight hours a day. You will ...'

25 January 1900. Patient dreaming in the state of semi-slumber. Time passes, the clock ticks. Tick tock, tick tock. Utters one word, 'Aleko.' I chant, 'you are stronger than Aleko, you are stronger.' Patient weeps. How he weeps. He begins to spit his poison – the secrets.

2 February 1900. Patient and hypnotist engage in relaxed conversation. Patient recounts having read Pushkin's poem about gypsies as a boy; stirred him to compose an opera based on it. He would call it 'Aleko', as in Pushkin. He tells Dal how he had wandered in an obscure lane in Moscow and found a copy on a bookstall. Aleko is the stranger in the camp who falls in love with the most exotic gypsy girl, the fiery Zemfira. She grows tired of Aleko after two years; rejects him for a fiery gypsy of her own tribe. In a rage Aleko kills the lovers. The patient is now deep in sleep. Dal begins his chant. You are stronger than Aleko ... stronger.

[a month later]

8 February 1900. Slower and slower. Very slow. '*Odin, dva, tri, chetyre, pyat. Ty snova budesh tvorit. Ty sochinish svoy veliky kontsert dlya fortepiano.*' Translated: 'You will finish your great piano concerto'.

22 February 1900. [Dal with a composition pad in his hand and composer's pen. The patient enters, hypnotist composing, remains silent, no acknowledgement of patient. The patient intensely watches from his hypnotic sofa, eyelids drooping. Time elapses. More time.] 'You now compose whole days ... entire nights. All the girls of Moscow love you.'

24 February 1900. The patient on his sofa seems awake. Eager to speak. Fragments about a gypsy woman who loved him; caressed his whims, stroked him. Charmed him as a sorceress when her husband was away. Bid him come closer, and closer ... until he could no longer resist, the wave that must crest.

27 February 1900. The patient has fallen asleep almost immediately. What has predisposed him? The hypnotist speaks: 'You have overcome your block; you are composing, you will become creative again, the new century has just begun, your concerto trumpets its arrival; everywhere it will be known as the 'twentieth-century concerto; your creative spur and the new century coincide, two stars in the firmament.'

2 March 1900. The hypnotist puts the patient to sleep. He describes a summer idyll. A family with the two most beautiful daughters in Moscow has a picnic. One daughter's name begins with 'N', she is sturdy with hands like a man's, the other clever and more nimble, her name begins with an 'S'. This is the dreamer's true family. 'They love you'. The hypnotist chants, 'VNS, VNS, VNS, all the A's, Varvara, Natalia, Sophia.'

3 March 1900. The patient sleeps. 'There was an Ancient Mariner ... and he stoppeth one of three.' The therapist delves into the act of creation. 'You are alone on a wide, wide sea. Only here the

imagination can create. You will finish the great concerto. Tchaikovsky has willed it from his grave.'

4 March 1900. The patient starts to reveal his secrets as soon as his head touches the plush cushions. The doctor has percolated coffee before the patient entered. 'VNS, VNS, will keep you warm in coffee.'

5 March. 'You will compose the successor of the great B-flat minor piano concerto of the master. Not Scriabin, not Medtner, not Glazunov. Rachmaninoff, Rachmaninoff, Rachmaninoff.'

9 March. 'Walk slowly, pace your steps, slow, slow, adagio, you are inside the Tretyakov Gallery, strolling slowly, slowly, observing the classical paintings of the great masters. They will inspire you to imagine the rest of your concerto. Their symbols calm your soul, their images arouse your imagination. Watch, watch, sleep, then wake … you will compose as well as the masters of the past painted.'

Dal did more than hypnotize Rachmaninoff – he bewitched him too. Rachmaninoff placed all his trust in him, sufficient even to spill out his narcissistic fantasies of grandeur. By March he took up Dal's gauntlet about gypsies and lakes at Oneg and Ivanovka, Dal who assured him he would return a happy man to those places if he finished the concerto. Dal greets him in the darkened room reeking of perfume. Rachmaninoff wonders if his master is carrying a small vial, but it is the scent of Dal's daughter whom the composer once espied in the shadows. Rachmaninoff falls into slumber lured by the good doctor's adagio repetitions: 'Odin, dva, tri, chetyre, pyat.'

He feels secure enough to banter with Dal about Vera Skalon and Anna the gypsy, conductor Glazunov and the failed symphony, about his former idyllic life at Oneg and Ivanovka. One day Dal inhales the perfume, his nostrils bulging outward to take in a quantity. He breathes heavily, then more heavily. The patient grabs the compositional pad and runs off... tomorrow he returns better.

Dal was a shrewder hypnotist than Rachmaninoff dreamed. His Saturday night séances frequently assembled instrumentalists who had played under Rachmaninoff's baton. He pumped them for biographical information, which they readily and unsuspectingly gave and Dal never let on he was hypnotizing the subject. A histrionic violist, full of himself, once described how he had seen Rachmaninoff in public drunk on the floor. The conductor-composer was in the company of his bohemian friends, who were also drunk and boisterous. Rachmaninoff drank all night and bellowed that he drank so much he could not compose. Dal never let on, just built the secret knowledge into his daily hypnotic routine. Alcohol was another specialty string on Dal's broad hypnotic bow.

By the summer of 1900 Rachmaninoff became sufficiently energized to return to the completion of his Second Piano Concerto, which he eventually dedicated to Dal. But Dal's greater gift was to pave the way for marriage. Whether he praised the Satins because they were paying for hypnosis, or because friend Grauerman had brought them together, is unknown. The fact is that within a year Rachmaninoff and Natalia were engaged and married, a knot tied in heaven even if it could never ignite the fireworks Anna did. Hypnosis had calmed Rachmaninoff's troubled psyche yet Natalia contributed far more than emotional placidity over four decades.

Dr Dal was the only hypnotist Rachmaninoff visited before leaving Russia, yet the composer returned to the hypnotic couch in the West many times. As late as 1929 a French hypnotist treated him 'lengthily'.[76] Rachmaninoff continued to display – it is reasonable to

---

[76] Bertensson cites the letter (p. 179) in which Rachmaninoff told Marietta Shaginyan, his already mentioned dear correspondent 'Re', with whom he was infatuated, that Dal was his *only* doctor for twenty years. Yet in a letter written to the Somovs and *also* cited by Bertensson (p. 259) Rachmaninoff further recounts being treated by hypnotists in France, after he left Russia, but were they French or Russian nationals? One is inclined to believe the latter. During the very same years in the *first* decade of the twentieth several central and Eastern European composers

conclude – chronic depression and a calamitous degree of worry most of his adult life. Perhaps Dal provided him with what neither Tchaikovsky nor Tolstoy could: an idealized parental imago figure whose hypnosis cure merely required future occasional visitations in Paris, Lucerne, New York, Beverly Hills – wherever the great pianist lived – as touchstones to health. Intermittent dabs for health.

RACHMANINOFF'S SECRETIVENESS IS MORE DIFFICULT to gauge. It endured throughout his life and appeared ingrained from early days; so rooted in, so native to his character it would be negligent to neglect. He himself commented on it; his family also knew; later his correspondents and managers too, and in time his secretiveness became something of an open secret, although its existence could not dissuade those refusing to acknowledge it. What was its source?

Literary semiotician Iurii Lotman has probed how the Russian aristocracy's adoption of European norms of social behaviour was historically neither predictable nor complete; and this would seem a starting point for Rachmaninoff's own aristocratic masks and camouflages.[77] Lotman describes the 'conscious theatricality' of the Russian nobility's sense of Western European comportment, especially their 'authentic difference' from native Russian manners. Yet if noble manners, gradually adopted among aristocrats in Russia, were transformed into theatrical masquerade, as Lotman suggests, their authenticity – what lodged behind the mask, behind the veneer of European customs – was also interrogated and doubted.

---

broke down, not merely Rachmaninoff and the Romantic Mahler who sought help from Freud, but others too – the times were out of joint. Six years after Rachmaninoff broke down Bartok sank into a depression, in 1906, from which he could not lift himself until he met Zoltán Kodaly.

[77] Iurii M. Lotman, 'The Poetics of Everyday Behavior in Eighteenth-Century Russia', in Lotman et al., *The Semiotics of Russian Cultural History: Essays* (Ithaca, N.Y.: Cornell UP, 1985), pp. 67-94, especially pp. 67-74.

Two popular Russian literary works written during Rachmaninoff's gloriously creative decade (1903-1913) edify the adoption of these Western social graces in the realm of masks, camouflage, and secrets. Leonid Andreev's 1907 play, *The Life of a Man*, is a dimly-lit production concerned with shadowy characters who thrive by hiding their darkest secrets. Russian critic Mark D. Steinberg has astutely commented that Andreev's play pierced straight to the heart of Russian Silver Age aristocratic nervousness:

> ... a reflection of the 'darkness', uncertainties, and 'masquerade' of identities often said to mark the character of modern urban life... The symbolism of the play's constant refrain, 'Who are they?' the repeated complaints about 'deception', and the talk of suspicious 'repulsive', but also often 'enchanting', masks on the faces of 'strangers' were all tropes to be seen again and again in stories about masks and masquerade, both in literature and, as we shall see, in newspaper reports about the masquerades of daily life.[78]

Another critic, also cited by Steinberg, observed that lies and masks prompted the upper-classes' nervousness: 'In everything is lies, on everyone masks', a position from which Rachmaninoff did not recoil, if his correspondence can be trusted. Andrei Belyi's then bestselling novel *Petersburg* (1913) – the second work – is even more striking in its compulsion to gaze beyond appearances into the authentic hidden essences of people, as were contemporary discussions of the current staging in 1911-1913 of Mikhail Lermontov's revived play, *Masquerade* (1835). One critic reviewing *Masquerade* opined 'it seems that life [today] is nothing but a "charade ... it is all deception."'[79] Secretiveness (or the presumption of others'

---

[78] Mark D. Steinberg, *Petersburg, Fin de Siècle* (New Haven: Yale UP, 2011), p. 89-91 for these observations.

[79] Ibid., p. 90; these points are noted in Steinberg's illuminating *Petersburg, Fin de Siècle* (New Haven: Yale UP, 2011).

secretiveness) grew to be the expected norm: a grim fact of Russian life permeating the period rather than an individuated psychological trait to be tagged on to composer Rachmaninoff. For Belyi, in *Petersburg*, the 'masks speak philosophically about surface illusion and the threshold beyond which lurks the individual's "hidden unknown" and psychological "abyss"'. One of Belyi's characters even declares "everything's real, yet not quite real".[80] In Russian aristocratic culture then suffused with these anxieties, and further compounded by the recent political wolf at the door – frequent disturbances – secretiveness would be a natural response, all the more noticeable in an emotionally fragile, post-hypnotic Rachmaninoff recently recovered from psychic collapse. He was creatively restored by 1903 but still lingered in the throes of emotional vulnerability. Is not the natural response, then, to conceal one's true self and present a different face, a different version of events, when one perceives widespread inauthenticity and illusion? Such camouflage at least provides some measure of protection against the 'perplexity, mystery, strangeness, confusion, illusion, phantasms, [and] the inexpressible chaos' found in novels like *Petersburg* and in Russian urban life during those years leading up to the 1917 Revolution.[81] For the hypersensitive and often hypochondriacal Rachmaninoff, camouflage also functioned as *amour propre*: self-love protecting him against these invincible deceptions. His frequently worn black concert attire – the proverbial 'cape'.

Links between the public and private man are always treacherous for acclaimed biographical figures. Yet I am cautiously suggesting, in addition, that Rachmaninoff was temperamentally secretive for reasons that can only be surmised. It is one of the loose ends in a life we cannot fully know, nor should pretend to. He may have shown himself to be covertly constituted even if born into a different Russian milieu protected by far fewer masks, for he seems to have gloated in furtive poses. For example, he wrote to his confidant

---

[80] Ibid., pp. 91-2.

[81] Ibid., p. 92. Steinberg makes these points without reference to composers like Rachmaninoff.

Morozov in the summer of 1906, characteristically, that he would 'begin with a *secret*.' He often did to others too. But the letter turns out to be a list of future concerts. Three years later, again to Morozov, 'there's something else – a *secret*', this one cryptically commenting that his American concert tour will not come off, but he gives no reason. Dozens of other letters commence with '*secrets*,' yet on close reading the secret's content can only interest the letter writer, not the recipient of the letter or future biographers. Why does Rachmaninoff so compulsively aim to conceal himself? Did the camouflages and masks discussed above persuade him his entire orbit was permeated with secrets he had best follow?

Rachmaninoff had been raised, as cousins Satins knew, in a family hounded by secrets: his father's dissipation, mother Lyubov's forbidding tyrannical rule, her own inner demons, their cash-strapped status, the Satins' *sotto voce* rescue and incorporation of him into their family. And its context was a riven socio-political milieu further driven by uprising and revolution. In these conditions the secretive personality could be seen to weather storms better than more open personality types. But even this is not the whole story.

Rachmaninoff's secretiveness was also compounded by his lifelong nostalgia. The two traits differ (one can be covert without being nostalgic), yet converged in his case as a consequence of his early narcissism and despair over loss. The life-narrative he told himself was, first that his family (papa Vassily) and their lands (Oneg) had been robbed from him; then his career lost (the severe critical reception his first major compositions received and his gathering awareness after the 1905 uprising that he would not be able to achieve the kind of career he wanted in Russia); followed by the loss of homeland (flight from Russia); and finally, after migrations westwards, the demise of his creative urge. He composed little after 1917, and – for reasons I try to edify in this book – his ability to compose in the same Romantic mode in which he had written so dynamically in Russia flagged. *All* the works for which he is most loved today were composed in Russia *before* 1917.

His list of personal losses was long, its litany compounded by his pessimistic melancholic disposition, prone to worry and sustained depression. Loss was the ballast of his predominant mood. The secretiveness embedding loss was also activated by his sense that *loss* had been the salient fact of his life, even when his earnings in America made him and his family rich.[82]

Cause and effect flourished in a reciprocal circle: secretiveness intensified his nostalgia and permitted it to swell so far as he felt he had to keep his nostalgia secret. The trait was not unusual among expatriate Russians in America, and practiced by other expat nationalities as well. Yet Rachmaninoff applied it with diligence that also served deep psychological needs.

The chain encompassed the quotidian rituals of a very private public figure who was practically a recluse when not concertizing. After all, he was a famous pianist with a biographical profile in the public domain whose main facts were printed in concert programs from the time he arrived in America. By cultivating this extraordinarily secretive life he could indulge in sustained rituals associated with his lost homeland: restricting his circle of friends to *Russians*, speaking *Russian*, writing in *Russian*, eating *Russian* food, using *Russian* china and samovars, visiting only *Russian* doctors and dentists – always aiming to keep the new foreign country at bay. He may have capriciously entertained the idea of returning to Russia someday, but after Stalin's 'Great Purges' of 1937-8 and then the Nazi menace he knew he never would.

Over the centuries psychological theory has generated much speculation about the secretive personality. Greek master-physician Galen judged it as one of four dominant personality types. Freud and Jung *both* associated it with versions of narcissism (however mild) in their different assessments, Freud classically relating it to the policing

---

[82] Rachmaninoff's bank accounts are not in the public domain and it is impossible to know precisely how rich he became. Nevertheless, it is significant that once he left Russia almost his entire annual income derived from concerts and recordings, and only a small portion earned from royalties from his compositions (sheet music). The latter was primarily from works composed before 1917.

super-ego and Jung explaining how it can act as 'psychic poison', alienating the possessor from the community.[83]

Much depends on the idealized parent imago and developing super-ego – the reason this now somewhat discredited construct (the super-ego) cannot be omitted from our (mine and the reader's) discussion. Clarification arises, especially about Rachmaninoff's secretiveness, provided we do not abandon the position that inner mental worlds are perceived as 'real'. A healthy infant hands over its infantile grandiosity to an idealized parental imago, whose power gradually converts this fragile super-ego into a good, sturdy one that is not overly severe. Dislike the super-ego as one may as an artificial psychological construct, but there is no eluding it when reconstructing the genesis of modern secretiveness. Moreover, good parenting, in contemporary parlance, amounts to enhancing the formation of a mild rather than severe super-ego. Creative artists (like Rachmaninoff) who aspire to a lead a good life, benefit from this mild super-ego. But ambitious matriarch Lyubov induced the opposite: she nagged and demanded greatness from her son.

More recently psychoanalytical theorists have specifically allied the secretive personality to narcissism and explained its role in the narcissist's life cycle in terms of deception. That is, the narcissist's *lies* are his unconscious transformations of grandiose claims formed in childhood in the interrupted – even disturbed – super-ego. It never develops into a *mild* super-ego; remains severe and crippling. 'But Rachmaninoff's behaviour', I protest, 'was modest, even humble'. I dare to complain further that 'he was not known to *lie*, was neither pretentious nor self-aggrandizing'. Perhaps true, but he made the most extraordinary demands on himself (policing super-ego): 1. on his pianism; 2. on his obsession to compose to the highest standard in addition to attaining unparalleled keyboard virtuosity; 3. on his granitic decree that he would never surrender his childhood's Russian way of life.

---

[83] Carl Gustav Jung, *Modern Man in Search of a Soul* (New York: Harcourt, 1933). Sissela Bok has, more generally, traced the cultural profile of secrecy in her book *Secrets: on the ethics of concealment and revelation* (Oxford: Oxford University Press, 1982).

This last was 'the white lie' while the first two made preposterous demands. His super-ego bellowed:

- you must become the greatest virtuoso alive

- you must compose as if you are the Russian Chopin

- you must live exactly as you did in Oneg and Ivanovka

These were his super-ego's prevarications: the fictions, as psychoanalyst Heinz Kohut, the preeminent explicator of narcissism in our generation, explains in his 'pseudo-logica fantastica', about the 'lie's undergrowth'.[84] Not the 'conscious lie': in Rachmaninoff's case the fabrication that he was wealthier than he was, or owned more Steinway pianos, Porsches and Arabian horses than he did, but that he was still an old-world Russian aristocrat, living and breathing in Russia's pre-Bolshevik past in America.

Dr Dal proved to be a salvo to Rachmaninoff's distortedly harsh super-ego: hypnotically calmed it, lifted the writer's block, and lessened whatever narcissism remained in the young man, which enabled him to marry his first cousin Natalia. This is a tall order for which the good hypnotist deserves more credit than he has been given. One wonders to what degree Rachmaninoff's narcissism remained intact; post-Dahl, it seems not to have been of the self-mutilating variety that caused his collapse in 1897-1900.

We tend to brand anyone we do not like 'a narcissist', but this is loose parlance and the world would burst with clinical narcissists if this definition were allowed to pass untested. Perhaps the world bulges with them anyway; yet every celebrity star-performer – not merely every successful concert artist – needs some amount to muster the confidence to sustain an international career. Once Rachmaninoff attained colossal international fame as a pianist in the 1920s, it was predictable he would turn even *more* secretive than he had been earlier. He did, but by now his super-ego had softened, mellowed into

---

[84] Heinz Kohut (n. 47), p. 146-48.

the mild, healthy type; allowed himself little pleasures, indulged fetishes, and bought more cars. He still courted his Russian past but to the detriment of his creativity.

Except that his post-1917 composing suffered. Somehow, his harsh pre-Dalian super-ego could still (before 1917) mandate great works unless its psychological force crushed him altogether. And Dal ushered in a period of creativity in 1900-1912. But when Russia afterwards came under threat, and then when he lost his country altogether, the old spark fizzled. He continued to try, but never again would there be another first, second, or third piano concerto; just the controversial fourth, composed in America, which so many concert pianists and connoisseurs have disdained.

Prominent American psychoanalyst James Grotstein has written about 'the splendor in the grass experienced by the fetus in its mother's womb,' and commented on the patient's later perception that his appreciation of, and ability to create, beauty arises in this 'watery, aery, abode of beautiful symmetry.'[85] Constant abandon to distant nostalgic memories, like Rachmaninoff's, taps into a repository of narcissistic recollections of basking in pleasure. The endpoint, according to Grotstein, is a dawning awareness of the beautiful mother – the mother idealized as lovely as the memory itself even if she (Lyubov) had been, in reality, a harsh castrating mother.

Perhaps this approach is too theoretical, yet Rachmaninoff could imagine Lyubov in this 'watery and aery' way in his unconscious despite his biographical mother having been so different – a disastrous parental imago figure who demanded grandiosity from her son's earliest youth and intercepted the formation of his mild, healthy super-ego. Lyubov told her son what Dr Dal would years later: 'you *will* become the world's greatest pianist, you *will* finish your great

---

[85] James Grotstein, MD, 'The Apprehension of Beauty and Its Relation to "O",' *The International Journal of Melanie Klein and Object Relations* 16(2) (1998): 273-284. Grotstein's 'splendor in the grass' does not merely refer to the 1961 film of that name and its two main underlying themes of sexual desire and sexual frustration, but also develops the relation of this desire-frustration to the child's aesthetic capability in later life. His theory's main concern is correlation of the child's later creation of beauty with his/her *memory* of what earliest life inside the mother was.

concerto'. But Lyubov's behests were dictatorially delivered whereas Dr Dal's were – symbolically in Rachmaninoff's imagination – those of the indulgent friend.

Small wonder then Rachmaninoff perceived his personal losses as ambivalent and ubiquitous: the loss of a mature and mild super-ego encouraging him to compose and live well; the loss of his creative urge; the loss of sociability and openness among friends; even the secret room he had longed for and indulged himself in. Little surprise too he was intrigued in real life by those who also kept their identities hidden. His biography abounds in such instances, not merely young female singers and poetesses, but the mysterious European lady – 'White Lilacs' he called her – who anonymously delivered flowers after every concert he gave in Russia before 1917.

Later on, in America, his holding back restrained him from teaching. He could have commanded huge, even princely, sums, and justified his refusal as lack of time. The truer reason was his entrenched secretiveness, which would have spilled over to his teaching. A teacher – no matter how great a performer – who cannot let himself go will never enrapture students. If your teaching manner is stiff and formal, your student suffers, even fails.

Rachmaninoff viewed the students he *might* have taught as guarded secrets, just as he did the works he was composing and their dedicatees. Acclaimed pianist Gina Bachauer (1910-1976) has documented her lessons with him; her concert programme-notes also do. But after Rachmaninoff's death, both widow Natalia and Rachmaninoff's perennial American manager Charles Foley denied it and made a noisy public row over her claims. Foley categorically asserted that Rachmaninoff never taught anyone piano from the year 1893 until his death fifty years later. Yet Bachauer is unlikely to have fabricated, or imagined, the lessons, even if they were far fewer than she claimed.[86]

---

[86] The printed evidence both ways is meticulously provided in Graham Wade, *Gina Bachauer: A Pianist's Odyssey* (Leeds: GRM Publications, 1999), pp. 10-14. Bachauer's letter of self-defence makes for sorrowful reading: 'It only remains for me to add how surprised and hurt I am that Mrs. Rachmaninoff has taken up this

Rachmaninoff's unwillingness to accept piano students was not fallout from abhorrent Zverev's tyranny but something more native to his secretiveness: as suggested, the teacher who holds students at bay and cannot let himself go out of fear. Yet the received sense of Rachmaninoff's profile today omits the entirety of his secretiveness – never holds its blended characteristics in a coherent container.

Besides, most listeners attracted to his music often forget that what they love was composed *before* he left Russia. His best music – the piano concertos, sonatas, preludes, also the *Second Symphony* and *Isle of the Dead* – conveys emotions of sustained melancholy and loss, from which listeners think he must have experienced these emotions himself, which he did of course. But here ends psychological specificity. Secretiveness, domestic life lived as if still inside the old pre-1917 Russia, the savage demands he placed on himself, the guilt that he was destined never to break away from the mould of late Romanticism – when these are invoked they are piecemeal.

Usually Rachmaninoff confided his darkest secrets in letters to well-trusted friends like Morozov. As he aged he relaxed the grip on his past, perhaps because the interior voice pathetically pleading inability to innovate had grown so familiar to him. Two years before his death he went public. He revealed his 'secret' this way to an unknown reporter in *The Musical Courier*:

> I feel like a ghost in a world grown alien. I cannot cast out the old way of writing, and I cannot acquire the new. I have made intense effort to feel the musical manner of today, but it will not come to me. … Even with the disaster of living [through] what has befallen the Russia where I spent my happiest years, yet I always feel that my own music[,] and my reaction to all music,

---

inexplicable attitude of casting doubts on all I have said about my studies with Rachmaninoff and waited until it appeared in print to do so when she had already accepted my statement so completely …' (Wade, p.13). Whatever the truth, a large part was owing to the Rachmaninoffs combined cult of secrecy.

remained spiritually the same, unendingly obedient in trying to create beauty...[87]

TO CLAIM WHAT HE WAS *NOT* – that Rachmaninoff was *not* a political animal – courts rhetorical understatement beyond its breaking point. He was a stranger to politics in ways Prokofiev and Shostakovich could never have imagined possible. The meagre pre-1917 politics he engaged in amounted to an affective politics of nostalgia; a psychological state of mind and body in which he experienced the wrenching away of the old Russia into the revolutionary new and felt the loss more acutely, and with heightened passion, than others did. Perhaps this is why, late in life, he could remember the composer he had been in this tautological, illogical fashion:

> I am a Russian composer, and the land of my birth
> has influenced my temperament and outlook. My
> music is the product of my temperament, and so it
> is Russian music; I never consciously attempted to
> write Russian music, or any other kind of music.[88]

Perhaps so, but professional politicians and revolutionaries of the second decade of the twentieth century did not experience the turmoil in Russia in any way proximate to the gut-feeling dislocation he did. Politics was a profession for them, or at least an ideology to die for; for him it verged on outrage, a cosmological disturbance conveying emotional disaster among its after-shocks. Of course he read newspapers and entertained political views, especially during the revolutionary period, and these intensified after the 1905 uprising. He followed the proceedings of the Duma, and learned about several of its members.

---

[87] Cited in Bertensson, p. 351.
[88] *The Etude* (December 1941), p. 7, in an interview given to David Ewen.

But even as an expatriate in America his politics dwelled on the *Old Russia* despite the presence of new leaders in *New Russia*: Lenin, Trotsky, Bukharin, Stalin, Communism, the working classes, the bourgeoisie, and expatriate White Russians. He conjured these rather than Calvin Coolidge, Herbert Hoover, F. D. Roosevelt and the American economic depression during his own last years (1941-43) as World War Two intensified. 'What economic depression', Rachmaninoff might have asked in 1932, or 1933, when its American nadir was approaching. The Rachmaninoffs' bank accounts were swelling, they took out American citizenship and voted, manoeuvres made for convenience and security rather than as political acts. And then, in 1933, Rachmaninoff betrayed the secret to the newspapers, not merely adding his name to a few letters carping about the new 'Soviets' but divulging who he was: 'You cannot know the feeling of a man who has no home. Perhaps no others can understand the hopeless homesickness of us older Russians.'[89]

The newspaper called a spade for what it was:

> Mr. Rachmaninoff still prefers to pretend that he is a subject of the Tzar of All the Russias. This tall, stooped man of sixty, who smiles seldom on his audiences, yet confesses that concert playing is his very life, can have spiritual integrity only by identifying himself with Russia's past ...

He might fault the new Soviets for banishing his music, condemn them by signing 'Letters from America' cautioning them, but only his lingering sense of the Old Russia's plight after the armistice of 1918 endured. His *déjà vu* cannot be isolated from his nostalgic sense of reality, which coloured everything. 'Mr. Rachmaninoff still prefers to pretend ...'

An artist's politics cannot be grasped in generalities or – worse yet – in the clouds. Historical fact and biography explain the reality more

---

[89] *The New York Evening Post*, 16 November 1933.

robustly. Perhaps a single correspondence, to confidant Morozov, begins to make the point about his *selbst politik*. The widespread unrest in Russia in 1905 touched him profoundly. Even the earlier revolts of the peasants in 1902, minor in comparison, disturbed him. He was able to compose but not as passionately as after Dr. Dal's hypnotic treatment. Something fundamental had changed.

Four years later his mindset has still not moved on. On 2 May 1906 he wrote to Morozov, his loyal friend from Conservatory days in Moscow who had suggested the famous second theme in the last movement of his Second Piano Concerto:

> My dear Semenovich, we have finally left Florence and Madame Luchessi's comfortable little pension and moved into a stone cottage at Marina di Pisa about five miles away on the sea. It has beautiful views and lapping waves are within fifty paces of its door. It contains five rooms and is very cheap. There is too little linen and almost no cutlery in silver, but the place is remarkably clean – such cleanliness I have never seen among the Italians. One finds such cleanliness in Italian villas just as rarely as one does in the compositions of all these modern composers, the Scriabins and their tribe. But there are no Russians in Marina and we live through our two Russian newspapers and the postman. Do come to visit us, dear Nikita Semenovich, you must come this season before we leave.

Six days later, on 8 May 1906, the reactionary daily Moscow newspaper *Novoye Vremya* called for demonstrations against all plans to liberalize Russia:

> A committee within the Duma has issued its report announcing that it has intelligence that the next uprising, after this last menacing one, will overthrow the monarchy. Men will be executed by

hanging, women and children sent to work camps in Siberia. Moscow and St Petersburg will cease to function as urban centers and will be transformed into clearing houses for assignment to other destinations. Schools and universities will close, hospitals no longer be staffed. The theatres and musical halls will be shut by decree.

Rachmaninoff began to envision the end of his career. Imminently 'home' would pose a much greater hurdle than these Tuscan rose-clad cottages. The leftists were bringing his performing career to a standstill. Strip a man of the ability to work, particularly a newly married man with an infant, and you emasculate him – this is what happened to Rachmaninoff. Worse yet, he could neither compose, conduct or practice. Then the insurrections of 1905 gave him a taste of what was coming but they proved to be small feed compared to 1917.

The turbulence of 1905 further derailed him, and the December insurrections in Moscow that year disrupted his routines as he saw queues of people begging for bread and then a general strike forming. He could barely bring himself to practice for his concerts. The news of Rimsky-Korsakoff's resignation as director of the conservatory in St Petersburg further demoralized him – old Russia was being sacrificed. He read Rimsky's much-published letter in the newspapers and joined him in spirit.

Czar Nicholas II did not take these uprisings calmly. Overnight he decreed draconian measures that punished intellectuals and journalists by throwing them into jail and even slaughtering a few as examples; but composers – men like Rachmaninoff and those of the School of Taneyev who had been his classmates and colleagues – were spared. Nicholas' retaliations served to raise the temperature of turmoil and hope for return to the status quo.

When revolution swept away the tsarist government in late February 1917, Rachmaninoff felt a dead weight in his heart – all hope gone. Nicholas abdicated on 2 March without a replacement, unwilling to pass the burden of power to his son Alexis, a boy of 12, weakened by chronic haemophilia and his nephew, the Grand Prince Michael unwilling to accept the crown, giving way to a Provisional Government the Rachmaninoffs could not imagine living in. Churches closed in fear, and by July Alexander Kerensky was named head of the provisional government. The old Russia, it seemed, was wearing down in just a few months.

Attention to miniscule details can reveal truths about an artist's politics. Rachmaninoff spent the summer of 1917 in the Crimea, too distressed to return to Ivanovka, whose ongoing refurbishments had bled him, to the point he was almost broke. But the political turmoil gave birth to the notion of flight: to anywhere, especially nearby Scandinavia, and he appealed to Siloti and his in-laws, the Satins, to help him obtain a passport, of which he alone was incapable. Siloti networked among concert managers and arranged for his nephew to be invited to appear in Stockholm, which opened the way for a passport. He was forty-four, and still imagining flight from Russia as redemption.

His mind ransacked recent political events. Russia had been drawn into conflagration that August 1912, when Germany declared war. By 1915 famine had become widespread throughout Russia, as sick and dying soldiers returned home to find political demonstrations and strikes against autocratic rule. Things worsened in 1916. Rachmaninoff gave a few concerts during these two years (1915-16) but their number shrank and he was reduced to playing for charity. 'Play for charity', his friends ruefully urged him as they watched his despair. By February 1917 the strikes intensified, and by February 27 the tsarist regime was toppled. This was the sequence.

Greater uncertainty was created during the so-called 'October Revolution' when the Bolsheviks seized power. Their seizure was astounding and ironclad even to those who had been observing events. It ripped the heart out of the tsarist government and intensified the political confusion. It dealt a further blow to any realistic hope of restoring 'the old Russia'. This was the event triggering Rachmaninoff's decision to depart for good. Within weeks he would be gone.

He kept rehearsing this sequence, like a broken record, as the train had pulled out, and did so too on his deathbed in 1943. His solution? Flight from his beloved homeland. It may have been one of the worst decisions of his life. Separation from Russia undid him in all sorts of paradoxical ways he could not imagine in 1917; nor could he have known he would never again return or again compose in the *Russian* way.

RACHMANINOFF'S NATIONALISM WOULD NOT BE an isolated concern if it had not made such magisterial difference to his composing-life. We saw him profess: he felt *Russian*, he responded to the world as a *Russian*, he composed as a *Russian*. Did not all Russians?

Not to his idiosyncratic extreme, as if *Russianness* was some sort of guarantor of greatness. His compositions, especially his songs and vocal works, are intensely Russian in sentiment, style, and native feel. He played the piano as only a *Russian* could, not in the melodramatic mania of Liszt (Hungarian), and not even an uninformed listener could imagine he was Italian (Busoni), French (Cortot), or Polish (Godowsky). In his musical appearances and keyboard technique, in the strangely withdrawn impersonality of his stage manner, even in his repertoire – as if Fate (*sud'ba*), about which I shall have more to say momentarily, invaded the performing stage when he was on it – he was distinctly *Russian*.

In public he played his own music coupled to a few other *Russian* composers, as well as a small smattering of Mozart, Beethoven, Schumann, Grieg, and a broad selection of the works of Chopin. But no early music, no Bach, no Brahms, no French impressionism – the absentee list is long. Even before exiting Russia he played primarily his *own* works in recital. And in North America his managers permitted him to play nothing else because the combination of man and his compositions, preludes in C-sharp minor and bumble-bees, sold seats – such was the new magic, in America, of seeing the combined *composer-soloist* at the keyboard. But his stock-in-trade repertoire was far smaller than is now imagined, limited to the selected works of a few composers and nothing proximate to the vast repertoire of internationally acclaimed pianists in other countries.[90]

'National character' thrives on stereotypes: the German, Frenchman, Italian, American, and — at the turn of the century — when Rachmaninoff was ascendant in both composition and performing career, he cut a decisively *Russian* figure: his facial expression, the tall and lanky physique, the brooding silhouette wrapped in black — as Chekhov noted, the black costume he wore on stage capturing his expression as lorded over by Destiny. Not even listeners who knew nothing about him could imagine the *man* or *music* before them as German, Italian or French. He stood apart from the Wagners and Mahlers, Mascagnis and Puccinis. His very name seemed synonymous with Russia: R A C H M A N I N O F F.

A generation later, in the late 1920s, Shostakovich — destined to become the greatest Russian composer of his generation — also began professional life as a virtuoso pianist-composer. Like Rachmaninoff's, his performing stage manner was also so impersonal as to abnegate the soloist and he replaced emotion with a riveting rhythmic drive. But that was in *Russia*. Rachmaninoff, too, had been typically aloof on stage, as if intentionally holding something back, playing as if the

---

[90] Chopin and Liszt also played their own works in public, of course, as did Beethoven and Mendelssohn before them. But they were not professionally managed in the way Rachmaninoff was. Had they been huge earners for American managers, they may also have performed almost nothing except their own works; in this sense Rachmaninoff was the last of the Romantic virtuoso composer-pianists playing primarily his own works in public, except that his forbears earned a scintilla of his royalties. In the decades 1890-1930 Russia produced a long list of virtuoso composer-pianists, including Prokofiev and Shostakovich, whose early careers depended on *both* activities, playing public concerts and composing. No other country than Russia then produced so many virtuoso composer-pianists or exported them in such numbers, even if unlucky Prokofiev's American career only lasted three years (1918-1921). After the 1930s a concert repertoire as limited as Rachmaninoff's, consisting primarily of his own compositions, would have been unthinkable for any internationally performing keyboard colossus of his stature. The fact further reinforces his incredible story of success in America.

listener were an imposter. Yet in *America* he gave the *Americans* what they wanted to hear: Romantic lyricism and melody performed by a visibly gaunt demigod from another planet.

Melody moves, melody sells, as American managers, symphony conductors, and concert promoters all learned when tallying their Rachmaninoff royalties. Rachmaninoff was a phenomenon not merely because he was luckier than other Russian composer-pianists but by dint of his cultivation of melodies that were identifiably *Russian*. One can never expatiate too extensively on this topic, both the sources for his best melodies and imaginative transformations of them, as the unforgettable opening themes of the second and third piano concertos make plain. Experts have traced them to folk songs and rustic idylls, yet despite all the speculation and scholarship inconclusiveness endures. Melody, above all else, captured his 'Russianness' as well as the mysterious quality embodying his old-world genius.

In 1905 – a symbolic year for the old and new Russia – the stereotypical aristocratic Russian, lamenting forfeiture of estate, land and serfs, pined for the old order and often conceptualized its disappearance in terms of Fate (*sud'ba*). The usual response to such deprivation was sustained melancholy (*toska* or, more medically, *melankholiya*). The historians have traced the case histories. After 1917 refugees like the Rachmaninoffs yearned for a homeland while lamenting the disappearance of the old order and its way of life. But their profile differs from its French or German counterparts whose history had been so different, or – geographically closer to home – from Polish nostalgics lamenting loss of their country multiple times in the last century. Musically speaking, one expects Chopin's nostalgia to differ from Rachmaninoff's, as well as its nationalistic underpinnings, and it did.

Compare melancholy and nostalgia in the piano music of Chopin and Rachmaninoff. Every listener waxes eloquent, intuitively, on the dissimilarities. Yet there are similarities too and something to the notion that Rachmaninoff strove to become, both in playing and composing, a 'Russian Chopin.' Or a 'Russian Chopin in America.' He has as many affinities with Chopin as with his *own* countrymen: Tchaikovsky, the Rubensteins, Scriabin, Rimsky-Korsakov. These composers, like him, also endured obstacles: Tchaikovsky his sexuality, Anton Rubenstein's Jewish origins and removal to Dresden, Scriabin's religious visions and mystical delusions. Yet they did not conceptualize their impediments as irretrievable *loss* to Rachmaninoff's degree.

Rachmaninoff's late Romantic style also differs from theirs' by its stubborn interpretation of Russian values. Rimsky-Korsakov – to latch on to the main figure – was thoroughly *Russian* and dedicated throughout his life to the creation of a national Russian style of classical music. His 'programme music' adhered closely to the selected libretti, or stories, and was well informed about national folk mythology and tradition. Like Mussorgsky's opera *Boris Godunov*, his popular *Scheherezade*, *Capriccio Espagnol* and *Russian Easter Overtures*, are as 'Russian' as anything Rachmaninoff composed, yet the two composer's stylistic and biographical differences are legion, not least Rimsky-Korsakov's inability to exalt the piano as the premier concert instrument. Furthermore, Rachmaninoff rarely taught piano and never taught composition; Rimsky-Korsakov did almost nothing else and educated more important composers – including Stravinsky and Prokofiev – than anyone else of his generation. Despite the nationalist character of his compositions, Rimsky-Korsakov's ideology was predominantly liberal, culminating in his support for the 1905 revolution shortly before his death in 1909 – another contrast with Rachmaninoff – and he was neither hypochondriacal nor narcissistic. Such biographical and compositional differences sum up in nutshell the issues implicated in national character. Otherwise, if either composer or his music is omitted, it is difficult to understand what is at stake in evaluating this formidable Russian national tradition.[91]

---

[91] In another key this 'Russianness' forms the argument of Richard Taruskin's important book *On Russian Music* (Berkeley: University of California Press, 2009), except that Taruskin dispraises Rachmaninoff for lack of stylistic innovation and resists acknowledgement of his musical contribution, however idiosyncratically neo-

But this is hindsight from the 1930s, even later after Rachmaninoff's death and his famous Russian composer-contemporaries': decades were needed to be able to see how Rachmaninoff functioned in the West before these differences and disjunctures could be clarified, as well as the making of these disparate Russian musical 'voices'. During Rachmaninoff's *Russian* years, during the first major political uprisings – 1905 – while other Russian composers were *abandoning* their national roots and going international, or at least becoming pan-European and innovative, Rachmaninoff drew inwards and rejected the new Modernism. In only five years *Firebird* (1910) would appear; in only eight *Rites of Spring* (1913). These works exist on another musical planet from Rachmaninoff's third piano concerto (1909), original as it is, by many counts his single greatest work and the one most professional concert artists still love to play.

RACHMANINOFF OBTAINED NO TRAVEL PERMITS by the time he fled Russia in December 1917, only exit papers. Desolately he held up in a hotel room in Petrograd. The Revolution's events – especially Lenin's army of workers attacking Kerensky's government – pre-empted all hope. He conjured an alternative plan. He would travel alone to Petrograd immediately. Not an hour was to be lost lest another uprising occurred like the one a few weeks ago.

Finland declared its national sovereignty on 23 November – ironically the very same day as Richard's death thirty-four years later in 1957 – and also abandoned the Julian calendar for the Gregorian. Parallel universes intensified: this was just a few days before Rachmaninoff himself left Russia. Besides, if there were further trouble down the road Rachmaninoff, a Russian national, might be

---

Romantic, to the national tradition. And Taruskin, despite the indubitable brilliance of his approach to Russian music at large, minimizes the creative value of sustained national nostalgia and appears to devalue the degree to which Rachmaninoff transformed himself into the 'Russian Chopin.'

unable to cross the Finnish frontier. So he departed Moscow alone in the rain at twilight on the last day of November; visibly quiet but the panic against the wolves of time simmering inside him. Only sister-in-law Sophia accompanied him to the Nikolayevsky Train Station and saw him disappear carrying one small suitcase containing none of his favourite manuscripts and certainly not the score of his great second symphony (today in the British Library). How fitting that she should be the last beloved face he saw in Russia. He had no clothes or other belongings and still no travel documents.

He pressed his chin to the cold glass of the carriage's window as the train pulled out of the Moscow station. It was wet, as if raining inside. He could not suppress the tears, which he tried to hide, and raised his hands to his ears as shields lest the other passengers see him weeping. He heard a male voice inside his head singing one of his earliest songs, 'Before my window'. This cold-carriage glass was his window now. Then flashed by the others: 'Morning,' almost the first he composed as a boy – and he recalled how it was inspired by the mornings on the lake, when Vassily would awaken him. And the other songs too: 'In the silence of the secret night', 'the field', 'water lily' and 'flower that had faded' and – the one he loved most – the 'isle,' a remote strange place he conjured in his imagination.

Departure was his fate – ripped out of the heart of his Muscovite city without dear wife and children. Just as the song titles augured, as if he had known decades earlier his fate: 'How painful for me,' 'Let us leave my dear', 'Again I am alone', 'Two partings' – the very thought of its melody brought flashes of 'Natalia, Natalia'. Thought and emotion blurred: he was leaving her, might never find her again, nor mother Lyubov whom he never did see again (she died in 1922 in the Soviet Union at seventy-six). He thought he might never write another song, was finished with musical composition – if he continued to ring his heart out in this pathetic way he soon *would* be dead, frozen on a railway track.

When the sobbing stopped he sobered up in the packed carriage. The plan was to await Natalia and the girls in Petrograd. They would follow in a few weeks. Once united the four would travel by train across the whole girth of Finland to the Swedish border, and from there – in that tundra at the edge of the Arctic Circle – by train south to Stockholm, a journey of many hundreds of miles.

Their exit flowed according to plan. Natalia arrived from Moscow with the children in mid-December. All four departed the Finland Station in Petrograd on 22 December, the same station where Lenin had arrived by train from Germany that April to start the October Revolution. Parents and children took one of the last trains out of the Finland Station before the Finns, who owned it, abandoned it in just a few weeks in the new year. Their train was bulging with Finns, fleeing like the Rachmaninoffs away from revolutionary Russia. Sergei was riven: he too was in flight – never again to see Russia.

Their first train, the Finnish train, gathered speed, dashing past Viborg in Russia up to the Finnish border en route to Tampere and Oulu and tiny Tornio. Tornio was the border ghost town, the two countries – Finland and Sweden – geographically separated by a frozen river with no bridges, only to be crossed by sledge in the dead of winter. Each country had its own railway station, four miles apart, separated by border guards, making the sledge even more crucial.[92]

They could not cross the Gulf of Bothnia from Helsinki because it freezes in winter – that simple ferry crossing of just a few hours was unthinkable. Instead they planned a fifty-hour trek from Petrograd to the top of Finland, covering hundreds of miles, including the sledge across the frozen river-border to Sweden, or miss the night train to Stockholm.

They made all their connections and arrived in Stockholm on a cold January afternoon. The po-faced Swedes were back at work, the streets almost empty. The weary Rachmaninoffs wondered how this could be on *Christmas Eve*. But it was *not* December 24th in Sweden; it was *January 6* and they had only been travelling for about fifty hours. It did not occur to them that New Style dates differed by thirteen

---

[92] Sophia Satina inscribed this vital detail about the sledge in her memoir of Rachmaninoff after his death and must have referred to it many times before then in the presence of her sister and brother-in-law when all three had migrated to Dresden and, later, to America; see Z A Apetian (ed.) *Vospominaniia o Rakhmaninove*, vol. 1, p. 48. Without its inclusion it would have been difficult to establish the exact escape route they took or work out the chronology of their departure from Russia.

days in the West. If less weary they might have reflected they were now on Swedish time, not Russian; and they were émigrés, Moscow now a distant memory. Soon a wide, frozen, ocean would separate them from Petrograd too.

It must have been eerie to enter the Swedish capital thinking this a *typical* Christmas Eve. Where was the gaiety, where the holiday shoppers? Why the solemn faces, not beaming with anticipation, their arms without ribboned presents, no church bells pealing?

The Rachmaninoffs carried few suitcases. The exile himself never felt more distraught, or lonely, than on this first day in the West; displaced, deluded about time, hearing a language he could not understand, cold in some strange hotel room, without a piano. Not even when despondently cringing on the stairs of the Mariinsky Theatre early in his twenties and listening to Glazunov's excruciating performance of his first symphony had he felt so unhinged. He was transfigured from himself in the Old Russia.

He had toured abroad many times, but always awaiting his return to the motherland. Now there was none; Russia was now a memory, recollection of it his future state. If that daunting thought kept pounding on him in Stockholm, it was for good reason. All he had now were his ten piano fingers and a wife who loved him.

An expatriate lives in a different country from where he is, or was, a citizen, and Bolshevik Russia produced thousands. Those who flee their country for political reasons are more commonly referred to as exiles. Expatriation refers to the state of exile, as for the many intellectuals denaturalized and deprived of their citizenship. But the Rachmaninoffs were never *forced*, or coerced, to flee – they chose to. They would have had to remain Muscovites much longer before they were compelled to flee, forced into flight, and their expatriation – which they long lamented – was voluntary. Other aristocrats – many 'White Russians' and other contemporary composers too, such as Prokofiev and Shostakovich – remained.

Moscow music critic and composer Leonid Leonidovich Sabaneev (1881-1968) understood the Rachmaninoffs' flight. He was soaked in Russian *fin-de-siècle* classical music, especially Scriabin's, and judged Rachmaninoff not to be the first order of composer. His reason? 'Some barrier', he wrote early in the 1920s, which 'prevents him from fully emerging'.[93] The impediment clarified itself a decade after the Rachmaninoffs had migrated. Sabaneev's reason is that it followed closely on the heels of the Rachmaninoffs' 1917 departure. It is worth citing again the 'barrier' he considered a 'tragedy':

> … apparently the tragedy of being torn away from his country [when Rachmaninoff went into exile at the very end of 1917] is still gnawing at his being [i. e., now in 1930 in the West]. Curious is this silence of the tomb, literally sepulchral, which has overtaken the creative genius of the composer since the moment of his departure [in 1917]. True, he has composed the Fourth Piano Concerto. But still a period of eight years of silence [1922-1930] is an enormous span for a composer. As if something had snapped in him at the time he parted with his native soil, his genius, rooted by mysterious ties in his fatherland, has no longer been able to issue a single sprout.[94]

This is the kernel of the matter – almost a succinct definition, if generalized, of destructive nostalgia. The *langueur* that descends on the artist sunk in despair over loss of the home: nothing sprouts because 'something had snapped in him at the time he parted with his native soil'. Sabaneev configured the nostalgic Rachmaninoff as a stricken

---

[93] Quoted in Bertensson, p. 202. Sabaneev wrote several books about Russian composers of the late nineteenth century, especially the Scriabin he so ardently admired. His 1930 *Modern Russian Composers* bears no similarity to the 1924 Russian-language version of a work entitled *History of Russian Music*. The Russian book contains just one paragraph on Rachmaninoff, within a section called 'Retrospectivism'. His *Vospominaniia o Rossii* ['Reminiscences about Russia'] (Moscow, 2004) documents his own imposed exile from Russia in 1926, first to Paris and then to Nice where he died in 1968.

[94] See p. 125 above; Sabaneev (1930), p. 117.

deer, 'an unstable and passive organism', psychologically compromised. The alibi that Rachmaninoff had little time to compose after migrating amounts to nonsense for Sabaneev, as it does to me. The Rachmaninoffs' departure to America wrenched an already excessively wistful Rachmaninoff more forcefully than he had been before 1917; further made him aware of the stark differences between *old* Russia – *his* Russia – and future Russia. Sabaneev's pronouncement can fittingly be the epigraph of this book for the way it pierces to the heart of Rachmaninoff's nostalgia.

His assignment of the composer's niche – neither too high or too low – praises without trashing, as the St Petersburg critics had done in the late 1890s. Sabaneev provides cogent psychological reasons too: a stricken nostalgic, who must forever be associated with Tchaikovsky (another stricken deer for his sexual frailty), cut down by revolutionary revolts, unable to compose anything important in the West, a barren talent whose nostalgia would not permit anything great to sprout there. How different this profile from other expatriates who flourished in exile, such as James Joyce who also went into voluntary exile, not to mention the dozens of expatriate intelligentsia fleeing Nazi Germany in the late 1930s who also found themselves, in varying degrees, creative abroad.

Putatively Rachmaninoff blossomed. He became rich, built residences, bought and traded costly cars, kept his wife and daughters in expensive furs, stayed in the finest old-world hotels, employed servants. But, as Sabaneev writes, he composed nothing great. Something snapped, the sprout would not grow. Is there an implicit 'tragedy' in all nostalgia as corrosive as his? Or just in narcissistic nostalgia?

KITSCH ART IS *IMITATION* ART whose primary purpose is the arousal of unbounded sentiment among the masses. Kitsch mimics its immediate predecessor without striving for originality and, unlike genuine art, is a utilitarian object, mass-produced, low-brow, elicits standardized response, lacks critical distance between object and observer who are conflated into a single unit. It fetishizes certain objects and gestures in the service of maudlin affect. It can court the nostalgic past shamelessly. Its chief function is collective mawkish sentiment and, as German philosopher Walter Benjamin has written, 'instantaneous emotional gratification without intellectual effort and without the requirement of distance, or sublimation'.[95]

Schmaltz also sells, as Theodor Adorno (1903-69), another German critic writing during the Nazi era, often called it. Rachmaninoff's variety courted longing, pathos, pity, sentiment and sorrow – the emotional realms of nostalgia – rather than *schmaltz's* more raffish characteristics. But *schmaltz* is a potentially confusing designation for its broad grip on the lower end of emotion's capacious spectrum: is it inherent in *all* kitsch or merely certain brands? In music, *schmaltz* usually permeates kitsch, but not all kitsch indulges *schmaltz's* emotional compass. Also, in the sister arts, especially in poetry and music, *schmaltz* particularly courts the bathetic and pathetic: the bathos in abrupt, unintended transitions in style from the exalted to the commonplace, as well as the pathetic mode arousing constant feelings of pity, sympathy, tenderness, or sorrow. Rachmaninoff excelled in the later, especially the lachrymose mode. Few of his works contain the stylistic bathos implicit in these extremes of emotional range – that was not a feature of his musical grammar as it was for other contemporary, and usually lesser, Russian composers. However, his cultivation of the pathetic, especially the *pathetic sublime*, was masterful for its full range and nuanced colour. And

---

[95] Quoted in Andrew Benjamin, *Walter Benjamin and the Architecture of Modernity* (Continuum, 2005) pp. 41-42. Another German sociologist of art, Arnold Hauser, contributed further to the definition of kitsch during the Nazi period by explaining how kitsch differs from merely popular forms in its insistence on being taken as *serious* art. In Hauser's view, kitsch should be construed as a type of pseudo-art whose essential attribute consists of borrowing from great art or indulging in parasitism, and whose chief function is to flatter, soothe, and reassure its viewer-consumers by assuring them that their instant grasp of the art work is the right one. See Arnold Hauser, *Sociology of Art,* trans. K. J. Northcott (Chicago, 1982), chap. 6. Valid historical grounds exist why German sociologists were first to comment at such length on kitsch art: Nazi art exploited kitsch imagery for its own political agenda, and many German critics and commentators who watched it from the sidelines were often appalled by its masquerading as serious art.

it may be that the yoking of both versions (the bathetic and pathetic) to *schmaltz* is unfair to his musical vocabulary and emotional sensibility.

Either way, Adorno's view of Rachmaninoff's music, however loaded, cannot be altogether disregarded.[96] Adorno, however opinionated, was no minor, armchair, music critic. An accomplished pianist, he had studied advanced composition with Alban Berg, one of Arnold Schoenberg's most gifted students, and could play difficult piano repertoire. In time Adorno became one of the twentieth-century's most original music critics – especially authentic for his novel positions – and demolished Rachmaninoff's claim to originality as a composer with an armoury of skills: first by explicating which of kitsch's many effects are found in his classical 'commodity music', and then by discrediting Rachmaninoff's universally loved Prelude in C-sharp minor as 'kitsch-parody':

> In the highest, as well as the most violent moments of great music, such as the beginning of the reprise of the first movement of the [Beethoven] Ninth Symphony, this intention [that great music 'is the way it is'], through the sheer power of its coherence, becomes directly eloquent. It resonates in lower works as parody, for example in the C-sharp Minor prelude by Rachmaninoff that keeps hammering 'That is the way it is' from the first to the last measure, while lacking that element of becoming that could lead to the state of being whose existence it affirms, abstractly and to no avail.[97]

---

[96] Richard Taruskin, already mentioned, thinks it can and should be neglected; see *The Oxford History of Western Music* (Oxford University Press, 2005), p. xiv. Adorno's attacks on Stravinsky's music – altogether different from Rachmaninoff's oeuvre – have not won him advocates, and his unabashed loathing of American jazz dented his stature as a music critic far more than his disappraisal of Rachmaninoff's kitsch.

[97] Richard Leppert (ed.), *Essays on Music: Adorno* (University of California Press, 2002), p. 292. Earlier in the paragraph Adorno has explained that music, both in great art and in kitsch, expresses intentions and judgements. Adorno further comments on kitsch in *The Culture Industry* (London: Routledge, 2001).

That is, Rachmaninoff's Prelude lacks formal coherence enabling 'greatness'; instead its gesture of mindless repetition from first measure to last – those same three notes, A-G sharp-C sharp, endlessly hammering out the doomed 'That is the way it is', as Adorno suggests – reduces it to kitsch. In Adorno's terms it has no authenticity and affirms nothing worthwhile because it possesses no 'element of becoming'. The fact that it was historically Rachmaninoff's most beloved piano piece constitutes further proof: the 4-minute work (and mercifully no longer) he was invited to play everywhere on the terraqueous globe, which earned him millions and was exalted by the last century's masses as the most popular piece in classical repertoire. This was – Adorno chafes – not art but vulgarity, gaudy, debased, hewn in bad taste just to offer instant gratification. It sounds difficult, Adorno demonstrates, but is easy to play. The disjunction enables its instant gratification in the collapse of distance between the object (Prelude) and observer (listener).[98]

Elsewhere Adorno commented on the Prelude more expansively than this, especially in 'Commodity Music Analysed', which he wrote in Los Angeles during the war years.[99] Here he treats the Prelude in company with three other kitsch works (by Gounod, Dvorak and Tchaikovsky) as 'commodities' by virtue of their terrific commercial popularity. And he embraces psychoanalysis, socioeconomics, and political theory to clinch his points. First and foremost is the 'Nero Complex', which he develops by combining Roman history and Freudian psychoanalysis. Emperor Nero 'fiddled away' among rooftops while he razed Rome to the ground; those who waste their time playing Rachmaninoff's *Prelude*, Adorno suggests, are also

---

[98] In fairness Rachmaninoff himself concurred, even before Adorno wrote, bewildered at the adoration of this musical composition and refused to perform it everywhere as if he were a circus puppet. Or was this protest just his public face?

[99] Reprinted in Theodor Adorno, *Quasi Una Fantasia: Essays on Modern Music.* Trans. Rodney Livingstone (New York: Verso, 1998), pp. 37-52. Karen Bottge has provided the fullest analysis I know of Adorno's approach to Rachmaninoff; see her 'Reading Adorno's Reading of the Rachmaninov [sic] Prelude in C-Sharp Minor: Metaphors of Destruction, Gestures of Power,' *Music Theory Online* 17: 4 (Dec. 2011); http://www/mtosmt.org/issues/mto.11.17.4.bottge. Accessed 23 February 2013.

'fiddlers' wasting their time. Nero was also a known narcissist who craved veneration; Adorno implies the same for Rachmaninoff. Composer, performers and admirers of the Prelude, Adorno writes, are 'dilettantes, megalomaniacs, conquerors'; labels one could not facilely place on the great virtuoso pianist.

Yet Adorno's narcissistic comparison ('megalomaniac') is telling. No one familiar with Rachmaninoff's whole oeuvre would reasonably apply a 'Nero Complex' to his pre-1917 works, but most of his American works qualify. His audiences, especially in the USA but not exclusively there, considered his Prelude the pinnacle of his accomplishment and paid up handsomely to hear him play its foreboding four minutes. The Prelude deserves this maltreatment as the insignia of the retrospective fame spanning his entire career: he was only eighteen when he composed it in 1892, long before he left Russia – the gene of kitsch was already in his blood.

Adorno devotes most of his space to the analysis of the three-note principal theme: what he terms its 'massive foundation' and construes as its chief 'commodity'. Readers can consult his pages to witness his job of demolition – or proof of kitsch. Here it is imperative to note how Adorno's commodity theory included fetishization as a major component, and his view that the repetitive three-note principal theme prophesying doom and gloom induced the listener's "over-attachment." The pith of his formalistic analysis is this:

Music	Labour and Economics
easy to compose	easy to make
easy to play	little labour required
easy to hear	instant gratification
little value	no worth

The only 'colossal' aspect of the Prelude was its composer-pianist's height.[100]

---

[100] Other composers followed suit, even if Rachmaninoff was among the earliest producers of kitsch music. Maurice Ravel's *Bolero*, composed in 1928, in time proved to be his most popular piece and displays the same kitsch elements of

Rachmaninoff defended himself by appealing to the Prelude's bell-tolling effect: 'All my life I have taken pleasure in the differing moods and music of gladly chiming and mournfully tolling bells. This love of bells is inherent in every Russian...'[101] It may be, but there is nothing cheerful or amusing in those bells. They toll 'mournfully' (as he writes) – as in his dozens of *Dies Irae,* Days of Judgement flavouring so many of his works – chiming for the burning, sacking, destruction, and dissolution prognosticating the annihilation of his beloved Russia. *Annihilation* is the clue, especially annihilation as repetition. The pleasure of annihilation is unrelentingly repeated, over and again, for the narcissistic pleasure it gives to the three principals of its production: composer, performer, listener. This narcissistic element of kitsch art unconsciously appealed to the psychologically self-centred Rachmaninoff – as if his super-ego commanded him to thump out those thundering chords, A-G sharp-C sharp.

The 'Rachmaninoff brand' became recognizable in America before the Second World War. Never lying far from movie narrative and suffused with elements of jazz, its basic mood was romantic lyricism propelled by gushing melody instantly accessible to listeners. The new entertainment industry thrived on garish moods plated over in antique hues – something Rachmaninoff's gushing melodies supplied. By the time he arrived in Beverly Hills the Hollywood studios were producing almost a film a week; each movie making its mark with its own well-developed music and most scores containing big piano parts sounding like concert pieces. The line between highbrow concert genre and more popular film score was blurred – rendered virtually invisible. Discerning composers were signed up, big names in both realms, with astronomical financial rewards. Why should a revered classical composer like Rachmaninoff not place his 'brand' in the service of the new medium, if lured with huge sums?

---

simple structure, repetition, fetishization, over-attachment, and commodity art. There were other kitsch Boleros, i.e., Jewish virtuoso Moritz Moskowski's (1854-1925) kitsch fifth Spanish Dance, a bolero, which David Lean used in a salon trio in his film *Brief Encounter.*

[101] Cited in Bertensson, p. 184.

Or put it otherwise: was the *new* Rachmaninoff, the Rachmaninoff *reinvented* after 1917, not altogether more interesting to Westerners – especially Americans – trying to add European cachet to their frontier cultural portfolio than the old Rachmaninoff, who may have perfected a backward-looking Romantic musical language but who basically had nothing new to say? Add to this his Russianness and what that connoted to early twentieth-century Americans and you have the figure – the 'brand' – that has more or less endured intact to this day among those who listen to music and attend concerts. All depends on whose view is adopted: in the post-1917 North American version, Rachmaninoff comes off (*pace* Adorno's kitsch and our best musicologists) rather well.

After Rachmaninoff's death during the Second World War, his 'Russianness' aroused further interest (after all America and the Soviet Union were allies for most of the War), as did his status as an entrenched Americanized émigré. His music, especially the Second Piano Concerto, which Dr Dal enabled him to write by calming his guilt, consolidated the trademark. Listeners instantly associated it with rarefied romantic sentiment, as do Laura Jessen and Alec Harvey in *Brief Encounter* (1945) where it is the film's backdrop music. Two figures in flagging marriages recognize they share 'something': not enduring love but the escapism of instant gratification.

But elsewhere, especially in Europe, the experts and cognoscenti recoiled. Nadia Boulanger (1877-1979), the famous French conductor and doyen of teachers who taught many great musicians of the last century, told her students to shun the 'brand' like the plague because it amounted to unrelenting evocations of self-pity.[102] She opined it arose from Rachmaninoff's psychological suffering during childhood but might as well have attributed his nostalgia to whisky and sex for all her non-existent compassion. Did she consider his terror of emigration? Instead she suggested absent fathers (Vassily), dominant mothers (Lyubov), and pederastic piano teachers (Zverev), but never

---

[102] The interview on which Boulanger's comments on Rachmaninoff are based is cited in Howard Pollack's biography *Aaron Copland* (New York: Henry Holt, 1999), p. 83.

chose which. Having enjoyed a happy childhood herself, Boulanger showed no charity to her contemporary musician.

The Boulanger line of attack continued throughout the latter half of the twentieth century, especially among academic musicologists who rattled their sabres at the Second Piano Concerto. But even the less kitsch-like 'Third' took its share of hits. A list compiled from the 1950s forward would make trenchant reading and cause dismay among concert-goers today who seek out these concertos so they can become drenched in tears and clasp their insides during emotional catharsis. Even happy listeners, with no history of black melancholy, respond in this way to his melodic music. But not our cognoscenti: the more distinguished the musicologist's rank, the fiercer – it seems – the indictments against Rachmaninoff have been. For example, Joseph Kerman, the late University of California at Berkeley professor considered to be the doyen of American musicologists, described the third piano concerto this way at century's end: 'Now [in 1999], nearly 100 years old, Rachmaninoff's 3's life expectancy goes up every year, and given the wonders of bioscience, the piece is likely to end up in some dismaying retirement home community of the 22nd century, toothless, creaky, scarcely ecstatic, but still ready to play and above all garrulous.'[103] Imagine Kerman's verdict about the much more glitzy 2nd dripping in Hollywood chintz.

In America, Rachmaninoff's hallmark-brand was not limited to escapist films and sentimental romances à la Adorno but also inspired others to follow him with further imitations: third generation kitsch, as it were, imitating second. Richard Addinsell (1904-77), a British composer of film music, was commissioned to write a 'Warsaw Concerto' (1941) in imitation of Rachmaninoff's Second Concerto for *Dangerous Moonlight,* a movie about the Polish encounter against the 1939 invasion by the Nazis. It aims to represent both the struggle for Warsaw and the romantic sentiment of the film's main characters. By 1950 Rachmaninoff's original Second Piano Concerto had initiated a trend for similar short piano concertos in the Romantic style, and in

---

[103] Joseph Kerman, *Concerto Conversations* (Cambridge, MA: Harvard University Press, 1999), p. 124.

time the original concerto's appeal as the backdrop for wartime films also did, films in *The Battle of Britain* genre voiced over with Churchill's words resounding in the background.

It was also predictable that pianist David Helfgott, who suffered a breakdown long before he appeared in the 1996 film *Shine* and spent years in mental institutions, would play both Rachmaninoff's Prelude in C-sharp minor and his third piano concerto in the film: kitsch and non-kitsch to demonstrate the differences. The film tellingly opens with Helfgott playing Rachmaninoff's virtuosic 'Bumble Bee'. Yet even Rachmaninoff's rendition *imitates* Rimsky-Korsakoff's '*The flight of* the Bumble Bee' – Adorno's 'kitsch-parody' again – whose first three words ('The flight of') of the original title Rachmaninoff suppressed to avert the possible narcissistic charge of self-delusions of flying. These films proved highly popular over a half-century, yet as early as 1919 Rachmaninoff explained to American music critic Olin Downes that he did not consider popularity and seriousness antithetical.[104]

Rachmaninoff was right: they are not. The greatest painters – Vermeer, Rembrandt, Turner and others – have also proved to be among the most popular. All the arts provide ample examples. The point about 'seriousness' and 'popularity' entails central poles rather than antipodes, yet the notion that kitsch was in Rachmaninoff's blood – and probably had always been – is intrinsically valid. The reasons for its late appearance in Rachmaninoff's career can be deceptive. One could wish Adorno had addressed their root causes. After all, Adorno had lived in Los Angeles much longer than Rachmaninoff, had been exposed to similarly diverse forms of American music (serious, classical, popular, blues, jazz, etc.). But he was altogether unwilling to abandon any notion that a developing American culture industry was manipulating the population, its

---

[104] Cited in Bertensson, p. 220. In music kitsch has long tentacles and extends back to the nineteenth century, certainly to the late part of that century with its wizard-virtuosi, such as Liszt, and further back to Mendelssohn's Christian kitsch that was quite something for a German Christian convert born into one of Europe's most enlightened Jewish families.

production of mass culture inescapably forming passive adherents. This was Adorno's attack 'from the Left', as more than one critic of the Frankfurt School has noticed, and it fit organically, even if positioned to stand against the taste of the masses, with the rest of his music criticism.

Adorno's concept of high art stood in opposition to the masses' values in popular art – kitsch. High art expresses 'truth'; was not an isomorphic, popular, commodity-driven imitation of it *sans* hard-won formal structure, subtle nuance, genuine innovation, and abstract meaning. The difference is the type of emotion evoked in each, as well as the kind of 'listening' (Adorno termed kitsch 'regressive listening'). Listening for edification versus listening for entertainment, and the sublime emotions of the individual suffering voice as distinct from complacent masses incapable of tragedy. The fact that Rachmaninoff's Second Piano Concerto might still fill a concert hall in the 1950s or 60s was no proof of its greatness. It merely attested to the masses' attraction to kitsch.[105]

Part of the double bind – again not the whole story – was our composer's *double* self, his *two* selves. Not all his music is soaked in the dye of kitsch. His works for piano – the preludes, concertos (except the Second), sonatas, Corelli Variations, cello and piano sonata, second symphony, many of the songs – are not. Kitsch elements

---

[105] No one has written more astutely about these differences than Peter Franklin, who has, additionally, defended Rachmaninoff from several of these deprecations; see especially his *Seeing through Music: Gender and Modernism in Classic Hollywood Film Scores* (New York: Oxford University Press, 2011). Despite Franklin's insights Rachmaninoff's American audiences remain understudied. When listening to Rachmaninoff play the piano they were doubtlessly dazzled by the solitary virtuoso-as-magician – the romantic Lisztian superman who mesmerized them in the concert hall. But it is less clear why they responded as they did to Rachmaninoff's *compositions*; specifically why secure Americans, with loving families and intact homes, who were not primarily melancholic audiences, responded so forcefully to such melancholic music. Perhaps these audiences should be separated into children and adults for further illumination of the reasons: children, who have been shown to be deeply attracted to Tchaikovsky's sunny melodies and rhythms (*Sleeping Beauty, Nutcracker* et al), and non-melancholic adults, who respond to Rachmaninoff's kitsch romanticism.

break out in most of his programmatic compositions – the *Bells* (based on a text by Edgar Allen Poe), *Isle of the Dead* (allegedly inspired by a painting by Swiss painter Arnold Böcklin), and trashy *Rhapsody on a Theme of Paganini* (imitating an étude by the Italian violinist but sentimentally also reflecting back on his own life by allegorizing the variations) – with the consequence of blurring their classification. But their degree of imitation, type of evoked sentiment, and audience's task in listening can be far more precarious to gauge than in works like the Prelude in C-sharp minor. Would Rachmaninoff have been better never to have composed it?

It is the wrong question to ask. Even before coming to America and on first hearing, in 1924, the Gershwin *Rhapsody in Blue* that so bedazzled him, he possessed, as I suggested, the gene of kitsch; and once his 'brand' took off and filled his pockets with gold, he could not desist from writing it. The 'double self', as I call his bicameral composing career for lack of better designation, places a different spin on his self-professed Russian loss: 'I feel like a ghost in a world grown alien'. His ghostly self *is* implicated in these blurrings. Yet the fact is that he had effectively suppressed kitsch on native Russian soil.

Rachmaninoff's kitsch cannot be abandoned before observing, paradoxically, the disparity between his and Adorno's émigré status. German-Jewish Adorno was a generation younger than Rachmaninoff and went into exile during the Mid-Thirties in flight from the Nazis. He followed his colleague-friend Max Horkheimer, another member of the Frankfurt School (German neo-Marxist social theorists), and, like Rachmaninoff, spent years living as an expatriate in Los Angeles. But Adorno happily remained there for almost a decade and worked creatively in 'Weimar on the Pacific', as Erhard Bahr has adroitly labelled Los Angeles during the war years:[106] an oasis of émigré culture where Adorno produced some of his best writing, including his *Philosophy of Modern Music*.

Rachmaninoff, in contrast, never settled in; lived as if still in the 'Old Russia' and to the end dreamed of returning. He was not merely

---

[106] Ehrhard Bahr, *Weimar on the Pacific: German Exile Culture in Los Angeles and the Crisis of Modernism* (Berkeley and London: University of California Press, 2007).

a 'ghost in a world grown alien,' as he described himself, but emotionally incapable of adjusting to America. 'I cannot cast out the old way of writing [composing], and I cannot acquire the new.'

KITSCH WAS, IN A SENSE, HIS RECURRENT DOOM-SONG; the portending three-notes of the famous *Prelude* coming to roost, as it were, in America: prophesying annihilation no matter how narcissistically pleasurable this potential destiny lodged in his subconscious. This as well as his kitsch Viking-religion. He drove past Valhalla Cemetery one Sunday afternoon while driving his girls around Westchester County, New York, in a shiny Buick Eight, fell in love with the sense of eternity in that Wagnerian heaven, but never bothered to ascertain what type of paradise it was. A place in Norse mythology consumed by repetitive cycles of battle, blood-drenched death, and grotesque feasting on blood-filled entrails: what practical person would long for such an eternity? Not Evelyn, but Rachmaninoff did – this was his double irony. In musical composition too he could neither break out of the old nor innovate in the new. What then was he to do? Give up – *die* – or pray. And then let his God judge him on the *Dies Irae*.

The biographical Rachmaninoff *did* pray, in all sorts of ways; not merely to his Eastern Orthodox god and saint – Saint Sergius – but prayed more privately. As a child Lyubov had chronicled how he was named after St Sergius, the saint of his birthday on 20 March to commemorate the monks John, Patrikos, and Sergius murdered at the monastery of St Sava the Sanctified in Jerusalem in the eighth century. Twice the Saracens tried to plunder its Lavra but God's Providence protected the monastery.

Lyubov demanded prayer of her favorite son as forcefully as piano practice, and daily prayer also became constitutive of his secretiveness. We have already glanced at premier psychoanalyst Heinz Kohut's theories of narcissism but not his accounts of the dicey role of religion in even the life of marginal narcissists. Kohut's versions do not judge narcissism – as good or bad – they explicate its dynamic rise in the young damaged super-ego. Kohut evaluates narcissism as an integral and natural aspect of human development; taken to extremes narcissism can nullify the possibility of a good life, or, when acting beneficially – as in Rachmaninoff's case – become a spur to creativity. Whatever Rachmaninoff's share, his narcissism was as propitious as harmful.

Rachmaninoff was putatively a card-carrying member of the Orthodox Church but he rarely went to church and never took the sacrament of confession, as perfervid in Russian Orthodoxy as in other Christian religions. His personal 'Church' embraced Orthodoxy's affective symbols sans its more ostentatious pieties and practices, which he sometimes mocked and even perverted. He thought nothing of bribing the Moscow priests to marry him to Natalia Satina, his first cousin, despite the then high interdiction on first cousins to do so. When he married Natalia, in 1902, first cousins were still required to petition the Tsar for exemption during the ongoing marriage ceremony itself. The Satins did so on his behalf, again, but if he had to pay off the Tsar he would have.

His religion was one of guilt for flight and failure, and in later life it drove his movements; his decision about what to compose, even the curious obsession to be buried in 'Valhalla,' the cemetery in Westchester County New York, where he once drove by with his daughters, in a flashy car, and became fixated on the dream of spending his eternity there among these Old Norse demigods who died in combat. His reason, similar to Wagner's, was profound distaste for everything in modern life. Both composers dreamed of a static, backward-looking national atmosphere sans evolution or flow, and preferred decay, if necessary, to the misery of modernity. Wagner set his operatic dramas in the distant realms of Medieval Norse mythology: temporal removal providing one of the chief attractions for the equally disaffected and nostalgic Rachmaninoff; his piano works composed in the manner of a prior generation, a gesture to annihilate time's flow. No wonder our Russian composer pined for the end of his own exhaustion in a great medieval hall honouring heroes of the past.

Rachmaninoff's striking *guilt* infuses his compositions too – before and after flight from Russia – except for the intimate songs and the great piano concertos. Little else in his music escaped it: all three symphonies, the *Isle of the Dead,* and *The Bells.* No other Romantic composer, in any country, ever inserted more 'days of judgement' into his works. *Dies Irae, dies illa:* 'The day of wrath, that day will dissolve the world in ashes'.

Remove these apocalyptic melodramas so ubiquitous in his works and Rachmaninoff's stock-in-trade imprint is lost. You might as well carve out melody from the connective thread suffusing his music. Both amount to religious kitsch: fear and trembling on show for the masses, then the pouring out of heart-throbbing melodies to allure them back. Rachmaninoff's personal guilt drove both (religion and surging melody), even if he experienced their pangs as poignant in his internal world. The affective toll on his psyche was distressing, yet, imaginatively speaking, his *Dies Irae* is another prop within (what Adorno had called) his ragbag of tricks. This is why Rachmaninoff never abandoned it, not even in the very late *Rhapsody* and *Symphonic Dances* where it returns with vengeance.[107]

Religion, for the deep believer, remains forever private; the soul's internal struggle with mortality and death. The kitsch believer parades the spectacle, dramatizes the strife, publicizes its devalued internal valence and puts it up for show – no wonder Rachmaninoff refused to attend confessions *a deux* and considered them the hocus-pocus of an Orthodoxy whose rituals he abjured. His religious music makes the point in nutshell: confident that his niche as a religious composer was assured, he superabundantly composed this music for public consumption – liturgies, night vigils, a *Liturgy of Saint John Chrysostom* – all celebrating his 'Russianness' too.

---

[107] Not even Paganini, that unrivalled Italian trickster, had included a single *Dies Irae* in his oeuvre, but Rachmaninoff could not resist the temptation; Haydn did only once when in a comic parodic mood, and Tchaikovsky twice; it features primarily among composers anticipating Adorno's kitsch music and Kohut's narcissistic religion: Bizet, Liszt, Saint-Saens, Myaskovsky, and Mahler (twice in the Second Symphony): all experienced religious 'crises' in one shape or another.

If writer Milan Kundera is prescient to observe that 'kitsch excludes everything from its purview which is essentially unacceptable in human existence ... [that] kitsch is a folding screen set up to curtain off death', his thought also demystifies Rachmaninoff's kitsch.[108] An arch narcissist, steeped in nostalgia for the Old Russia, Rachmaninoff swelled his apocalyptic props to mask death and defend him against its terrible finality.

Yet death was not the sole barricade in his religion; love and romance were also. Early in life he ardently abandoned himself to both – his escapades with the Skalons, the gypsy Anna, perhaps even seductive singer Nina on a lesser scale – with the effect of his narcissistic libido culminating in hypomanic activity.[109] He composed brilliantly for three years. But when those loves crumbled, he crashed. Rehabilitation with Dr Dal produced romance anew in his music, as in the opus 21 and 26 songs (1902 and 1906), but after emigration and immersion in the American scene it was impossible for Rachmaninoff to replicate the miraculous quality of composition he had in the long decade (1902-1916) before flight. Afterwards, America elicited *another* Rachmaninoff: neither stylistic innovator nor fully-fledged film composer. And even if he did not explicitly compose music for Hollywood films, his compositions tended to move in that direction. Yet even a decade earlier the gene of kitsch exposed itself: not in the high-brow Mahlerian abstract Eros of that composer's second to fifth symphonies, but in compositions such as the Second Piano Concerto seemingly constructed for the masses and too sentimentally gushing to be authentic (in Adorno's sense). On balance, the miracle of Rachmaninoff's complete piano music is the series of preludes (opuses 23 and 32) and third piano concerto, all written before 1917 and avoiding these extreme pitfalls and antipodes while retaining his indelible 'brand'.

---

[108] See Kundera's meditation on the concept of kitsch in *The Unbearable Lightness of Being* (1984).

[109] Kohut, *Analysis of the Self* (n. 47), p. 151, explains why these terms that seem like jargon when invoked here are necessary to explain immensely difficult psychodynamic processes.

Rachmaninoff's songs also eschew kitsch and to this day remain discerning creations whose romantic elements do *not* elicit pretty sunsets, artistic flower arrangements, and snow-covered mountains – a *Sound of Music* Hollywood Arcadia produced for crowds. He was hauntingly obsessed with death, as narcissists of his cloth usually are – and saying so must not be seen as depreciation of his great creative musical talent. But the heart of the matter is not what he told himself about his set of beliefs – this eviscerates the point. It is rather the overlap between biography and creative representation, and the specific shapes imbrication of the two took in his musical composition. To glance back at Barenboim in my epigraph, this is a composer about whose life it is important, even essential, to have intimate knowledge.

Had there been multiple Rachmaninoffs? Kitsch Rachmaninoff and non-kitsch, and other types too? The characteristic of each was a penchant to yearn, to long, to weep: when extreme nostalgia grips these different Rachmaninoffs he abandons himself to kitsch piety, kitsch devotion, kitsch creed.

FINALLY FATE, THE GREAT RUSSIAN DISCIPLINARIAN. Rachmaninoff's relation to Fate had less to do with philosophical Fatalism or Destiny than with local Russian national character. He unrelentingly tried to shape his own destiny and did not lay much stock in the metaphysical notions of Fate promoted by Schopenhauer and Nietzsche, or, more recently in his lifetime, Verdi in his opera *The Force of Destiny* (besides, Rachmaninoff was not a fan of Verdi's music). No, his version of Fate must be sharply demarcated from ours'.

To an educated Russian of this period – as Rachmaninoff during the 1890s was – the embrace and acceptance of *sud'ba* (Fate) was an essential attribute of the peasantry; not of his own aristocratic landed class, or even of urban workers, but of the Russian peasantry, considered – in the words of a prominent contemporary historian –

'the true bearers of national character'.[110] The peasantry's *sud'ba* was intrinsically linked to their view of Russianness. Neither could be construed without the other because *sud'ba* was – wholly and entirely – a *Russian* state of mind, and to be *Russian* was to adhere to *sud'ba*.

But *sud'ba* also comprised an ambivalent and incongruent set of beliefs for Rachmaninoff's contemporaries. Peasant fatalism was paradoxically a sign of irrationality and ignorance, as well as one of spiritual purity, uncorrupted by the excessive rationalism of Western culture as Tolstoy preached. It was often understood as a form of passive submission to the authority of Orthodox Christianity, while simultaneously tied to the heretical ('superstitious') elements of popular religion. Intellectuals and savants like Rachmaninoff might lament the age-old peasants' resignation to hardship and oppression and found it paradoxical, but in their pious acceptance of *sud'ba* the intelligentsia also detected an enviable stoicism. The same *sud'ba*, or 'Fatalism', also defined how educated Russians saw themselves: their mission to bring to the common people the values of rationality, activity and enlightenment. More often than not the intellectuals and policy makers were nevertheless plagued by doubts about whether this was a realistic goal and whether they themselves were too beset by indolence, vice and greed (all linked to the spiritual chasm of Western individualism) to be able to bring it off.

Fate was forever conjoined to death in Rachmaninoff's psyche. For much of his life he felt overwhelmed by hopelessness, pointlessness, the sense that Chance *is* Fate (*sluchainost est sud'ba*). The Russian poet Marina Tsvetaeva's (1892-1941) psyche resembled his: as a young girl she studied piano at the turn of the century and heard him play his own Second Piano Concerto.[111] His Imperial Age piano music fired her imagination with already forming doctrines of Fate and Death – she sensed the composer's plangent heart. Tsvetaeva

---

[110] Maureen Perrie, '*Narodnost*': Notions of National Identity', in Catriona Kelly and David Shepherd (eds.), *Constructing Russian Culture in the Age of Revolution, 1881-1940* (Oxford: Oxford University Press, 1998), p. 29.

[111] Discussed and cited in Alyssa W. Dinega, *A Russian Psyche: The Poetic Mind of Marina Tsvetaeva* (Madison, Wis., 2001), p. 186. She committed suicide after her husband's execution in 1941.

once said: 'I'm going out for a few minutes.' In 1905 either figure could have said that: 'jump, jump.' Suicidal ideas were then never far from the tip of the imagination.

Rachmaninoff's idiosyncratic view also emphasized *sud'ba*'s 'Russianness'. Again, as in the *amour propre* of his secretiveness, his chief hurdles centered on being able to position himself in relation to his geographical homeland. So, on 27 April 1906, when the effects of the 1905 uprising were still reverberating, he bared his soul to his longtime confidant Morozov, who was both trusted friend and cherished sounding-board because he was so knowledgeable of music: 'If I choose the "two birds in the bush," I can live abroad, but only if I can control my longing for Russia.'[112] *Always Russia* – longing for the homeland. 'Birds in the bush' referred to the works he was composing, and at the time there were two. But the 'crisis' his letter refers to is whether to work in *America* – and even before he has decided, before he has left, the mere possibility precipitates intense 'longing for Russia'. He loves her *more* for the prospect of leaving.

The letter includes a postscript anticipating the inevitable. While composing it the doorbell rings, the postman conveys a contract to conduct a season in St Petersburg. Relief – did he break into tears? The peasants know best; *sud'ba* has saved him. He concludes the letter with the words 'Fate knocks at the window. Tap. Tap. Dear friend, cease striving for happiness' – this because *sud'ba* determines all.

The same words appeared in his song 'Fate', the very one he sang for Tolstoy at the nadir of his collapse on his second visit. Rachmaninoff's predicament, encased in his superstition and irrationality as well as the *amour propre* he developed as protective armor, was that he could not exist without being on *Russian* soil. Practically speaking, in 1906 he needed either an American or Russian contract to make ends meet. But he had not yet heard from the Americans – hence the panic. He suspected the American contract, if it could just arrive, would be more lucrative than the Russian, but thought he might be 'cheated there' – in America – and 'compose nothing.' His logic is flawed but his intuition prescient; his notion of

---

[112] Quoted in Bertensson, p. 122-23.

being bilked and not composing elusive, both no less superstitious than the *sud'ba* of the peasants.

His *petit cri* of 1906 — where to live in relation to where to compose — was to plague him all his adult life, unless he could have remained at Ivanovka. The momentary flap was the microcosm of a larger psychic universe governed by person and place in relation to country and homeland. '*Where* to compose' was quintessential because it determined, he thought, whether he *could* compose. The toll his imagined *sud'ba* took was no less consequential than his hypochondria and secretiveness. He had loved some of the peasants at Oneg and Ivanovka (which his wife owned but which he loved more or was at least more psychically attached to); he had incorporated their versions of piety into his obsessions with church bells, the seasons, and Days of Judgement.

Viewed in perspective his obeisance to *sud'ba* was heartfelt — a life-jacket — especially the *sud'ba* whose Russianness engulfs other components. For the fact is that the Rachmaninoff who migrated to America never relinquished *sud'ba*, prayed in Beverly Hills California to Russian gods, still entreated Russian spirits of the place, even surrounded his bed — the symbolic zone of well-being — with icons of Saint Sergius. A supplicant, he died under the sign of his Saint's embrace.

Does it desecrate him too far to suggest that even this version of his Fate may have been *kitsch sud'ba?* Some kitsch invades his practice of it, especially his ordinary daily fears and fetishization of Russian objects, Russian things. Why did he not think more practically of the art of composition and what would endure the test of time? Of the way he would be remembered? Such a small output for such an immense talent. And such intractability — as he himself concedes throughout his life — to alter himself, to innovate, to write the new music. Let us be honest, be brutal: remove kitsch and what is left of the late Rachmaninoff for the camp of Beethoven and Brahms?

But we must also never lose sight of Rachmaninoff's total oeuvre. The plain fact is that not everything he composed was kitsch. Much was, but not all. As music critic Damian Thompson has written: '…his rhetoric conceals ideas of unsettling originality, presented in dark colours, snapping rhythms and strange textures that yield a little extra reward every time you listen to them.'[113]

These disparate voices, on either side of his fate, come and go. *The inventive Rachmaninoff, the yearning Rachmaninoff, the kitsch Rachmaninoff. The composer surprising you, the composer moving you, the composer incapable of innovating.* Nostalgia is the most secure key to unlock his psychological mindset – his secret chest. Please turn the key all the way to the right.

Is Rachmaninoff dreaming of Russia in his tomb in Valhalla? Then he has had the last laugh. He has not died at all. He need not so broodingly have feared the islands of the dead and their macabre figurines overlooking coffins draped in white. Even here, among the cadavers, he lives. His piano concertos still fill the largest and most prestigious concert halls worldwide, performed by the greatest pianists alive. These works will not die or go away, unlike Medtner's or Nicolai Rubenstein's, even if Medtner, forever jealous, quipped that Rachmaninoff sacrificed himself to the mighty dollar in the Western entertainment industry. If numbers of devotees counts for anything, if wisdom still exists in the *vox populi*, Rachmaninoff will be remembered as long as classical music is played.

Even this version of his nostalgic life constitutes an 'In Memoriam.' Fate of a different type.

---

[113] Damian Thompson, reviewing Michael Scott's biography of Rachmaninoff in *The Telegraph*, 2 August 2008.

Part 3: Evelyn's Rachmaninoff

Rachmaninoff was dead, dead in his grave, but what became of Evelyn — the Evelyn who could no longer unhinge herself from his memory?

AFTER HER MARRIAGE DISINTEGRATED Evelyn and Sam became estranged, but the 'Rachmaninoff thing' — as she called it — lingered. Not a day elapsed without her thinking of the composer-pianist. Only he remained fixed in the front of her consciousness from her 'former life': her past years (as she referred to them) filled with 'multiple mishaps'. She lapsed into reveries, remembered playing his works, even that rueful day in Town Hall; kept fantasizing about his own divided life into Russia and America and thinking she must read more about him.

One afternoon Sam returned early from work, around 2PM, while she was practicing Rachmaninoff's second sonata — the work she *should* have played in Town Hall. She bathed that morning, washed her hair, perfumed herself, and dressed in the Town Hall red velvet gown.

Sam parked the car in the garage, entered through the back door, as he always did, heard the racket, marched into the living room, and looked at her in shock. He had never seen her dressed in the 'symbolic dress' before — shunned so definitively since her debut day — nor watched her playing Rachmaninoff so bombastically as if on a concert stage.

He stared while she continued. Evelyn stopped, in the middle of a phrase, lifted up her hands, spread out the folds of her red gown, remained on the piano bench, and looked at him agape.

Wife and husband froze, as if having made a major discovery. After a long interval Sam silently turned around, marched out, got into his car and drove away. Evelyn had no clue about his disappearance, but it marked the beginning of a new phase. Two people, barely speaking, living under one roof.

Sam returned a few hours later and moved into Richard's bedroom. Evelyn wondered whether he snapped. Was it her simulated dress rehearsal – decked out as if on stage – or did his antics entail more? For the first time he saw his wife in this pose: energized by day, the depressive she had become at night.

Afterwards everything degenerated. Sam became gradually incommunicado, then he started to date women. They'd phone up and ask to leave a message (Evelyn wondered if they knew Sam was married).

About three months later, Sam packed a suitcase and walked out after making his own breakfast. He was gone that whole night, and Evelyn phoned him at the office the next day several times. His secretary said he was out and he never returned her phone calls.

'Is Sam in the office today?' Evelyn politely asked the secretary. 'This is his wife.'

There was always an excuse: he's out to lunch, he's with a client, he'll return the call but never did. Evelyn was persuaded he was there rather than under a truck and did not call the police. Two weeks later, a letter arrived from his lawyer requesting that all communications to his client Sam Amster, including business pertaining to the house and bank accounts, be channelled through his law offices.

Sam never returned. His lawyer sent Evelyn three or four communications a week about bank accounts and stock dividends, and in a long letter explained that his client did not want a divorce, just needed to be by himself for a while.

Evelyn was relieved. She too needed time alone, time to practice the piano again, as well as the leisure to stare into space, reflect and figure out what Richard's 'vanishing act' meant. It was her new circumlocution for death. How can Richard have been here one day, living in their house on Dartmouth Street, and gone the next day? What was life if everyone checks out so quickly?

Then Evelyn altered. Manically she threw herself back into the piano, practicing for hours each day; systematically working up her technique, playing hours of exercises trying to overcome the technical difficulties she had experienced with Adele. Her hand was less powerful now than it had been at twenty, but she was slowly returning to the point where she could play the works on her debut programme: Chopin, Liszt, Rachmaninoff. If Sam returned she would take him back, but if not, teaching would fill vacant hours and provide income with which she could attend concerts in Manhattan.

A few months later she heard about Sam's new woman, a twenty-something-year-old travel agent who had recently returned to Queens after having been posted abroad. An older lady who frequented the same beauty parlour told her. Evelyn had met the younger woman several years earlier, and she took pity on her during Richard's illness. When Evelyn told her Sam had walked out on her, she wept.

Sam had apparently joined a dating agency and worked his way through several women until he 'clicked' with Joyce, who was everything he was not: proactive, assertive, quick-moving, and capable. She wanted an older, established man in his forties.

According to Evelyn's friend in the hair-salon they were living in an apartment in East Elmhurst, close enough to the City for Sam to drive in to work. Joyce also still worked and they had been seen – her friend said – at a nightclub in Brooklyn, on the other side of the Williamsburg Bridge.

Evelyn was relieved to know Sam was being cared for. He had become helpless during Richard's illness and the death reduced him to an almost puerile state. But her sympathy ended here. It was sufficient that Sam was not in trouble or suicidal.

Her search to find good piano students panned out. Word of mouth circulated and within six months she had a cadre of different level students to fill up the day. Practicing and teaching restored a purpose, even if they could not expunge her loss. She could feel in her bones that something else was coming... this was temporary.

Sam's lawyer wrote about a year later to say that his client had developed stomach cancer and dictated his burial wishes. Sam had made a new will leaving everything to Evelyn and implored her to follow his wishes to be buried in a plot next to Richard. He wanted an orthodox Jewish funeral presided over by a rabbi.

She civilly replied and inquired about his condition; correspondence followed, making plain Sam was fairly far-gone. The cancer manifested itself late, beyond the point when much could be done, and spread to his lymph and bones and was inoperable.

She also wrote that if summoned she would visit him, at home or in hospital. His turn of fate seemed less to level justice to an adulterer than unfairness to a decent man in his forties. He had been a caring husband and father; he deeply loved Richard and was broken when progeria struck; his sudden departure and extramarital affairs were the results of confusion and desperation rather than abnegation. The more Evelyn reflected, the more she pitied Sam: having seen his son die only four years earlier, now death summoned Sam himself.

A nurse at Queens Hospital contacted her rather than Sam's lawyer a month before his death. Evelyn drove to the hospital so familiar to her, and found Sam just three floors below Richard's room. His mouth was filled with tubes – he could not speak. She held his hand. It was a pathetic scene of a man in pain; he cried intermittently and tried to say how much he loved both son and wife – the only two things that had mattered in his life.

This was the last time she saw Sam, but sitting at his bedside revivified Richard's death. She made arrangements for his funeral, still smarting from the hospital's terse account of Richard's death, and buried them side-by-side in the Jewish Cemetery in Forest Hills. Richard had died in the month of November, Sam in April. It was still cold and she wore the same black dress and black belt. Two of his cousins and a few partners from work returned to the house afterwards. They brought flowers and chocolates, stayed for a couple of hours, lamented the loss of this 'young' man, and were then gone.

Suddenly the emptiness on Dartmouth Street became welcome, broad-beamed in its daylight finality, like Richard's disarmingly glum expression, she recalled, when he had finally emerged from her belly. Sam's death triggered memories of their courting and marriage and the happy months they enjoyed before Richard's birth. But Evelyn was a different person then: a talented girl in love with the piano who had frozen up at her debut recital, a 'daddy's girl' too who had received little education other than on the keyboard. Richard's illness had transformed her, for the first time in her life, into a researcher of magnitude: someone who combed libraries for information about his rare medical condition and who, as a by-product, turned to books and journals for edification. Sam never read, just watched TV.

Of course she did not welcome his death but they had been separated for over three years, and even before then, while Richard was alive, they had grown so far apart their marriage amounted to little more than ritual habit. Besides, she was dealing with her own demons. The piano again became her lover to whom – in this luminous vacuum on Dartmouth Street – she wished to return. Richard's memory haunted her and, increasingly, the specter of Rachmaninoff too, for reasons her diaries indicate she was trying to comprehend.

I WAS SHATTERED WHEN EVELYN DIVULGED all this in telephone calls. To think – an entire chapter of my past obliterated, the mirror of my idealized childhood vanished. Richard dead, Sam dead, their stately home in Queens with the shiny concert grand piano lost – only generous Evelyn lived on in this forlorn psychological state. I wondered if other people would be able to relate to the strange facts of her life – would they too be incredulous of its significance if told? I reflected that Evelyn was especially worthwhile because so unusual, despite being somewhat incomprehensible herself. She said she had more time now for the 'R thing' and claimed to be coming round to the view Adele had been right all along; but even if Evelyn had selected the easier programme, her concert career – she told me – would have faltered. She placed little stock in psychological explanations, certainly not the unconscious reasons for frozen nerves. Her fingers told the truth.

The 'R thing', Evelyn continued to believe, would have set in whether or not her debut was successful. One sentence in her notebooks for 1963 intrigued me: 'My fate in failing has been marvellous, and my new determinism to discover who R really was is now energizing me.' I could never imagine myself writing that sentence. She was then forty-five.

What haunted her, she believed, was the ghost of a man, 'R', who had been the century's greatest virtuoso and who could produce tones no one else could. Her 'R thing' was not limited to piano technique, or even to his pianism, but to her sense of a man searching for a 'home' while alive. Not because he was nomadic, or an outsider, or just because he was obsessed with death – his sought-for life in Valhalla – but some geographical home capable of replacing Russia. Evelyn was no scholar yet she seems almost to have imagined Rachmaninoff in a Nietzschean struggle where the soul searches for a fixed abode in a pilgrimage to which she could attach no name.

Once, in a telephone call, I asked her where she got her information. 'What books do you read'? 'Nothing much,' she replied, 'newspaper articles, concert programmes, this and that.' Yet I knew she had been addicted to libraries ever since Richard was diagnosed. She was getting her information somewhere.

She kept repeating, even in letters to me, that now both Richard and Sam were dead she was finally free to discover who Rachmaninoff *really was*, even if she had to pursue his memory to the end of the earth. She even left me dumbstruck once when she said 'this is more worthwhile than having succeeded in my career.'

Evelyn aimed to remake herself – not easy for a forty-five year old widow who had endured multiple traumas. She painted her house in different colours and changed the wallpaper. She bought a new car. Her teaching distracted her but was no substitute for Sam and Richard. She walked compulsively, short strolls four or five times a day, puttered in the back garden, shopped and cooked when her three friends in Queens called around, and she read furiously. She read with pencil in hand, highlighted passages, made notes, stuck chewing gum at page bottoms, and generously spilled coffee on them, as her diaries show.

Once she underlined a sentence in a magazine affirming that 'marriages were formed in the unconscious'. These six words buzzed around in her head, like an indefatigable fly. The author's lack of source fazed her not; indeed the idea attracted her and she ruminated on its significance. Did it mean that predestined attraction was based on unconscious factors about which no one could ever know anything?

The idea gripped her and she became more philosophically engaged with it, thinking it was the key to everyone married she knew. Vita married Barry because their unconsciouses were … Brenda married Jerry because their unconsciouses were … her parents too and her parents' friends. Everyone except Sam: why *did* she marry Sam?

She became absorbed in her own unconscious mind; interrogated it – as a sleepwalker does the waking world – and never again blithely wandered into another marriage. If she had only understood her *own* unconscious, she told me once, her marriage would not have been as empty as it was with Sam. One idea segued into another, until each was dethroned. The past haunted her too. She read an obituary of Benno Moiseiwitsch in the *New York Times*, the great Jewish Ukrainian-born pianist who took British citizenship; clipped it, wondering what her life would have been like if she had not frozen up at Town Hall. Adele Marcus loved Moiseiwitsch's Chopin and took her students to hear him just before Evelyn's aborted debut in 1939.

She experienced these tantalizing ideas as intellectual immersions, pleasures too as fulfilling as fine food and drink. A few years later, in 1966, she became engrossed in a new Pulitzer Prize playwright: Edward Albee's play *A Delicate Balance*. Three years earlier, in 1963, she had gone to Broadway with her friends and was bowled over by Albee's play *Who's Afraid of Virginia Woolf?* Later she read how it scooped the best drama awards. She followed its nomination for the Pulitzer Prize in Drama, and was dismayed when the advisory board — the trustees of Columbia University — eliminated it on grounds of 'profanity and gross sexual themes'. In objection she drafted a letter to several newspapers that was not published, which intensified her disgust. She was forming independent ideas.

Her preoccupation with *A Delicate Balance* pierced, she thought, to the heart of her dilemma about the continuing deprivation of human happiness. That October, in 1966, she watched it performed at the

Martin Beck Theatre on Broadway and was so agitated she gave herself a Christmas present: a front row seat in December. 'The acting was magnificent', her notebook reads, 'and Jessica Tandy as Agnes outstanding'. Main characters Edna and Harry began to haunt her. She repeatedly rehearsed the plot in her mind, eventually putting it into her own words in her diary. From her jotting I composed this account:

> Edna and Harry arrive at their best friends' – Agnes and Tobias – house with suitcases in hand. Something intangible (but what?) has frightened them and they are too afraid to return to their own home. They ask to move in with their best friends. Tobias welcomes them and puts them in daughter Julia's bedroom, where they hide for most of the play's duration. Harry is Tobias' longest living friend and, after many decades of friendship, says he is entitled to move in. Daughter Julia has also returned home, just having left her fourth husband. Each time Julia divorces she returns to her parents; this time becoming hysterical that Edna and Harry have usurped her room. She demands them to leave, claiming they have no entitlement with her. Eventually they pack up but not before making a scene before the family. Harry explains, once again, why they have come: they were frightened at home. In Act Three Tobias and Harry have a conversation à deux in which Tobias recaps that the couple are entitled to stay – they have the right. Tobias adds that it is his responsibility to look after his friend Harry – friendship is defined by responsibility. Tobias' wife Agnes asks the couple if they would have accommodated them – Agnes and Tobias – if the tables had been turned. Edna replies 'no', which startles Tobias and Agnes. The disruption has caused both couples to lose something vital in their lives: their 'delicate balance'. But what is it? The

loss centers, undeniably, on home. Even friendship, which embodies the play's main philosophical quandary, is configured as a domestic matter: one couple leaving their own home to move into their best friends' home. The action suggests the fright they experienced was located inside their own home. Can it be that they were at home alone in an empty house?

This was Evelyn's strange plot summary and she scribbled she may have got it wrong, so she stayed on red alert about Albee's repetition of the word 'entitlement' – especially in the theatre in December. Afterwards she combed newspapers for reviews to answer her question but found nothing. The *Delicate Balance* contained no filthy language or sexual overkill to eliminate Albee, and she rejoiced when she read that he won the Pulitzer. This was how her mind was developing.

Then she found a sentence in Scott Moncrieff's translation of Proust's *In Search of Lost Time*, which she dissected in the same way. It is the moment where Swann establishes parallel universes between everything and everything else: male and female, love and death, microcosm and macrocosm, which she also thought led to the unconscious:

> 'She' – he tried to ask himself what that [word] meant: for it is a point of resemblance between love and death, far more striking than those that are usually pointed out, that they make us probe deeper, in the fear that its reality may elude us, into the mystery of personality. (p. 305)

EVELYN HELD OUT THIS WAY for four years after Sam's death, from the summer of 1963 to 1967. Then the tenth anniversary of Richard's death came on 23 November 1967, which she observed alone on Dartmouth Street. It fell on a Wednesday, the day before Thanksgiving, when America closes down and everyone flees her office for family and home.

She drove her new car down Queens Boulevard to 164th Street, parked it in the hospital car park, strode down the walkway to Richard's hospital room window and viewed the very spot where he must have fallen … jumped? She moaned until an old, sickly man peered piteously at her from the fourth-floor window and then absconded.

She also told me that during that summer of 1967 she had bought a thick new biography of Rachmaninoff by Sergei Bertensson published in 1956. She slowly read it over three months and marked the margins in her newly acquired fashion. Some facts were revelations, she said, but she doubted the interpretation.

'He's got the wrong pulse of the composer,' she wrote in agitation to me, and 'he doesn't understand what mattered most to him'. In telephone conversations that autumn she twisted any comment I made to Bertensson this, Bertensson that. She became obsessed with Bertensson's five-hundred page book.

I relayed the little I knew about Bertensson-the-man: that he had lived in Russia and known Rachmaninoff, burrowed for a long time in Russian archives, then moved to America, befriended the Rachmaninoff family, especially sisters Natalia and Sophia, and only a few years earlier – in 1962 – died in LA after having seen his biography through the press.

Evelyn still lived alone, of course, on Dartmouth Street. She could have learned more about the 'real Rachmaninoff' close by, in Apartment 9b on 170 West 73rd Street, in Manhattan, where Rachmaninoff's cousin/sister-in-law Sophia Satina was living, but Evelyn was unaware. A spinster, Sophia was then pushing towards ninety, the living authority on the facts of her cousin's life.

Sophia had remained in Moscow after the Rachmaninoffs fled Russia in 1917, taking academic posts in botany at Moscow's Higher Women's Institute and then a similar job in Dresden; but when she pined for sister Natalia and Rachmaninoff late in the 1920s she crossed the ocean and found a high-powered research post at the famous Cold Spring Harbor Science Centre on Long Island. Here she remained until World War Two broke out; then, shortly before the Rachmaninoffs moved to California, she moved to Northampton, Massachusetts, where she headed up Smith College's Genetics Experiment Station and bequeathed her papers to them.

From Northampton Sophia gathered the most important reminiscences about Rachmaninoff to appear since his death, in 1943, by those who knew him in a privately published book called *Vospominaniia o Rakhmaninove* to which Evelyn's newly found biographer Bertensson contributed. And here Sophia remained until 1966, still a spry eighty-seven year old, when she moved to West 73rd Street and wrote a still extant letter (about Edison and Rachmaninoff) to the husband of an American pianist requesting where he could hear the great pianist's voice. She told him Edison tried to reproduce it on records around 1920. Sophia could have told Evelyn a great deal – except that Evelyn never knew Sophia was alive. Bertensson's biography was silent about Satina after Rachmaninoff's death – the woman so central to Rachmaninoff's story dropped out of Bertensson.[114]

Sometime in 1968 Evelyn wrote this entry in her diary as an imagined reply to Bertensson:

> GOOD for you, Rachmaninoff, not surviving the War into the 1950s. Your fate might have been as troubling then as Bolsheviks, suicidal son-in-laws, and unquenchable nostalgia had been earlier. Your letters to Russia in the 1930s, the outraged one published on 15 January 1931 in the New York

---

[114] In hindsight it is easy to fault Evelyn for failing to perform a full search for Sophia Satina, but trial-and-error communications in 1966 were slow and required snail-mail patience. Nothing in Bertensson's biography provided Evelyn with any clue about Sophia, not even indicating whether she was still alive. Besides, Evelyn was remarkably intuitive and sensitive but was no scholar. She read whatever she could find and combed libraries but her approach was haphazard. She would become immersed and then obsessed, as she had been with Albee's play, and then move on to the next obsession. Only Rachmaninoff remained, after Richard's death, from beginning to her own end.

Times denouncing Russian education, might have placed you under suspicion as some type of Russian double-agent. Nothing you could have said during the Cold War might have dispelled the notion. If you were called up in the McCarthy Era – while Bertensson was placing the final touches on his biography and cousin Sophia Satina watching Bertensson's every move from Northampton, Massachusetts – you might have been interrogated for un-American activities. The publicity would have disturbed you, and wife Natalia too, and sent you to the grave as quickly as any deadly melanoma did.

Spot on, I thought – McCarthy would have done in Rachmaninoff. But why did Evelyn never suspect that Sophia Satina might still be living? His letter to the *New York Times* she found on p. 271 of Bertensson, and its effect was the ban on playing Rachmaninoff's music in Russia for the rest of his lifetime. As I poured over Evelyn's diaries I remember being astounded by the intensity of her reading and recall of detail. I was moving posts that summer in 1968, from Harvard to UCLA, and forgot to ask her why she overlooked Sophia.

I settled into LA early in the summer and phoned Evelyn in Queens: *she too was heading out west,* she said. Nothing could keep her any longer in metropolitan New York. Mihaela and Cezar had both died. Everyone close to her was dead. Her conversation was confused. Was she following me?

We must have spoken for an hour. She said she was moving to Beverly Hills so she could follow up leads Bertensson had not – he could not, he was dead. She was coming by train; had sold the house with everything in it, including the big grand piano. She would buy an upright once settled and bring just two large suitcases, one filled with notes and books, especially her annotated copy of Bertensson. She kept comparing her anticipated train journey to Rachmaninoff's trek from St Petersburg. Could I meet her at Union Station and take her by taxi to the Beverly Wiltshire Hotel on Santa Monica Boulevard because it was so close to Elm Drive where Rachmaninoff had died?

She held up there for a few weeks until she found an affordable apartment in Venice Beach. I remember seeing little of her in the ensuing weeks. We were in term, committees were convening, examinations awaiting marking, and the city still recovering from the shock of Robert Kennedy Junior's assassination on June 5.

But we did speak on the phone. Evelyn claimed she gave up her former life because she wanted to understand what lay at the base of Rachmaninoff's melancholy – this was her word – and through his plight she might begin to comprehend her own. If he could move across an ocean in an era before airplanes she could travel cross-country. She also said she was now an émigré – she used that word – a lifelong émigré from her anticipated concert career, her son, her husband, and, now, her native New York.

Her tone on the phone modulated from initial confusion to eventual calm; if anything now she was too sober, almost as if drugged into passive reason. I told her I was going to London for the summer to do research, and would return at the end of September. She wrote me a few brief letters containing no revelations, just the fact that she had settled in well and made the right move.

When I returned to UCLA she was more unpredictable, one week calm, the next manic. Term was starting and I knew there would be little time to spend with her. It was my first year teaching in California and I was not doing too well. I was an Easterner at heart and – unlike Evelyn – unable to make the transition. I sensed I might even need to leave, which never happened.

We never really lost touch although our visits diminished. I was still a very young man in my late twenties, finding my way personally and trying to establish an academic career. I would cross town to see her three or four times a year, usually thrashing out the 'Rachmaninoff thing' until late at night. She had become immensely learned about him, in ways I was not. It seemed to me she knew more 'facts' about the man and his music than anyone I had met.

On one visit, around 1975, she waxed eloquent about Victor Seroff's *Reminiscences of Rachmaninoff,* republished two years earlier in 1973. She annotated it as prolifically as she did Bertensson but was less critical, maintaining he understood more of the man behind the music – the man who could compose 'like this'. She meant soaring and surging. I was at a loss to challenge her, not having read Seroff, but nevertheless indulged her theories, hour after hour.

There was another reason too, which I did not know at the time. As I indicated, we slowly lost touch and by 1980 she receded into the hinterland of my personal universe; only revived when I began to study the history of nostalgia as an abstract category and province of cultural history.

EVELYN'S RATIONALE POINTED TO ELM DRIVE where Rachmaninoff lived and died. Ever since Evelyn moved to LA in 1968 she made a habit of walking in its neighbourhoods. I viewed it as her needing exercise, she as activity central to her mission. Within a few years she knew every landmark like the back of her hand: Carmelita, Foothill, Maple Drive; she recognized each mansion, its vintage and architecture, and could have given historical tours of the vicinity. She peered into gardens and porches and invented imaginary lives for the occupants – all in her somewhat mad pursuit to reconstruct how Rachmaninoff had fared there in his last few years.

Some time after reading Seroff's *Reminiscences* she met a woman walking her dog. Her diary entry records the day as 18 May 1975. This was Daisy Bernheim, about Evelyn's age – Evelyn was fifty-seven in 1975 – who claimed to have been born in the house on Carmelita she still lived in.

Daisy was a young widow who had inherited a fortune. Her late, much older, husband was the principal jeweller of Beverly Hills – the 'diamond king' was her sobriquet – his magnificent shop on Rodeo Drive the equal of small diamond centres in Paris and Amsterdam. Daisy's hobby was playing the piano. She was fifteen when the

Rachmaninoffs moved into Elm Drive and exhilarated at the prospect of living so close to the world's greatest pianist.

As a student at Beverly Hills High she rode her bicycle past 610 North Elm Drive almost every day: crossed Santa Monica Boulevard, took a shortcut into Durant Drive, crossed over Santa Monica, made her way up Carmelita, turned left into Elm Drive, and then – applied her breaks at the fifth house on the right.

That was 610, with its long concrete path leading up to a dark green door. Two massive windows, floor to ceiling, one above the other on each floor, flanked the whole left side of the door to the roof. Here, on the ground floor, was Rachmaninoff's music room containing two Steinway concert pianos. Daisy was never invited inside (the Rachmaninoff's were far too secretive for that) but she told Evelyn she learned to creep unnoticed into the high hedges to the left of the path. There she waited, inert, breathless, for piano playing.

Evelyn and Daisy had converged almost in front of 610, passing each other as if each had something to say to the other.

'She's just turned nine and knows her own mind,' Daisy chuckled, pointing to Mina. 'Mina leads me on our daily walk.' Evelyn looked down scornfully. 'I would have called her Gorgi, but not Georgie, which I loathe, but that sounded too close to Corgi and she is no corgi.' Evelyn wondered where this conversation was leading.

Daisy continued.

'She always stops here, at the house where the great pianist used to live, as if he might return from the dead and play again.'

This woman knows all about Rachmaninoff, Evelyn mused to herself and replied, 'do you think dogs distinguish different kinds of music?'

Daisy laughed: 'I don't know.'

'Have you been walking this way long?' Evelyn asked.

'Oh yes. I was born around the corner, on Carmelita, almost a half century ago. I was almost fifteen when he moved in.'

'You remember it?'

'As vividly as if yesterday.'

'Tell me, please.'

'I was taking piano lessons and my teacher said that Rachmaninoff already lived in Beverly Hills. Then my parents heard he was moving here, so I kept watching every day on my bike rides.'

'Did you see him move in?'

'Yes. It was a cloudy June day. I came home from school around three o'clock, took out my bike, and as soon as I turned into Elm Drive from Carmelita could see two huge moving vans. They were enormous. I rode up to the house, and watched from the other side of the street. I wanted to see how many pianos he had.'

'Did you?'

'Yes. Two large black cases came out, tied up in straps, like gigantic coffins at a funeral. Three men in another smaller truck walked them up the ramp. The other moving men did not touch them. The piano men seemed to warn them, with clenched fists, not to touch the big black bellies.'

'You must be one of the few people who ever saw that,' Evelyn assured Daisy.

'Do you know who Rachmaninoff was?' Daisy asked as if just awakening to the fact that she was speaking to a stranger who may never have heard of him.

'Oh yes, very much so.'

'Then you play the piano?' Daisy inquired in an almost childlike way.

'I do,' Evelyn replied, 'and I've walked down this street many times before, but never met anyone who knew him'.

'I know lots of people who did,' was Daisy's emphatic reply. 'All of us who were then teenagers are now fifty-ish. Everyone of that age around here knew about these weird Russians living here.'

'Weird?'

'They protected their privacy with iron fists. I rode by every day. I used to see the wife going in and out, but she never even smiled at me.'

'What did you expect?'

'I hoped she would let me listen inside, but she never did. She gave me a cold shoulder. If looks could kill.'

'Did you ever see him go in and out?' Evelyn was quick on the uptake.

'Once. He jumped into the taxi. He must have been going to play a concert somewhere. He was wearing a black cape.'

"I'll bet it was the *same* cape I saw when I heard him.'

Daisy appeared puzzled. 'Maybe he always wore black capes?'

'I heard him twice,' Evelyn rejoined, 'he was wearing a black suit, and the jacket appeared to be a cape. It clung so naturally, but I was too far back from the stage to see what he looked like.'

Daisy smiled, her nose changed shape, as if she were about to inhale through her nostrils before replying.

'He was huge. Taller than six feet, with a somber expression on his face. His skin was pale. Almost sallow. No trace of a smile. I wanted to hear him play but not meet him.'

Evelyn could not explain her good luck. She thought their meeting ordained. This was the opportunity she had been waiting for since her arrival in LA. She had combed articles and program notes, read Bertensson and Seroff, but Daisy might be able to tell her much more.

'Look, my name is Evelyn Amster and I live in Venice by the beach. Would you like to have coffee some time?'

Daisy understood why she was being courted. 'I can tell you a lot more than this. Like the day they brought him home from the hospital shortly before he died.'

Evelyn's face became flushed. This meeting entailed more than serendipity; it legitimated her *raison d'etre* for migrating. Did Daisy notice the change in the stranger's expression?

"Tell me something about yourself. You seem very keen to know about him."

'I am keen, believe me. I tried to become a concert pianist but failed. God gave me a prodigiously talented son who was destined to become a great concert cellist, but he died young, at fifteen, of a rare genetic disease. Then my husband left me and he died. I had nothing to do with the rest of my life, so I moved out here from New York.'

'Why?' again that inquisitive childlike voice.

'In search of Rachmaninoff.'

'Are you serious?'

'Absolutely.'

'What do you think you'll find?'

'The secret of myself, of my failure, of my life.'

'How can that be?'

'You see, I tried to play a Rachmaninoff programme at my debut recital but then froze up on stage. Then everything in my life went downhill, as it did in his.'

'Downhill?'

'Yes, the Bolshevik Revolution came to Russia, the Rachmaninoffs fled, they migrated to America, and he lost his drive to compose.'

'But he was the world's greatest *pianist*.'

'Maybe, but a great *composer*, like Bach or Beethoven, is worth a lot more. Pianists, even when great, are a dime a dozen.'

'You must be kidding. They're the greatest celebrities.'

'Well, I exaggerate, ok. But great composers are in another league to pianists,' Evelyn rejoined.

'But he *was* a composer. He played his *own* works here, in concerts, I heard them, especially that famous prelude.'

'His great works were all composed in Russia, before they fled.'

'So why did he lose his drive'?

'That's a sixty-four thousand dollar question. I don't believe he burned out or had no time.'

Evelyn's voice was rising; now she was declaiming rather than having a friendly conversation. 'You see', she continued, 'I have this thing in common with Rachmaninoff. We both lost our "homes". He lost Russia, which was the most important place to him in the world, more important than any person, and I lost my son Richard who was everything to me, my career, my life, my home.'

Daisy began to recognize the troubled waters she had drifted into. A thought flashed through her mind that she had better cut this conversation off. But Evelyn soldiered on:

'People create when their homes are intact, and homes represent more than literal things, they're symbolic and abstract too, and homes can be "times" as well. Like when you say "I was so at home at that time of my life."'

Daisy was getting the point: 'like the different homes right here on Elm Drive, each one with its own personality, each reflecting everything about the occupiers.'

'Yes, and when you lose your home, or homeland, your talent dries up and your inspiration disappears.'

'I don't understand. What about those émigré writers who wrote great works in exile? Some of them were here in LA.'

'They were the majority, Rachmaninoff was the exception. He was a relict of another era, could not adjust to the new émigré world, neither in Russia or America, so he just kept playing the piano, compulsively, and of course perfectly – his only remaining joy in life. Having lost Russia there was nothing left for him to do.'

Daisy pulled Mina back who was by now impatient to keep walking and tugging and starting to bark.

'I'd best be off,' Daisy said, 'I have a few errands to do.'

That night Evelyn drank a half bottle of red wine with cheese and crackers, sat in her favorite cushioned sofa near the window overlooking the Venice boardwalk, Bertensson's biography in hand, and rehearsed the day's main event. She reread the pages about Rachmaninoff on Elm Drive a half-dozen times. What could Daisy tell her that she did not already know? Daisy probably never heard of this book. Who was Daisy anyway?

She did not stir for a few hours. The wine made her drowsy and enhanced her serenity; she gazed at the liquid sky and saw how it folded into the Pacific. A few nascent stars could be seen, and they twinkled as brightly as the small ships on the ocean. She was on to something big; Daisy was a godsend. Intuitively she sensed discovery coming.

A week later they met in a café on the beach. Daisy was happy to drive over – her days were not busy and she had not seen the beach once this summer. The weather had turned warmer, as it often does in LA early in the summer, and Daisy was wearing a colorful orange bandana in her hair and a short skirt that almost looked like a bathing suit.

'This is a nice cosy place,' Daisy said, 'how about this table?'

Evelyn was amenable to anything her guest wanted. She reminded herself a few days earlier that if Daisy had been fifteen in 1942 she would have been born in 1927. Then Daisy was nine years younger than Evelyn; a small gap that would not jeopardize their friendship.

They ordered filtered coffees and two pieces of carrot cake, then Daisy began to talk.

'I used to hide in the side bushes,' Daisy said, 'and saw a lot but I never heard him play. The piano was too far away. But I could see inside the big window downstairs.'

'Weren't you afraid of being caught?'

'No,' Daisy chuckled, 'those Russians could never have charged an adolescent with being a spy. I was only fifteen. I could see them moving around, sitting down for tea around four o'clock, just when I used to ride my bike and hide.'

'Was it just the two of them, the pianist and his wife?'

'No, there was an old lady who wore a long dress. I wondered about her; whether she was a relative or maid or companion.'

'Did you ever find out?' Evelyn asked.

'Not her name but I recognized her face the next winter; around the time he was brought back from the hospital.'

Evelyn was *au fait* with Rachmaninoff's last months – his winter exhaustion, the collapse on his last tour, their spending Christmas at 610, his hospitalization in LA – but the 'old woman' piqued her curiosity. Bertensson briefly mentions a Russian nurse, Olga Mordovskaya, who was called in at the very end. Could this the same person? When she asked, Daisy drew a blank.

'I'll bet that old lady in the long dress was Russian,' Daisy said, 'she lived there for a long time.'

'You mean from the time they moved in, when you saw the pianos carried in?' Evelyn pursued.

'No, not that long,' Daisy chortled as she took another piece of cake, 'but I remember seeing her through the window during those holidays when school was out and I was riding around a lot. She had a strange face. I wondered who she could be.'

Evelyn's mind backtracked. This was Christmas 1942, two months before Rachmaninoff was taken ill the following February. By now Evelyn knew the final chronology well and Bertensson's account too: how the Rachmaninoffs spent that Christmas on Elm Drive, then left in January 1943 for an American concert tour, Rachmaninoff taken ill in February, wife and husband abandoned the tour in Atlanta on 17 February, Rachmaninoff hospitalized at the Good Samaritan in LA on 26 February and did not return home until March 2. Nurse Olga Mordovskaya – assuming Bertensson had her name right – cannot have been the same person Daisy saw at Christmas, unless she had moved in earlier.

'Are you sure you saw an old Russian lady then? Was she the same person you saw there later that winter, in March?'

'Oh yes,' Daisy assured her, 'I'll tell you why.'

Evelyn perched herself to listen attentively.

'I remember the day he was brought home in an ambulance. His wife exited the ambulance first, then two men carried him out in a wheel chair. It was in the late afternoon. They did not knock on the big green door. It opened from inside and there she was, the same old lady in the long black dress. I recognized her shape although I could not distinguish her face. She was the same person. Definitely.'

'What about Rachmaninoff's death?' Evelyn probed.

'I remember my piano teacher telling us that Rachmaninoff had gone back into the hospital. That would have been soon after I saw the ambulance bring him back home. But I never saw an ambulance again. If they brought him back a second time I missed it. I only remember my teacher saying – around the end of the month, in March – that he had died.'

'And the old lady?'

'She and the other lady, his wife, remained in the house for a long time after he died. I would see them packing up when riding around.'

'How long?'

'Months and months.'

EVELYN'S MIND ASSESSED DAISY'S CAFÉ NARRATIVE. That night she spun her own Ariadne's web:

> The Rachmaninoffs insisted on everything 'Russian' to the tea. Rachmaninoff never trusted American doctors, refused to see one. Whenever he became ill he found a Russian doctor – whether in New York or Beverly Hills or even when on the road concertizing – to treat him. He also told correspondents he consulted with hypnotherapists after Dr Dal, in Paris and New York. Evelyn asked herself why this Russian nurse now? Because Rachmaninoff's depression flared, was her answer.

Evelyn continued her interior dialogue:

> 'Olga Mordovskaya must have been her name and she was also Russian. Bertensson calls her a 'nurse' – he was accurate. But suppose Olga also fulfilled other roles. Suppose she was a very special type of nurse. A year before his death Rachmaninoff continually moaned about his fatigue and despair. Suppose his depression flared again and Natalia intervened to find him this very special nurse. Call her a nurse or anything else you like. Olga Mordovskaya could have been that person. Nurse and companion – the two had been linked from time immemorial.'

Where did Bertensson discover the information about Mordovskaya? Evelyn was clueless ... Natalia may have engaged Mordovskaya by Christmas 1942 but someone had to introduce her to the Rachmaninoffs. Natalia would never have advertised for a Russian companion. She was too proud and secretive.

Evelyn pondered the dilemma for a couple of weeks and mentioned it to Daisy, who hadn't a clue. Daisy relied on memory for everything, wrote down nothing. She remembered her bicycle rides, the seasons, the old lady's strange face, the ambulance, the two ladies in the aftermath packing up, but read no books or articles.

Evelyn thought the clue to be a 'Doctor Golitsyn', who Bertensson mentions as having been brought in around that time, but he leaves the door open as to *when*. And who was Golitsyn? Bertensson asserts Golitsyn had been looking after Rachmaninoff for 'the last two or three years' but documents little beyond that and says nothing about the man.[115] Yet he cites one of the last letters Rachmaninoff wrote, on 22 February 1943, to the famous Russian-biologist Nikolai Petrovich Rashevsky (1899-1972), when he abandoned his American concert tour and returned to LA aware of how very sick he was.

Rachmaninoff and Rashevsky had met in Paris early in the 1930s, the least likely friends-to-be, the one a mathematical biologist, the other composer-pianist. But these Russian expatriates were bonded by similar 'White Russian' backgrounds and values (Rashevsky had actually served in the White Russian Navy and after the Bolshevik revolution had to flee for his life to Constantinople). It is impossible to know how well the two men knew each other but this letter's tone suggests intimacy. Except that Rachmaninoff's message – far from being witty or cheerful – almost beggars belief.

The great pianist almost never cancelled concerts, yet now, in New Orleans, he tells Rashevsky how run down he is and how gravely ill: 'I should see a doctor, but on this question I am a narrow-minded nationalist: I recognize *only Russian doctors*, and there is one I can see in California'. So the criterion is nationality rather than expertise or specialty. Even in these throes of pain at the end of life his nostalgia calls the last shot and the letter plaintively concludes: 'I'll talk with

---

[115] See Bertensson, pp. 380-84 and note 116 below. It is not superfluous to reiterate that neither Daisy nor Evelyn knew the nurse's name as early as 1975-78. Daisy perhaps never knew it, unless Evelyn enlightened her during the 1980s; Evelyn reconstructed it from Bertensson's biography by putting two and two together, meshing Daisy's narrative with Bertensson's account. Evelyn died persuaded, as we shall see, that Nurse Mordovskaya was Golitsyn's dependent, and she was right.

him [the Russian doctor] about my side, and we can recall old times. It will be good for both body and soul.'

His nostalgia will calm the pain – the lethal cancerous melanoma – puncturing his side. Can Rachmaninoff really have been so naïve? Did he think an internationally acclaimed scientist, as Rashevsky was in 1943, would find recalling old times funny or sunny? Rashevsky himself was unknown to be nostalgic. The further twist is that the 'Russian doctor' proved to be none other than Golitsyn, corroborating the time frame Daisy had all along suggested to Evelyn: Rachmaninoff had been under his care for several years, since arriving in California – a typical ploy for Rachmaninoff to enmesh himself in the new émigré scene there. Yet no matter when Golitsyn was brought in, he was the likeliest link to introduce Mordovskaya to the Rachmaninoffs. And if he did, as Daisy and Evelyn thought, the whole chronology fit beautifully: that is, late in 1942 Rachmaninoff is clinically exhausted and despondent, he has already been consulting Dr Golitsyn for several years in Beverly Hills, Golitsyn diagnoses chronic fatigue and depression, Natalia requests a *Russian* live-in nurse-companion, Golitsyn introduces them to Mordovskaya.

Evelyn spelled out her theory to Daisy and they thrashed it out for weeks over coffees on the beach.

But Daisy had a talent for unwittingly posing tough questions. 'What's *against* your theory?' she asked.

'Well', Evelyn said, 'quite a lot. Natalia may not have permitted anyone to live with them. But if she were just the right *kind* of old Russian nurse, the right vintage, the right age, the right class, the right feel, Natalia may have acquiesced.'

'Why didn't the doctor prescribe pills rather than a companion-nurse?'

'There were no antidepressants then – in 1942. Just amphetamines, which Rachmaninoff never would have agreed to take as a consequence of their side effects, especially memory loss. Tranquilizers were around but he didn't need them.'

'So the depression killed him in a few months?'

'No, no', Evelyn said emphatically. 'Depression doesn't kill people; he died of melanoma, a skin cancer, which appeared later.

When Golitsyn first diagnosed him in 1941 he detected no sign of cancer, just fatigue. Later, at the end of 1942, Golitsyn thought the fatigue may have been producing other illness too. That's where Mordovskaya came in. Golitsyn identified her as the ideal nurse-companion.'

'Wouldn't Rachmaninoff have tried more hypnosis first?' Daisy rejoined.

'Probably not', Evelyn assured her. 'By this time he was so tired and burned out he didn't think it could any longer help. Besides, he was too old. He would be seventy in just a few months. His thoughts lay elsewhere. Natalia realized this too, so she preferred the nurse-companion. She was tired of all the traveling over decades and was no longer a spring chicken. The nurse idea may even have been her idea.'

'I see', Daisy said, still searching for objections as her mind's inner eye recalled the old Russian lady staring from the window.

Evelyn continued: 'she was with him to the very end … to the last hours, holding his hand.'

Daisy's girlish voice rose in excitement as she wondered what new information was found. 'Evelyn, could he have told her secrets he never told anyone else?'

'Maybe,' Evelyn said, already chasing those secrets.

EVELYN SEQUESTERED HERSELF during the ensuing weeks. Slowly, drinking brandy in her window, peering at burning red globes setting over the Pacific, often mumbling to herself — a habit that intensified with age and over which she was almost proud — she processed her 'discovery' that the face Daisy saw was Mordovskaya's. Biographers Bertensson and Seroff were silent about this detail, and other biographers too. Evelyn was persuaded Dr Golitsyn was the clue: she wondered why Bertensson said so little about him and why he mentioned Mordovskaya only *once* on p. 382. By now she had eclipsed her personal obsession and became absorbed in the fetishistic quest for biographical relics.

She noticed Bertensson's footnote reference to an article Golitsyn wrote a few weeks after Rachmaninoff died, entitled 'Illness and Death of S. V. Rachmaninoff' and published in English in a local magazine in San Francisco intended for the Russian community.[116] Evelyn's diary describes her trying to obtain an interlibrary loan copy, but she never indicates its arrival. She had made a discovery, she thought, by connecting Golitsyn to Mordovskaya in this intimate way; linkage that Rachmaninoff's biographers knew nothing about, and she was unprepared to abandon it.

Evelyn's diaries about Rachmaninoff break off in the mid 1980s, except for one long extract I shall come to momentarily. She continued to write in her notebooks after the 'discovery' about Mordovskaya, but less consistently and her jottings are punctuated by long gaps. Was she preoccupied with some matter whose account does not survive? Daisy's name appears until the early 1980s and then drops off. Did Daisy move away? Did they fall out? I could not help imagine Evelyn was drinking, a suspicion borne out in our phone calls.

Once, around the time of her 'discovery' – to which I am coming now – she asked me if I knew anything about 'a Dr Golitsyn'. 'No,' I said, 'what should I know about an obscure Russian physician who

---

[116] Alexander Golitsyn [Golitsin], 'Illness and Death of S. V. Rachmaninoff,' *Russkaya Zhizn* (San Francisco), April 14, 1943. I Anglicize the spelling throughout to 'Golitsyn'. The article provides details of Rachmaninoff's last days, focusing on the medical aspects of his melanoma. However, more crucial for the connection with Rachmaninoff was Golitsyn's pedigree, as we see in the ensuing pages. Rachmaninoff knew the Golitsyns in Moscow and was summoned to play at their palaces after 1910. Evelyn, who read no Russian, could not have discovered any of these connections, nor were Prince Alexander Golitsyn's papers yet deposited in the Hoover Institute at Stanford University in Palo Alto, California. They were sent there in the 1950s, unbeknownst to Evelyn, who could have consulted them had she known; they were donated in the decade after the death of Prince Alexander and his wife Lyubov (1882-1948) as part of the Hoover Institute's ever-growing archive of unpublished material about Russian affairs. Eminent American historian Douglas Smith has recently published a moving biography of the lives of both these great aristocratic families based on far-flung archives, including those at Stanford. Smith also had access to private manuscript collections I have not been able to see; see his *Former People: The Last Days of the Russian Aristocracy* (New York: Farrar, Straus & Giroux, 2012).

had migrated to America in the 1920s?' In those days long before the Internet you could not google anyone who ever lived and discover what you wanted in a jiffy. After that conversation I think we spoke only three or four more times before her death.

I never expected to find what I did in the last few years of her life: her solution to the puzzle about Rachmaninoff's final days and his much-lamented nostalgia for Russia. I still register my amazement, more than two decades after her death, since then having assembled every known fact I could about his last days. But first I need to backtrack: if Dr Golitsyn was the lynchpin, who was he? How could I understand nurse Olga Mordovskaya if I did not know who Golitsyn was? Suppose he was not just another White Russian émigré doctor? The fact is that Golitsyn and Mordovskaya were the only two people, other than wife, daughter and sister-in-law, with Rachmaninoff at the end of his life.

I tracked some of Golitsyn's papers to the Hoover Institute at Stanford University, immersed myself in them and constructed a skeletal life. His archive revealed almost everything I needed to know except for the resolution of one mystery, but this one depended on Evelyn rather than Golitsyn or Mordovskaya. So I start at the beginning.

ALEXANDER MIKHAILOVICH GOLITSYN (1876-1951) was the second oldest son of Prince Vladimir Mikhailovich Golitsyn, the famous 'Mayor of Petersburg' on the eve of the Revolution. The Golitsyns were one of the two most powerful landed aristocratic families in Tzarist Russia (the Sheremetevs were the other), but both families were of another order of aristocrat than the Rachmaninoffs: far more influential, wealthier and exerting direct influence on the Tzar. Alexander grew up at Petrovskoye, near Moscow, in a seventeenth-century palace so revered by all the Golitsyns that no piece of furniture or object could be moved from its original spot. A family political squabble ended in Alexander's inheriting the palace, rather than his older brother, which he and his wife Lyubov Glebov (1882-1948) took possession of in 1901. The area surrounding Petrovskoye was home to thousands of peasants and villagers who ransacked the palace top to bottom after the Revolution. Today the house still stands in ruins.

After the events of 1917 Alexander trekked eastward across Siberia into Manchuria and Harbin with Lyubov. He was taken prisoner of the Reds in 1920 in Irkutsk, a train stop on the Trans-Siberian line near Lake Baikal, and thrown into prison. Here he contracted typhus and nearly died. But he was trained at Moscow University in infectious diseases, and knew how to save himself. His younger brother Lev, another 'Prince Golitsyn', was also captured by the Red Army and incarcerated, but less lucky than Alexander he died a miserable death from typhus in the arms of his medical brother.

Lyubov and the children continued eastwards to Harbin, then a Manchurian city filled with White Russian émigrés. The train divided near the Mongolia-Manchuria border, and Lyubov made sure they were in the carriage continuing southward into Manchuria and on to Harbin. Harbin's development had begun when the Russians invaded Manchuria towards the end the 19th century. The Russo-Manchurian treaty of 1897 granted Russia a concession to build the Chinese Eastern railway and Harbin became its administrative centre with a fifty kilometre wide zone along the railway. It also became a cultural centre: during the 1920's and 1930's famous Jewish actors gave frequent performances there, which promoted the spread of western music in China, a development in music education still evident today. These exiles and refugees required medical treatment, which Dr Golitsyn provided in the new hospital opened in 1920.

While Golitsyn himself recovered in prison in Irkutsk he helped the Red prison officers treat their sick soldiers; for this they released him and he too continued on to Harbin. Lyubov was shocked to see him so gaunt but better feeble than dead. Eventually recovered, Golitsyn returned to the bustle of Harbin and slowly charted the family's departure. He would volunteer for the Red Cross who would post him somewhere; given a choice, he would select America. Lyubov preferred to return to Moscow but the prospect of again trekking across Siberia over months – over years? – was too daunting and perfidious to ponder.

Their wish was fulfilled in the spring of 1923. Golitsyn's plan bore fruit; by then the Red Cross relied on him as their chief medical officer for infectious diseases in Harbin. When they required their representative to find an American home for thousands of their refugees, he was selected.

He crossed the Pacific Ocean with three-hundred dollars in his pocket and chose to be based in Seattle; far better off than Rachmaninoff fleeing westward with Natalia and their girls without such a stash of dollar bills, with only his piano fingers. Golitsyn wrote memoirs about his life, especially his migrations during the Bolshevik Revolution, but they are silent about his medical patient Rachmaninoff.

Golitsyn became disenchanted in Seattle. He had renounced his Russian citizenship immediately upon arrival (something the Rachmaninoffs would never have done). Quickly he took to the American way of life but found Seattle provincial and unexciting and dreamed of migrating further south to the reputedly edenic 'El Dorado' California symbolized.

A few years later he did, together with Lyubov and their adolescent children, first moving to San Francisco and then LA, which both husband and wife preferred for its milder climate. In southern California he built up his practice during the 1930s, cashing in on his expertise in infectious diseases and was in demand to treat the hundreds of patients still dying of measles in this era long before a vaccine became available early in the 1960s.

By the 1930s Golitsyn – now approaching sixty and at the crown of his medical career – was widely known in LA medical circles. Within the Russian émigré community he was the most distinguished *Russian* doctor irrespective of specialty. Thus when the Rachmaninoffs migrated to Beverly Hills and searched for a family doctor who *must* also be Russian, their natural choice was Golitsyn.

Rachmaninoff was an international celebrity who would be a feather in the cap of any practicing physician, émigré or otherwise.

The likelihood is that they met in the summer of 1941 through LA's large Russian network of émigrés. The Rachmaninoffs and Satins knew all to well who the 'Golitsyn princes' were, and when the prospect arose of having one as their family doctor in LA they were delighted. Doctor and patient shared so much in common – Imperial Russia, fellow aristocrats, pedigree, flight from the Reds, birthdays only three years apart – that even the secretive Rachmaninoff was comfortable with this fellow.

It is impossible to surmise whether Rachmaninoff revealed his early nervous collapse and breakdown to Golitsyn as part of his medical history, but he probably explained his fatigue and the new blockages he was experiencing in relative old age as he approached seventy. Even so, Golitsyn remained silent: his papers say nothing whatsoever about his patient. We shall never know.

Wives Natalia and Lyubov were also contemporaries with husbands who both lived through hell – this common ground binding them when they visited each other and took Russian lemon tea. The doctor-patient relation then had none of the formal constraints practiced later in the twentieth century, even in America; among these White Russian expatriates the codes were even looser. The women shared samovars, reminisced, frequently rehashed the past and the new world they had inherited on Hollywood's doorstep.

Golitsyn must have listened rapturously to his celebrity patient during the rare visits the great pianist made to his dark office covered with exotic burgundy rugs. Golitsyn understood the sources of his patient's deep secretiveness, expressed in hushed Russian cadences, and sympathized with his burnout. Rachmaninoff told him he had been tired for many years – crisscrossing the world – and by now his body was showing signs of deterioration. Yet Golitsyn was no psychiatrist, no Dal; he empathized, he understood the plight of the nostalgic expatriate before him, and he tried to be helpful, but he was an infectious diseases doctor, not Sigmund Freud. They were lancemen, of course, even if Rachmaninoff was the confidant who barely opened up, sensing his good luck in having hitched up to such an old-world Russian doctor rather than the medical upstarts surrounding Hollywood.

Among Golitsyn's symbolic gifts to his patient was one Rachmaninoff never anticipated.

I PROVIDE THIS BACKGROUND because Evelyn's notebook includes the disjointed sketch of a diary of nurse Olga Mordovskaya's last days with Rachmaninoff. The incoherent account is written in Evelyn's own hand and records no source or origin. Where did Evelyn find it? Did Daisy tell her? Did Evelyn reconstruct it from Daisy's story? Did both women fabricate it? These questions cut to the heart of the mystery.

Whatever its source it remains Evelyn's most capacious remainder. Notwithstanding the diary's significance for Evelyn's life, it also provides a touchstone for Rachmaninoff's internal sense that he could not shed his lifelong malaise: the nostalgia I always believed to be the most explicit source of his compositional failure after migration. None of his biographers has ever doubted the effect of his psychological nostalgia: certainly not Bertensson, Seroff, or any of the two-dozen others. What was in question, and what remains to be understood, is the *effect* on his post-1917 compositions: their paucity and poverty of imaginative leap, their inability to innovate stylistically.

I concluded that Evelyn herself composed 'The Nurses Tale' in her last decade of life – that was the reason she withdrew into herself and became reclusive – she was thinking and jotting. First she connected Daisy's recollections to Bertensson's brief account of the nurse; Bertensson who gave the nurse a name, which Daisy could not. Then Evelyn kept reworking the diary as one writes a novel: an all-consuming passion that drained her residual energy even if she went nowhere with it. When Evelyn finished, she died – mildly sated, reassured she had made a 'discovery', fulfilled in having compiled a fragment.

To backtrack – Daisy filled Evelyn's ears with her memories of Rachmaninoff's last days. What Daisy did *not* say – could not recount because she did not know it – were the conversations between Rachmaninoff and his nurse. These awaited reconstruction by someone with a fecund imagination, which Evelyn possessed. So Evelyn set herself this task (not knowing, of course, the end was coming so soon). She managed to finish it and then rested content she had understood something profound about her own life, and perhaps Richard's too. All this enabled by Rachmaninoff-the-filter.

Evelyn wrote out everything in longhand, even business letters. Her hand was never clear, but as she aged it grew feebler and more garbled and she pressed increasingly less on her pen (I remembered how arthritic she was the last few times I saw her, pressing down on her pen hurt her). The final paragraphs of the Nurse's Diary are much murkier than the opening ones.

Another possibility remains. Imagine such a 'Diary' physically existed; that is, nurse Mordovskaya compiled it while she lived with the Rachmaninoffs on Elm Drive, and cousin/sister-in-law Sophia Satina eventually inherited it after Rachmaninoff's death and Mordovskaya's too, as Sophia did the rest of Rachmaninoff's archive, passing from husband to wife to sister-in-law. Mordovskaya was already 'old' in 1943, and did not live much longer. But her 'Diary' is nowhere to be found. Sophia Satina's papers form the base of the Rachmaninoff Collection in the Library of Congress in Washington, and no Diary is among them or at the already mentioned Hoover Institute. Suppose it never went to Sophia Satina but remained in LA and made its way to a dealer who advertised it in the 1970s. Evelyn could only have purchased the Diary if it was cheap, which it may have been considering that interest in Rachmaninoff was still negligible. Evelyn's cash reserves had been dispersed by the late 1970s: the shabby furnishings in her Venice Beach pad made that perfectly clear and she lived on a shoestring. If a Diary existed in Russian, and *if* she purchased it, she could not have afforded to pay a Russian translator to translate it into English.

All this hypothesizing is far-fetched; it begs too many questions and leaves too many loose ends unanswered, not least its disappearance. Why would someone who had found and purchased a manuscript of this rarity, so precious to her, then destroy it or lose it? Why would Evelyn not have kept it intact with the rest of the remains she sent me?

The greater likelihood is that no written diary ever existed; that Evelyn pieced together an *imaginary* 'Diary' from various sources – just as I have pieced together this memoir from her jottings and notes and many other sources too, including her wide reading, Daisy's recollections, and my sense of Evelyn's punctured life. Evelyn's internal world inhabited with, and for, both Richard and Rachmaninoff was so ripe she could easily have invented a 'Nurse's Diary'. Her personal psychology was stamped with triple-tragedy: aborted career, Richard, Sam. Rachmaninoff alone – the man and his music – connected all three, even in her blackest despair. And Rachmaninoff permitted her to rescue herself. Now, in her last jottings, she gave him her best shot: she invented a 'Nurse's Diary'.

Evelyn's sentences are inchoate, unformed and filled with ellipses. Few can be cited as she left them because they make little sense. Only by stitching together the rest of her remains and decoding her handwriting could I reconstruct a 'Nurse's Tale'. But I have taken liberties in finishing it, and it is now as much my Nurse's Tale as Evelyn's. While reconstructing it I wondered whether Evelyn took notes – now lost – while Daisy dictated and, later on, perhaps over a number of years, Evelyn transcribed the notes on to the pages she sent me. Or whether the Nurse's Tale was wholly and entirely of her own fabrication: barely prompted by Daisy, occupying Evelyn over several years, reflecting on, and replying to, her own reading about the biographical Rachmaninoff.

THE NURSE'S TALE

Nizheopisannyi tekst – opisanie poslednikh dnei Sergeia Vasil′evicha Rakhmaninova, sestroi miloserdiia O. G. Mordovskoi. [The following text is a written account of the last days of S. V. Rachmaninoff, by nurse O. G. Mordovskaya].[117]

I am Olga Mordovskaya, nurse, born in Petrovskoye in 1881. I worked as kormilitsa for the princes Golitsyn from thirteen and learned trade of midwife. In 1898 the young Prince Golitsyn, Alexander, third son of the great Vladimir Mikhailovich who was then still vigorous although ageing, encouraged me to elevate myself to proper nurse through apprenticeship. In Ivanovo, near Petrovskoye, I was apprenticed to experienced women who taught me technique and

---

[117] The reader is reminded that this is the *same* Olga Mordovskaya who contributed to M. B. Dobuzhinskii's volume of reminiscences about Rachmaninoff, the *Pamiati Rakhmaninova*; see above, p. 144, n. 49. But 'The Nurse's Tale' produced here is an entirely different fragment from the memories Olga Mordovskaya produced in 1946 at Sophia Satina's command, which merely comment on the composer's daily medical symptoms and diagnoses. Evelyn was unaware of Dobuzhinskii's volume and Mordovskaya's chapter within it. If – a *big* if – Evelyn came upon a manuscript Mordovskaya wrote, it was unlikely to have contained the same material as the chapter published in Dobuzhinskii's volume; and it seems even more far-fetched to hypothesize that Evelyn found a handwritten manuscript somewhere in Los Angeles, either in Russian or English, which had been the basis for Mordovskaya's 1946 published chapter. I feel almost certain that Evelyn fabricated the idea of a 'Nurse's Tale' based on her dissatisfaction with Bertensson's 1956 account of Rachmaninoff's last days and Daisy's memories. It is not impossible that the same Olga Mordovskaya who published a brief medical memoir, also wrote a more extended personal unpublished account of her celebrity-patient which Evelyn found. However, it seems improbable. Evelyn more likely wanted to piece together an end-of-life account of Rachmaninoff as the symbolic counterpart of her own life grounded in nostalgia, loss, and – then – stalking. Her 'Tale' fixes the house at 610 North Elm, the house she walked around for so long, as a container for her personal nostalgia where she could imagine her destiny as finally meeting Rachmaninoff. I believe that 'Nurse's Tale' formed an integral part of her stalking as the final object of her nostalgia.

trade in a college of nurses. I remained with them until 1901. Then I returned to Golitsyn Palace until uprising of 1905. After these civil disturbances my beloved Golitsyns moved to Moscow, in fear went into hiding, plotting their escape, and I fled with them after the bloodsheds.

Prince Alexander considered me almost as daughter although he was not old enough to be my father; so too his wife Lyubov, who was Lyubov Glebov before she married the Prince, around turn of century. They had four children – I was nurse to all. Everything was confused in the first years after 1900: Lyubov bringing up the three children (the fourth was born just before Revolution in 1917) and the terror of political disturbances. Petrovskoye was changed after 1905 and never returned to the former tranquillity I enjoyed in my childhood there.

In 1917, years after the war with Germany broke in 1912 and five years later the Red Revolution, the Prince escaped eastward and took me with him as far as Manchuria. Lyubov was brave, she never cried. The train journeys lasted for two years through Arctic freeze and ice. We slept on cold floors in carriages, like animals, and ate weeds and flowers we picked when train stopped. Harbin was filled of White Russians, like us. We could have remained there forever, like oasis after train migrations through Siberia and Manchuria. Later we crossed to Pacific Ocean by train and in big American Red Cross ship to Seattle. After train, the boat was like hotel. Delicious food, elegant waiters, comfortable beds. This was in 1922, when we left Harbin. We went to Washington State and Alexander settled there as doctor. He and the family were happy and found a nice house but the culture was poor. Americans very kind people and friendly but had no understanding of our old world Russia.

I was forty years old in 1922. I took English classes and attended a college for training of nurses. Two years later I had a degree, in spite of poor English. Three years later Alexander told us Russian immigrants in San Francisco needed nurses. Would I go? I said yes – no husband, no children, nothing to stop me, and San Francisco had more Russians than Seattle. But I would miss the Golitsyns. And where would I live? He said he would fix everything.

I was sent to a rich family on Russian Hill, devout Orthodox people who took me with them to every liturgy at Holy Grace Cathedral. ... such beautiful church. They were getting old, their children moved out, they had grandchildren, and when Raya's husband died I moved to another Russian family near Lombard Street. Russian people were everywhere in San Francisco and wanted nurses familiar with their old practices who could also speak their language fluently.

In California we lived as if still in Old Russia, cooking and eating in the former ways, speaking our customs, praying, following daily rituals, with icons, crosses and triptychs, samovars, dark bread, and long supper parties with Russian friends.

Around 1925 a letter came from Alexander announcing he and Lyubov too were moving to San Francisco. I rejoiced. A homecoming for me! My Russian Prince had become a prominent doctor in America and was being called to San Francisco. Once arrived, he and Lyubov bought big wooden house near Russian Hill district to be close to his patients. He visited hospitals to see Russian patients but was not a scientist in a laboratory studying the infectious diseases about which he already knew so much.

I asked Alexander if I could live with them and he agreed. He was almost fifty now, Lyubov too, and the children adolescent. With them I could learn really good English. Lyubov suffered from often migraines and I nursed her and prayed for her. But on many occasions Alexander assigned me to his ailing Russian patients as private nurse.

We continued this way for four or five years until Alexander announced we were moving to Los Angeles, four-hundred miles away. I was anxious, having grown accustomed to Russian Hill and feeling at home with my own White Russian people with whom I spoke Russian, ate Russian food, prayed in Russian and imagined I would some day die. But Fate said not.

After so many migrations since Moscow the removal to southern California was not hard. The Golitsyns had not gathered so many possessions in San Francisco and the two oldest children remained there in colleges. But living in so many different houses began to disjoint my memories. I thought of Petrovskoye, Ivanovo, back to Petrovskoye, Moscow, Harbin, Vladivostok, Seattle, San Francisco, and now the new city still foreign to me.

Los Angeles by the ocean was warmer than San Francisco and more beautiful. We moved to a quarter called Pacific Palisades overlooking the ocean. The climate was like paradise but the atmosphere could not compare to the European quality of San Francisco. Russian people lived there too, especially in nearby Santa Monica, but there was no Russian Hill and no Grace Cathedral.

This town urban centre had about same number of people as San Francisco, and earthquakes too. Just before we arrived was small earthquake in Santa Barbara. But people here seemed much richer. Many people drove big cars, some gold cars with huge windows. Alexander told me I would be in great demand among Russians.

So I found too. I could pick and choose my family, even among the most Russian of the Russian. I was growing old, now more than fifty. I chose families with few children. Besides, the elderly needed me most. Those who, like me, had migrated from the Old Russia yet kept their way of life and customs intact.

But this period was not happy. The rest of America was suffering economic hardship, much less in rich Hollywood film-land. Still the unemployed workers increased – more every year. We heard the Nazis in Europe were rising, and Stalin still oppressing and torturing our people, with millions starving to death. New wars were coming. We were lucky to be here, across the ocean, far-far-far from Europe. To think, if we had remained in the Old Russia and had to face Stalin after the Revolution.

The situation became worse in 1937. Alexander, who listened to the radio all the time, told us about the Great Purge and the hunger strikes. Thousands were perishing across the whole width of the Soviet Union. Especially people like me who had been attached to one place, but soldiers everywhere were imprisoned too, thousands of Communist officials murdered. The police were everywhere, fear and terror ruled.

By 1939 we heard war was coming, although California was so far away it could never reach us here. But after the Japanese invaded

Pearl Harbour, America must go to war too. I prayed not for another catastrophe of the kind we had with the revolutionaries. Where would we go this time?

But still I worked as professional nurse and was in much demand. I went to Santa Monica for several months as nurse to one of Alexander's dying patients who owned a big car dealership, and then in Hollywood Hills for a rich Russian film producer. That was in summer 1941 some months after Pearl Harbour when I celebrated my sixtieth birthday.

Soon afterwards I explained to Alexander I should work no more. I was tired, becoming old. I liked the little room overlooking the garden he assigned me in Pacific Palisades and would quietly retreat there, which I did until the day the next March when Alexander summoned me to his house office.

The samovar was ready, and beside it a plate of syrniki [i.e., cottage cheese pancakes] with cream and jam. I could not imagine what was so pressing and thought we must be moving again, as we had fled Moscow so many many years earlier. Kind and wise Alexander sat me down.

'Olga, u menya k tebe ochen vazhnaya prosba. I have something important to ask of you.'

'What?'

'My patient is Sergei Vasilyevich Rachmaninoff, the greatest living pianist.'

'Rachmaninoff!' I well knew his name, had heard it many times before in great houses in Los Angeles. He was legendary.

'What is wrong with him?'

'We don't know, but he is very sick.'

'Is he dying?'

Alexander was an optimist and said no, but I knew better.

I said I was ready to do anything for Sergei Vasilyevich. Did he require a nurse and companion?

'Yes,' Alexander said, 'you must go immediately and you must be everything to him. There is no cancer diagnosed but he is failing. He is chronically exhausted and low of spirits.'

'What is the diagnosis?'

'Maybe heart failure, maybe something else, but the greatest happiness for Sergei Vasilyevich would be to die when held by someone like you.'

I remember moving my arms to my chest, feeling cold and crossing myself. I understood Alexander's prophetic words.

'You will be my gift to that suffering family. You must protect Sergei Vasilyevich from intruders and visitors; you know why he hides from the light of day and turns away from outsiders.'

I understood my role. Alexander continued:

'You will calm him, even more than Natalia Alexandrovna, at the end. Your role will be more than nurse. Was Pushkin's nurse not the most important human being to him during his exile?'

The next morning Alexander drove me from Pacific Palisades to a big house on Elm Drive in Beverly Hills with one suitcase. It was a wide street with great tall palm trees along sides. House was recessed, with enormous front windows, but seemed dark inside despite bright sunlight on street. Natalia Alexandrovna, his loving wife, had visited Golitsyn household once I was told, but I never met her. Now she awaited me at front window, peering like princess.

She greeted me with warm civility and showed me to room I would occupy on ground floor near the garden. I saw how distraught she was – at the end of her straw. She could not imagine life without Sergei Vasilyevich who had come to the end of his life and she would travel to the end of the world to help him – she said – but he was profoundly sick.

I was instructed to recreate complete Russian atmosphere for him now that he had returned from hospital; everything must seem as if we were still on his estate at Oneg during his childhood.

'V kontse dolzhno byt nachalo. In the end is the beginning,' Natalia whispered to me soon after her instructions finished. I followed her to sick chamber. She was frightened but hopeful he might recover. Sophia Alexandrovna was on her way from the East. The train would take three days. Sergei Vasilyevich would feel better as soon as he saw her.

She emphasized that I must not repeat that we were so close to the Pacific Ocean coast. I should pretend this was the Old Russia thirty years before the revolutionary time. I must do everything for him. Administer medicine, feed him, make his bed, wash him, never leave his side.

I had never met the great Sergei Vasilyevich until now, and was amazed by his courtesy and degree of charm and even his jokes. He looked washed out and ill, gaunt and emasculated, but kept speaking of his love for Russia and the Russian way of life.

No one else would be routinely admitted to his sick chamber but I must not remain there more than necessary. If he spoke, or reminisced, I must listen and offer brief comments, but I must say nothing that could possibly arouse him. Most of all, I must not tire him. Sophia Alexandrovna would read to him after her arrival. I must only listen.

Sophia Alexandrovna arrived a few days after me and went straight to him. This was still early in March. She flung down her case and made for the sick chamber. He embraced her and said they were now united: 'My vmeste, kak byly v Rossii. We are together, just as we were in Russia'. Two days later she was reading Pushkin to him.

In this first week home he was lively, interested in everything, the news, the war, Russian music, his garden, he even moved his fingers in mechanical exercises and practiced piano on the cardboard keyboard in his bed.

But I don't write to enlist his medical details, how such a great man quickly became so depleted. It is too sad to explain. Within a week his appetite disappeared and swellings began to appear on his body. They were everywhere, especially on torso. They were almost pale red and smooth but elevated. I was disheartened to see how my profession of medicine could do nothing. Alexander came twice a day, yet had hands tied before the giant of this illness. Chaliapin visited every day – but Sergei Vasilyevich was too fatigued to speak much with his old friend. He raised his eyes each time but said little. Only to me he spoke.

Now the days flowed more slowly than before. By middle-March he had changed. The swellings increased, his energy decreased, and he ate less. Below I copy only what Sergei Vasilevich told me near his end, before he lapsed into the comas of his last three days. For Sergei Vasilyevich said many things future ages will want to know, and he whispered them to me as only two old people from the same Old Russia could understand, two people who looked into each other's deep eyes and knew there is never cause for fear if your memory is intact. I wrote everything he said in my notebook before I went to sleep.

First, Sergei Vasilyevich repeated how happy he was he could die at home. He said he would have died much sooner if he had remained in hospital. The pain in his side eased as soon as he returned to house.

Second, he was very independent in the sick chamber. Did not like anyone to fuss over him, not even me. He begged me not to force feed him, so often having no appetite. He was tired of bed and asked me to help him walk to the garden where he sat in a chair under the warm sun. He would stare at the sun for hours, gazing at it through the rustling tree branches.

Third was homeland. When Sophia Alexandrovna read Pushkin to him every day he pressed her hand and only asked her about the war in Russia.[118] I always remained in sick chamber when she was there and I heard everything. How eager he was to know about the Russian victories over the Germans. Sophia Alexandrovna recounted the fierce fighting in Kharkov in the Ukraine. The Germans had retaken the city and murdered thousands of Russians. Every day he asked her about Kharkov. He relapsed when Sophia Alexandrovna reported the Germans had retaken Kharkov. Whenever it appeared the Russians were on the verge of taking back the city Sergei Vasilyevich sighed and would say 'Thank God! God give them strength.'

---

[118] The 'Nurse's Tale' never recounts Rachmaninoff using the word Soviets or Soviet Union as the country was known after 1917; Evelyn's version, and perhaps Rachmaninoff's as filtered by Evelyn, is always 'Russia' and the 'Russians'. It is as if time has stopped marching.

Often I held his hand, grasping the legendary fingers that made him so famous. Once, when pointing to one of the icons surrounding the walls of his bed, the one of his saint, Saint Sergius, he whispered to me he wished all the American Russians would keep their vigil for Russia alive. His voice lowered, his tone quivered as if touching on the holiest of holy subjects.

Fourth was sickness. After all I am medical nurse. Many times he cried 'Ya skuchayu po domu' and 'toskuyu po rodine' when Natalia had left the room. 'I suffer from homesickness.' He mentioned other illnesses too. Even when famous, before fleeing Russia, he was sick. His dear 'Re' – Marietta Shaginyan – knew. He loved her, he said, and many other young women too. He named them 'dear Re, Nina, a poetess, a lady in white, like lilacs.' I cannot remember all their names. They were also his children, he said. I stroked his head and said 'be quiet, Sergei Vasilyevich, do not exert yourself.' But he kept repeating, 'toskuyu po rodine, toskuyu po rodine, I suffer from a yearning for the homeland,' and he held up his hands to his head as if in anguish. 'That is my illness. Nostalgiya is killing me.' He kept incanting, almost as if crying 'nostalgiya, nostalgiya, nostalgiya.' For half hour I calmed him down.

Fifth was family. He always spoke softly and slowly about them, as if watching a faraway star. He said his love for Russia had carried over to his girls. Their residences in Paris and Switzerland made them no less Russian than if they remained in motherland. He said love of your country knows no boundaries for old or young. It is like blood passing from mother to child and then to grandchildren, down through generations. Only Russians would understand this.

By now he could no longer sit in his chair in garden – the swellings hurt him too much. But he spoke about the future: his children more than compositions would be his legacy. He referred many times to his firstborn, 'Irinochka' (Princess Irina Wolkonsky), sickly as child, but she survived into womanhood and suffered her own tragedy when her husband killed himself just before their baby was born. I held my silence. I understood the reason why a young man pulls the trigger because he cannot tell his wife his secret …

He said Tatania, their younger daughter, was luckier. She and her husband survived Nazi occupation and fled to Switzerland. My frail patient stared into space and seemed prophetic about his girls. He called them 'two anchors during every migration'; through each bout of illness in his life, he said he pictured them in his mind running with him in the fields around Oneg.

Dr Golitsyn visited his patient at least once a day, and gave him injections. Then he came twice and gave him two injections per day. Natalia entered more often, but Sophia Alexandrovna no longer read Pushkin to the patient, Sergei Vasilyevich could not concentrate or hear her words. Soon Natalia no longer left his side, but we were not yet at that point near the end.

The injections eased his pain and made him even more tired. He slept much and dreamed and murmured utterings while dreaming. Sometimes they sounded like a child's search for his mother. 'Russia, my mother, rodina-mat, my motherland.' I thought he must be delirious. He had already suffered delusions for some days.

Often something he said hung unfinished in the air. I would return to the room and wonder which sentence he would finish, for he seemed to remember he had not. But he was no longer a storyteller looking back at his life in his last days. By now he could only speak a few words. My duty was to listen and record.

The day before he died, on 27 March, he suddenly grew silent in the middle of a phrase, as if drawn to some interior place incapable of beholding anyone than himself. Like an island inhabited only by the dead. Could this be his end, I wondered? Natalia had left the sick chamber, said she would return momentarily.

He continued, whispering, incomprehensively, slowlier and slowlier, his eyes closed. His words were garbled. But I knew my patient, I could disentangle them. He asked me, why are we leaving Russia? I said we already left long ago, but he heard me not. He repeated the question two or three times, each time softer, as if renewed of spirit. When I replied once more that we left long ago, he almost laughed with sudden energy. 'A-a-a-h,' he said, 'you tease me, Olyushka, I will tell you what I have never told anyone. We have not left Russia, we will never leave Russia, to leave Russia would be the biggest mistake I could make.'

Then he was dead, but his words echoed in my ears. They repeat themselves, like a broken record. 'We will never leave Russia.' As he lay dying he judged this error the greatest tragedy of his life. I continued to think about his secret. He never told anyone – this was his self-knowledge, which he knew throughout his life. That he loved Russia more than his own life. Only me he told. But Sergei Vasilyevich was different from other Russians. They loved America, like me; they could bring Russia into America with them. Even Dr Golitsyn and his family adjusted to the new country, and other Russians I worked for. Not my last patient, Sergei Vasilyevich, who died broken-hearted because he had wandered for so long without finding the permanent home he had lost.

This was his enigma. To be such a great man, to write such beautiful music, to play the piano so well, and to think he could never return home. Why could Sergei Vasilyevich not imagine a return? He could have returned to Russia through his music. But he said the instrument inside him was broken. I looked at my Saint's icon. My own return home would be to God. Did Sergei Vasilyevich not trust in his God? If only I could have helped him remember more of his life's beginning in the end.

Did he find peace at last beneath the rolling fields of Valhalla Cemetery when they buried him a few weeks later?

Note on Sources and Literary Form

This memoir relies on two types of material: the first – Evelyn's story – contained in manuscripts, oral accounts and personal contact over four decades; the second – my proposed life of Rachmaninoff and discussion of historical nostalgia – in printed books and digital storage websites. Evelyn's notes and diaries are in private hands, and although I cannot attest to the historical veracity of the New York she describes between the wars, I allow her scribblings to speak for themselves. Besides, they have enabled her 'story' to be reconstructed as completely as it can be. My memoir derives primarily from almost a half-century of friendship with Evelyn, especially face-to-face meetings and telephone conversations; and while I quote verbatim very few sentences from her jottings, the greatest portion of my narrative is necessarily the work of reconstruction and interpretation. In this sense, the 'truthfulness' of Evelyn's version of events – her music lessons, music teachers, and historical view of musical life in New York; her analysis of Richard's progeria and untimely death, and, even more fantastically, her 'second life' in Southern California and meeting with Daisy Bernheim – plays an ancillary role that can only be verified by external corroboration. Its degree of veracity is a biographer's, or historian's, arduous task that I have been unable to undertake, nor have I any desire to perform it.

My main interest is in setting forward a set of complex parallel universes between a great composer and an aspiring concert pianist who played his music. For this reason principally, Evelyn's 'universe' in Part One and Part Three has few endnotes or bibliographical sources. The proposed new 'Life of Rachmaninoff' occupying the whole of Part Two has copious notes citing sources. I realize that by telling Evelyn's story, for the first time, I may inadvertently have paved the way for future scholars interested in the cultural and musical life of America in the first half of the twentieth century to confirm or discredit her accounts.

The second type of material, essential for Rachmaninoff's life and times, is different despite obvious chronological and geographical overlaps with Evelyn's universe. The new type of life presented in Part Two does not yet exist in academic Rachmaninoff studies: I have imagined it over the years in response to Sergei Bertensson's benchmark biography of 1956, which continues to be the yardstick of all measurement. The materials necessary to construct any new sense of Rachmaninoff-the-man are found in printed, manuscript and digital documents, and many of these have been cited in the footnotes; notes that aim to suggest the range of materials that *could* be consulted in any full-scale, new biography. I have also tapped into a small body of literature about Rachmaninoff published in the Soviet Union and post-Soviet Russia during the last few decades, as well as new material that has appeared in the West. The sources for nostalgia – medical, scientific, psychological, historical, literary and cultural – are also mostly printed and form a vast archive on a subject I have been tapping into for more than two decades.

Rachmaninoff's Cape consists of a blended genre of memoir and biography narrated in the first-person to capture my own voice. This voice, I discovered while writing, is emphatically lodged in the crossover from memoir to biography and vice-versa; and if genre conventions are disturbed by so doing I take responsibility for crossing those borders. It would be disingenuous, moreover, not to acknowledge that I have written *Rachmaninoff's Cape*, in part, to locate myself within the symmetry of these other musical lives: Rachmaninoff, Evelyn, Richard, Adele Marcus, and my contemporaries at Chatham Square. Even more thirstily to understand how I made the slippery transition, in my own life, from aspiring concert pianist to professional academic; a passage I apparently navigated so undramatically, so uncannily, and so unwittingly, that ever since I have wondered whether some trickster, lodged in my memory, enabled it without my noticing.

Considering the role I played in Evelyn's life – as her son's only friend, as an *alter ego* during the decades she lived in California, and, more palpably, through the archival remains she bequeathed to me – it was predictable I would want to situate myself somewhere near the centre of the memoir's two parallel universes: Evelyn and Rachmaninoff. For good reason I cite sparingly from Evelyn's remains – diaries, letters, notes, jottings, even phone conversations during which I took notes – and only when her notes cry out to be heard for a distinct sense of her character. Otherwise the words enabling this reconstruction are wholly my own. In the end it was impossible to tell her story in any other voice than my own.

But Evelyn could only imagine Rachmaninoff as the result of her obsession with the man and his own profound biographical melancholy and nostalgia, which she intuited from her early piano-days. Her sympathy for him, like his for Russia, arose from an empathic imagination enabling the creation of characters almost by inhabiting them. This sympathy formed the basis of *both* their ingrained nostalgias. Evelyn sympathized with Rachmaninoff to the point of imagining she *was Rachmaninoff*. She was, of course, nothing of the sort. She was the daughter of poor Eastern Jewish immigrants in New York City, but the young Evelyn was also a latter-day Romantic stereotype – like Rachmaninoff himself – capable of interiorizing another pianist. Baudelaire, the great French poet and doyen of early Modernism, captured the essence of this Romantic process in 'Les Foules': 'Le poète jouit de cet incomparable privilège, qu'il peut à sa guise être lui-même et autrui. Comme ces âmes errantes qui cherchent un corps, il entre, quand il veut, dans le personnage de chacun.'

Acknowledgements

This memoir began life on the day I accidentally broke Richard Amster's cello in 1949, although I did not view the catastrophe at the age of eight that way, and the memoir significantly advanced, more tangibly, in the aftermath of his mother's death forty years later. Since then it has been transformed many times into the present version that calls itself a 'nostalgia memoir,' deliberately titled as such to suggest both the virtues and defects of nostalgia within this type of life-writing. Perhaps the title 'an anti-nostalgia memoir' would have described it more accurately, calling attention more dramatically than I do to the corrosive influences nostalgia bestows on its devotées. But such a title would have risked confusing the reader about nostalgia's multiple meanings and the memoir's equally important parallel universes between Evelyn and Rachmaninoff.

Many friends and colleagues, my American friend 'Helen' mentioned in Part Two, as well as Margery Vibe Skagen in Norway and John Thacker in England, have thrashed out with me both pro-nostalgia and anti-nostalgia positions, as well as confronted the cruxes inherent in proposing a new critical biography of Rachmaninoff. I have also discussed this Russian composer with dozens of musical and cultural critics, and academic musicologists too numerous to name here; and I have relied on the published work of many, especially Karen Bottge, Svetlana Boym, David Cannata, Yuri Druzhnikov, Natalia Fedunina, Emanuel E. Garcia, Dan Healey, Catriona Kelly, Richard Leppert, Geoffrey Norris, Francis Maes, Alex Ross, Tatiana Soloviova, Richard Taruskin, and Andreas Wehrmeyer. Slavic scholar Simon Pawley of Oxford University was especially helpful in tracking down and assessing various strands of the Russian archive and ensuring that no relevant Russian materials had been overlooked. To all I am grateful, although I alone take responsibility for the construction of Rachmaninoff's enduring malaise and mindset I call *nostalgia*.

I also profited from the medical community's input in dealing with Richard's progeria: especially various members of the Progeria

Acknowledgements

Research Foundation of America, formerly located in Boston but now in Peabody Massachusetts, and the Great Ormond Street Hospital for Children in London. And I could not have understood Rachmaninoff's emotional collapse and creative breakdown without the expert input of several psychiatrists and psychoanalysts, including Emanuel E. Garcia, M. D., as well as Peter Agulnik in Oxford and Norland Berk in New York, the latter an accomplished musician himself. I would like to thank all.